Ethical Teachings of Abū Ḥāmid al-Ghazālī

Ethical Teachings of Abū Ḥāmid al-Ghazālī

Economics of Happiness

Sami Al-Daghistani

ANTHEM PRESS

Anthem Press
An imprint of Wimbledon Publishing Company
www.anthempress.com

This edition first published in UK and USA 2021
by ANTHEM PRESS
75–76 Blackfriars Road, London SE1 8HA, UK
or PO Box 9779, London SW19 7ZG, UK
and
244 Madison Ave #116, New York, NY 10016, USA

British Library Cataloguing-in-Publication Data
A catalogue record for this book is available from the British Library.

Library of Congress Control Number: 2020941207

ISBN-13: 978-1-78527-530-2 (Hbk)
ISBN-10: 1-78527-530-5 (Hbk)

Cover image: Serge Zimniy / Shutterstock.com

This title is also available as an e-book.

For Lina.

Earning is not the aim of human life but only a means to an end.

(Al-Ghazālī, *Iḥyā'*, Vol. 2, 62)

CONTENTS

EDITOR'S PREFACE

It is an honor and a privilege to have been involved in the publication of this volume - a study of the past and from a different world, where Abū Ḥāmid Al-Ghazālī, a man of faith and knowledge, thought hard about the intricacies between ethics and the mundane realities of economic life. His faith forced him to confront the inequities of human societies, and his religious quest urged him to find wisdom from the philosophers of the past. He explored Greek philosophy which laid the groundwork for a new synthesis between the moral imperatives of Islam, the force of logical thinking, and the precarious conditions of human life and our common vulnerability. Al-Ghazālī's thought became a bridge between religion and philosophy, and a source of knowledge for those who are thinking hard about the essential contours and conditions of a more just world.

Al-Ghazālī is famous for many achievements, not least his research into what constitutes human happiness. To achieve insight into human wellbeing, he concluded that rationalism was not in itself sufficient to guide humans to self-knowledge and at the same time that religious piety was more than a collection of rules to guide the faithful. As a Sufi philosopher, he acknowledged the force of everyday experience, and the inspiration of music and dance. We moderns can benefit from his teaching, because in our world happiness is often degraded to mean merely selfish satisfaction.

The 2020 pandemic has highlighted the iniquities of the contemporary world and the depth of human suffering. His philosophy has forced us think deeply about the intersections between morality and economics. This publication is the first volume in the series *Religion and Society* with Anthem Press. Sami Al-Daghistani has established a level of intellectual excellence which will inspire future authors and develop a deeper understanding of the complex relations between the secular and the religious.

Yuri Contreras-Vejar and Bryan S. Turner

ACKNOWLEDGMENTS

This work has been a profound interest of mine since my graduate studies at the University of Leiden, spanning many eras and places. Though commencing in Leiden, it traveled through Sarajevo, Münster, Rabat, Montreal, New York, and Oslo. Al-Ghazālī continues to occupy a unique space in my academic and personal life, ever since my initial discovery of his work in relation to Islamic sciences in general, and on classical economic thought in particular. Time and again I have returned to his work, reflecting on his life, philosophical and *ṣūfī* insights, ethics, and especially economic ideas. It is therefore no surprise that his ethical economic teachings have become a primary field of inquiry for this project. Al-Ghazālī's proposal that economic philosophy and engagement not be isolated issues and be treated separately from overall human reasoning, behavior, and sensations lies at the core of my understanding of economics.

Many scholars, professors, family members, and friends have been pivotal to my journey of reading, thinking about, and writing this work. I would like to thank my former MA graduate advisor at Leiden University, Mohamed Ghaly, who inspired me with his intellectual rigor and ethical demeanor to delve deeper into conceptual history and Islamic ethics, and who guided me throughout the two years spent at Leiden University; Maurits Berger, who would later guide me during my doctoral studies and provide comments to the initial draft of this volume; Asghar Seyed-Gohrab for reading one of the very first drafts of this manuscript and for supporting my book project from the get-go; and Petra Sijpesteijn, who offered useful advice during the early years of my graduate studies. I am also indebted to Wael Hallaq, who became a mentor and co-advisor during my doctoral studies and who opened my eyes wider into the world of Islamic intellectual history, law, and ethics. In addition to his invaluable comments on this manuscript, I will always recall with fondness our discussions on *Sharī'a*'s moral law and the role of the human. Likewise, I express my gratitude to Hossein Kamaly, Souleymane Bachir Diagne, Alexander Knysh, and Seyyed Hossein Nasr for their insights into classical economics, al-Ghazālī's thought, Sufism, and epistemic shifts. I also greatly appreciate my colleagues and friends for their intellectual engagement at the Norwegian School of Theology, Religion and Society in Oslo—which also provided institutional support—the Brooklyn Institute for Social Research, and the Institute for Religion, Culture and Public Life, and the Middle East Institute at Columbia University.

At Anthem Press, I would like to sincerely thank the series editors, Bryan S. Turner and Yuri Contreras-Vejar, for believing in my project and for our gap sessions on society, economics, and ethics. Megan Greiving and her team have also been crucial to this project, and I thank them for their overall support and editing process as well as the two blind reviewers for their valuable comments and suggestions.

On a more personal note, my warmest gratitude goes to my beloved father, Nabil Al-Daghistani, who helped in translation, especially of some key passages from al-Ghazālī's *Iḥyāʾ*, and to my mother, Marija Al-Daghistani, for her consummate love and sacrifice. I would also like to thank my brother, Raid Al-Daghistani, with whom I have exchanged numerous—and at times opposing—thoughts and ideas on philosophy, Sufism, and al-Ghazālī's life. Last but not least, I express my heartfelt appreciation to my wife and companion, Kristin Soraya Batmanghelichi, for her immense love and support. As for our daughter, Lina Jocelyn—she is a beacon of light—her presence is a constant reminder to perfect my own ethics.

INTRODUCTION

Modern economic science as it is known in the West is intricately linked to an eighteenth-century European division of natural and social sciences, yet economic philosophy dates back centuries if not a millennium. Various civilizations and religions contributed to economic thought, including some of the most prominent classical Islamic jurists, theologians, and *ṣūfīs*. *Ethical Teachings of Abū Ḥāmid al-Ghazālī* studies the interplay of ethics and economic philosophy as reflected in the writings of one of the most renowned scholars in Islamic history, Abū Ḥāmid Muḥammad ibn Muḥammad al-Ghazālī (d. 1111).[1] Imām al-Ghazālī, nicknamed "the proof of Islam," contributed immensely to Islamic theology, philosophy, and Sufism or *taṣawwuf*. He also made seminal contributions to the field of what is nowadays broadly called economics. Scholarship has largely neglected this particular contribution, despite the fact that al-Ghazālī dedicated many chapters in his books to the topics of justice and *Sharī'a*-based economic conduct in Muslim society. The academic silence toward al-Ghazālī's economic contributions goes hand in hand with a claim made by several Western scholars (e.g., J. Schumpeter), albeit refuted by various Muslim scholars such as Mohammad Ghazanfar and Abdul Azim Islahi, that classical Islamic scholarship did not offer any significant development or contribution in the domain of economic thought during Europe's Middle Ages. It goes without saying that al-Ghazālī was well studied in Western and Muslim intellectual circles. In the past decades, numerous works have appeared on his life, cosmology, ethics, philosophy, and even gender studies, but surprisingly few and relatively small and incomplete studies analyze his economic postulates, especially in light of his ethical theory of happiness.[2] Furthermore, no full translation from Arabic into English exists

---

[1] All Arabic terms and concepts in this book are used in accordance with the *Encyclopaedia Islamica* ("System of Transliteration of Arabic and Persian Characters," Brill Online Reference Works, accessed March 2017, http://referenceworks.brillonline.com/entries/encyclopaedia-islamica/system-of-transliteration-of-arabic-and-persian-characters-transliteration). At times, the letter "h" is omitted at the end of certain words—e.g., *ḥisba*, *Sharī'a*, and so forth. In the bibliography, "al" in front of names of scholars is positioned alphabetically.

[2] Scholars have written various books on ethics in Islamic tradition and al-Ghazālī's role therein, yet few have looked into the convoluted universe of economics and ethics in

of his economic opus, which spans several books and treaties. To my knowledge, only one complete translation is available in English of the third book of the second volume of his encyclopedic *Iḥyā' 'Ulūm al-Dīn*, which is nonetheless only one source of his overall economic thought.[3] This indicates both a relegation and a general disregard by contemporary scholars of one, al-Ghazālī's economic teachings, which form the backbone of his ethical theory of happiness, and two, of analysis of economic theories driven by human agency and ethical behavior, which is pertinent especially for humanities and Islamic studies scholars.

As a work of intellectual history, this book is primarily concerned with the ethical aspects of al-Ghazālī's economic ideas, his engagements, and his activities. It analyses what is largely an understudied contribution of his economic teachings positioned at the intersection of *Sharī'a*'s moral law, philosophy, and *taṣawwuf*—all of which constitute his overall ethics of happiness (*sa'āda*).[4] This work centers on al-Ghazālī's theoretical accounts and economic philosophy, offering an analysis of passages from his economic corpus that present him as a scholar of heterogeneity who positioned himself across two domains not typically understood as interlinked—namely *taṣawwuf* or *ṣūfī*-mystical thought[5] and *Sharī'a*'s law[6] as part of his overall ethics of happiness.

---

light of al-Ghazālī's theory of happiness, which is the present work's major concern. The book by Zahra Ayubi on ethics and gender came rather late to my attention—that is, after concluding this manuscript. Ayubi's book analyzes three key ethical texts by classical Muslim scholars, including al-Ghazālī, on constructed ideas of the self in relation to the family and the society. While Ayubi asserts al-Ghazālī's ethical epistemology and language are hierarchical and male-oriented, and that his idea of an ethical human was achievable through a male elite, given the gist of al-Ghazālī's ethical and metaphysical themes, his position can perhaps be seen as part of the overall male-dominated culture of the time that found its way into textual sources, rather than his particular a priori disregard of woman's rationality. For an erudite analysis of the subject, see Zahra Ayubi, *Gendered Morality: Classical Islamic Ethics of the Self, Family, and Society* (New York: Columbia University Press, 2019).

3 See Adi Setia, *The Book of the Proprieties of Earning and Living* (Kuala Lumpur: IBFIM, 2013).

4 For more on al-Ghazālī's notion of happiness in light of economic teachings, see Chapter 3 of this book. For a more general view on ethics and philosophy of happiness, see, e.g., Aristotle, *Nicomachean Ethics*, trans. F. H. Peters (London: Kegan Paul, Trench, Trübner, 1906).

5 *Taṣawwuf* is often translated as *Sufism* in the English language; however, it should not be equated with mysticism. *Taṣawwuf* was throughout the history of Islam a dynamic movement composed of various strands and sects and often opposed by religious orthodoxy. However, it was mystical only in certain instances. For more, see, e.g., Alexander Knysh, *Sufism* (Princeton, NJ: Princeton University Press, 2017).

6 *Sharī'a* is nowadays understood as a religious law and is often equated with corporal punishment. I use the term *Sharī'a* first and foremost as a "moral cosmology" born out

Linking Economics with Happiness

Al-Ghazālī's ideas are embedded in the notion of *dīn*, in English translated as *religion*. Yet the content of his writing surpasses purely religious practice, and thus his usage of *dīn* entails a rather broader, more comprehensive meaning that incorporates social and economic systems of inquiry. In this regard, Worland states that:

> [T]here is a close correspondence between ethical values presupposed in welfare economics and the conception of economic activity implied in scholastic philosophy. […] Welfare economics can be considered a corollary of scholastic natural law. […] A deliberately metaphysical interpretation of welfare economics may have some plausibility, a validity greater than may be realized by the present generation of economists—accustomed to think of their discipline as a strictly scientific organon.[7]

Why should a twelfth-century Islamic philosopher and *ṣūfī* devotee appeal to a twenty-first-century crowd of intellectuals, social scientists, and economists? Studying intellectual history advances the idea that the past is as important as the present, or rather, that without past knowledge it would be impossible to comprehend the predicaments and contestations of late modernity. Given the nature and historical development of economic science, this holds true especially for (classical) economic thought. Tradition is not only a method that operates between the boundaries of language and thought. It is also about the ruptures emerging from within a tradition and between different modes of knowledge. Without studying, analyzing, and, whenever possible, applying ideas from intellectual history—especially in the context of economic deliberations—theories and economic predispositions can slip into oblivion or be discredited as unworthy or unscientific. A scholar like

---

of the metaphysical and theological qualities of the Qur'ān, which provided an early Muslim community with a particular worldview. In the context of this book and the writings of al-Ghazālī, *Sharīʿa* is moral law, whereby the legal quality is a derivative from the moral norms and thus secondary. See Wael Hallaq, *Sharīʿa: Theory, Practice, Transformations* (Cambridge: Cambridge University Press, 2009); Hallaq, *The Impossible State* (New York: Columbia University Press, 2014); Hallaq, "Groundwork of the Moral Law: A New Look at the Qur'ān and the Genesis of *Sharīʿa*," *Islamic Law and Society*, Vol. 16, No. 3/4 (2009): 239–79. The phrase "moral cosmology of *Sharīʿa*" explains the totality of moral economic activities and behavior patterns predicated upon a particular cosmology as conceived by classical Muslim scholars. See Sami Al-Daghistani, "The Making of Islamic Economics" (PhD diss., Leiden University, 2017).

7 Stephen Theodore Worland, *Scholasticism and Welfare Economics* (Notre Dame, IN: University of Notre Dame Press, 1967), vi.

al-Ghazālī generated further complexities and meanings for a particular discourse and worldview. Reading his (as well as other classical or premodern Muslim scholars') work through a critical lens should nonetheless be repeated time and time again. He envisioned an economic modus operandi based on ethical development, whereby philosophical reasoning and the teachings of *taṣawwuf* went hand in hand with socioeconomic well-being. Sadly, this particular scheme has been cast in modern times as undesirable or impossible to achieve. Nevertheless, al-Ghazālī's work offers clear links between the ethical sustainability of economics and the very condition of being human; the latter's weakness lies in one's ethics and spiritual demeanor, in which all things are materially done.

The rapid popularity and enduring influence of al-Ghazālī's theological philosophy and his accounts on eternal happiness are directly related to both his personal story and his thoughts on humanity as a whole. How have we arrived at notions such as ethical economics, the locale of intellectual tradition, *Sharī'a*'s moral law, and above all, Islamic metaphysics? Despite its premodern, classical, and for some perhaps even "outdated" views, his economic philosophy presents a rather fresh look at the relationship between economic growth, ethical considerations, and abstract reasoning geared toward eternal life within an Islamic discursive tradition.[8] *Sharī'a* as a moral law teaches us in light of al-Ghazālī's economic thought that human reason can discover faculties complemented by spiritual uplift. The human ego should give space to more profound and complex qualities of belief, reason, and inner-worldly orientation when dealing with economic activities. Hence al-Ghazālī speaks to philosophers, theologians, economists, and social scientists alike; the versatility of his work and his mastery of various rational and traditional sciences may provide answers to trends beyond the confines of his life and the century in which he lived.

While al-Ghazālī might have not anticipated the modern trends of economics, he did envision an economic agent or rather economic subjectivity based on inward or psychological traits that surpassed the technical-legal nature of economic engagements. If in modern economics capital plays the key role in managing markets, in al-Ghazālī's view, capital would be replaced by an ethos based on the psychological-spiritual stations of *maqāmāt*, such as awareness of God, spiritual poverty, renunciation, and reliance on and

[8] For more on Islam and Islamic orthodoxy as a discursive tradition, see Talal Asad, "The Idea of an Anthropology of Islam," *Qui Parle*, Vol. 17, No. 2 (2009): 1–30. For al-Ghazālī's thought within the Islamic discursive tradition as a multifaceted space, see Ebrahim Moosa, *Ghazālī and the Poetics of Imagination* (Chapel Hill: University of North Carolina Press, 2005), 56–57.

trust in the divine order. These formed the basis for his theory of eternal happiness. The technical-legal economic decisions an individual faced necessarily involved the navigations of one's moral compass, spiritual values of common good, and overall ethical considerations. In light of the objectives of *Sharī'a*'s moral law, whereby a moral position is not disassociated from an ethical system, al-Ghazālī firmly believed an individual could attain such happiness by emphasizing common good and social justice, and do so without damaging society. Classical Islamic economic thought, especially al-Ghazālī's, underlines economic relations critical to ethical reasoning whereby economic activities and behavior are judged by moral laws through a set of spiritual actions.

The interpretative-critical approach engaged in this book positions al-Ghazālī as an Islamic thinker who merged Islamic legal tradition, philosophical reasoning, and Sufism under the banner of the science of the hereafter (*'ilm ṭarīq al-ākhira*).[9] It praises his contributions to European scholastics and the phenomenon in the West known as (secular) economic thought, though it does not regard him as a premodern economist. This particular approach supports interventions into the realm of economic theories and ethical behavior whereby academic discussion returns to the table, so to speak, when invoking economic theories and engagements in relation to the notion of an ethics of happiness.

On Modern Islamic Economics and Intellectual History

Modern Islamic economics is predominantly concerned with licit and illicit conduct, or what is lawful or unlawful according to *Sharī'a*'s legal tradition: How should economic transactions be incorporated into the commercial economic system? How does an Islamic banking system operate and deal with other predominantly juridical-technical and financial matters? Islamic economics has been regarded as one of the subsystems of *Sharī'a*, although it cannot be exclusively equated with only legal precepts.[10] For various contemporary thinkers, the main premise of Islamic economics originates from the two main textual sources—namely the Qur'ān and the Sunna (the tradition

[9] Adi Setia, "Al-Ghazālī on the Proprieties of Earning and Living: Insights and Excerpts from His *Kitāb Ādāb al-Kasb wa-al-Ma'āsh* for Reviving Economies for Communities," *Islamic Sciences*, Vol. 11, No. 1 (2013): 19–62.

[10] Farhad Nomani and Rahnema Ali, *Islamski ekonomski sistemi* [*Islamic Economic Systems*] (Sarajevo: El Kalem, 1996), 75. For more on the notion of Islamic law and its relation to *Sharī'a* as the divine ordinances and *fiqh* as human understanding and interpretation of it, see Hallaq, *Sharī'a*.

of the Prophet Muḥammad).[11] Additionally, the contribution of the *fuqahā'* (Muslim legal specialists or jurists) is also significant; how they constructed the sophisticated system of Islamic law and jurisprudence is an elaboration of the Qur'ān and the Sunna. Since Muslim jurists argue all conduct must be in accordance with the fundamental principles of *Sharī'a* as a moral domain, Islamic economic thought is a crucial part and thus indispensable for understanding wider aspects of human conduct.[12] This includes commercial transactions, monetary exchange, purchases of licit goods, and the general economic behavior of mankind. They are all embedded within the very basic concepts of *tawḥīd* (the Unity of God), *'adl* (justice) and *iḥsān* (benevolence), *maṣlaḥa* (social well-being), *zuhd* (renunciation or abstinence), and *tazkiyya* (purification). Thus, al-Ghazālī's writings on economics are relevant for today's analogous discussions, unlike modern Islamic finances which often addresses only the technical aspects of financial transactions. Moreover, in addition to pursuing one's own introspection, which he advocated, the applied ethical teachings exercised by Islamic governance are fundamentally important to achieve fair economic conduct for the ideal Muslim society.

The Aims and Outline of *Ethical Teachings of Abū Ḥāmid al-Ghazālī*

Since al-Ghazālī's contribution to economic thought is perceived within his theory on an ethics of happiness rooted in self-knowledge, this book aims to investigate his theoretical stance on the intricate relation between economic reasoning and ethical propositions.[13] The main questions that drive the research are: "What was the main theoretical premise of al-Ghazālī's economic thought and how did he apply ethical teaching to it?" In order to address these two questions systematically, I have divided them further into sub-questions. Each is addressed in individual chapters—namely, "Who was al-Ghazālī as a Muslim scholar who merged various fields of inquiry and how does his biography reflect his works on economic thought?" "What was

---

[11] See, e.g., Syed Nawab Haider Naqvi, *Ethics and Economics: An Islamic Synthesis* (Leicester: Islamic Foundation, 1981); Muhammad Umer Chapra, *Islam and the Economic Challenge* (Herndon, VA: International Institute of Islamic Thought, 1992); Masudul Alam Choudhury, *Islamic Economics and Finance: An Epistemological Inquiry* (Bingley: Emerald, 1992).

[12] Hallaq, *The Impossible State*, 115–16.

[13] See, e.g., al-Ghazālī, *Alchemy of Eternal Bliss*, trans. Bilal Muhammad Asim (Lahore: Kazi, 2001). For more on al-Ghazālī's ethics, see, e.g., Richard Gramlich, "Muḥammad al-Ġazzālīs kleine islamische Fundamentaldogmatik," *Saeculum*, Vol. 31 (1980): 380–98; George F. Hourani, "Ghazālī on the Ethics of Action," *Journal of the American Oriental Society*, Vol. 96, No. 1 (1976): 69–88; Mohamed Ahmed Sherif, *Ghazali's Theory of Virtue* (Albany: State University of New York, 1975).

al-Ghazālī's contribution to classical Islamic economic thought?" "What are the main sources of Islamic law and how are they related to his economic philosophy, including the notion of *maṣlaḥa*?" "What is al-Ghazālī's ethics of happiness and how it is associated with his economic thought?" and "Does the role of Islamic governance with respect to the preservation of just and *Sharī'a*-based economic conduct entail also wider socio-ethical teachings?" This book is divided into five chapters in addition to an introduction and conclusion. The first chapter discusses al-Ghazālī's personal and intellectual life, including his political involvement with the Saljūq empire, while the second chapter briefly looks into the history of economic thought in Islamic tradition. The third chapter constitutes the gist of this book and interrogates al-Ghazālī's economic philosophy and his ethical and legal thought, as well as his views on Islamic governance. In order to position his economic philosophy in modern discourse, the last two chapters deal with a historical-comparative analysis of classical and neoclassical economic thought as they emerged in early modern Europe. In the fourth chapter, I present postulates of classical economic theory from early modern Europe and compare them with al-Ghazālī's views, whereas the fifth chapter explicates neoclassical economic theories and tries to position his economic philosophy in modern debates on economics and ethics. It is not assumed that al-Ghazālī anticipated the modern trends of Western economics; however, due to his importance and influence, he set forth the study of ethical axioms of knowledge and action within economic teachings. Hence, a rather specific reading of al-Ghazālī's economic philosophy is necessary, one that engages with moral principles and metaphysics, for he conceived his economic analysis as an edification based upon ethical teachings as a means toward achieving a divine end. In the conclusion, I advocate reestablishing and reinvigorating the notion of ethical-economic teachings in the contemporary era as a field of inquiry geared toward higher ends.

Though researchers have completed much scholarship on al-Ghazālī's philosophy, cosmology, ethics, and Sufism, this research relies predominantly on economic analysis through primary sources: *Iḥyā' 'Ulūm al-Dīn* (*The Revival of Religious Sciences*), *al-Munqidh min al-Ḍalāl* (*Deliverance from Error*), *Mīzān al-'Amal* (*Criterion of Action*), and *Kitāb Naṣīḥāt al-Mulūk* (*Counsel for Kings*). The passages from *Iḥyā'* on economic thought translated from Arabic to English are mine unless otherwise indicated. On other occasions, I have referred to already translated passages in English, such as his *Revival*, *Alchemy of Eternal Bliss*, *Counsel for Kings*, and *Deliverance from Error*, as well as to Ghazanfar's and Islahi's *Economic Thought of al-Ghazali*.[14]

---

[14] Mohammad Ghazanfar and Abdul Azim Islahi, *Economic Thought of al-Ghazali* (Jeddah: Scientific Publishing Centre, King Abdulaziz University, 1997).

In addition to other secondary literature, for the theoretical analysis of his writings, I consulted several works, including those of Ghazanfar and Islahi. Their analysis, however progressive and novel, is rather technical in nature and does not exhaust the ideas on the intricate relation between ethical-economic thought, *ṣūfī* teachings, and *Sharīʻa*'s moral law, an important correlation this book explores in the following pages. While Ghazanfar and Islahi propose a particular division of al-Ghazālī's economic thought and refer to state rather than to governmental authority in premodern Islamic tradition, their book does not position his economic teachings at the intersection of law and the tradition of *taṣawwuf*, congruous with the concept of "mystical Sharʻism" put forward by Wael Hallaq.[15] It is the intricate correlation of and between philosophical discourse and *taṣawwuf*, and the psychology of the ethical self and *Sharīʻa*'s moral law, that I believe needs to be interrogated when reading al-Ghazālī's work on economic thought. It is an essential part of his overall theory of happiness. By discussing classical economic and legal thought in Islamic tradition, as well as other classical scholars on the genre of ethical-economic teachings—including, for instance, Ibn Abī al-Dunyā, al-Muḥāsibī, and al-Rāghib al-Iṣfahānī—one can appreciate the complexity and value of al-Ghazālī's economic epistemology. Furthermore, Ghazanfar and Islahi's text neither positions al-Ghazālī's economic ideas in the broader context of ethical-economic thought in Islamic tradition nor places him in dialogue with modern economic theories. Addressing this omission would potentially be relevant for today's (lack of) discussions on economics, ethics, and fair conduct. As secondary literature on the historical contributions of al-Ghazālī's economic thought, I refer to Ghazanfar's book *Medieval Islamic Thought*,[16] as well as Ahmed El Ashqar and Rodney Wilson's *Islamic Economics: A Short History*.[17] For al-Ghazālī's personal and intellectual accounts, in addition to his own works, I often invoke works by Frank Griffel, Kenneth Garden, Avner Gilʻadi, Eric Ormsby, Mohamed Ahmed Sherif, Ebrahim Moosa, and M. ʻUmaruddin, to name but a few scholars. Consulting these sources, among others, allowed me to scrutinize al-Ghazālī's main ideas, terms, and theoretical premises in relation to his economic thought. Further, they helped me to see the cosmology of ethical principles and economic activities. By investigating al-Ghazālī's influence on economic teachings along with his views on

---

15 See Hallaq, *The Impossible State.*

16 S. M. Ghazanfar, *Medieval Islamic Thought: Filling the "Great Gap" in European Economics* (London: Routledge, 2003).

17 Ahmed El Ashker and Rodney Wilson, *Islamic Economics: A Short History* (Leiden: Brill, 2006).

religion, philosophy, inward mysticism, and governmental injunctions, this book aims not only to present al-Ghazālī's historical contribution and his economic philosophy but also to discuss his ethical-economic terminology and definitions related to philosophical and *ṣūfī* teachings as part of applied ethics.

Chapter 1

ABŪ ḤĀMID AL-GHAZĀLĪ

BETWEEN POLITICS, PHILOSOPHY, AND SUFISM

1.1 A Life Outspoken

This chapter begins in part with a linear examination of the events of al-Ghazālī's life that structured his ethical-economic worldview. Pinpointing some crucial moments in his life may explain how the eminent scholar came to understand the concept of divine knowledge and the political-intellectual environs in which he lived. On some level, his biography assists the reader in navigating what might appear to be contradictory views on philosophy, Sufism, and ethics, which are directly correlated to his views on economic subjectivity. In the second section of this chapter, I delve into al-Ghazālī's own intellectual-autobiographical work, focusing on how he constitutes philosophical reasoning and *ṣūfī* introspection, while in the third section, I introduce his major work *Iḥyā' 'Ulūm al-Dīn*. This monumental text is both a work of science of praxis or *'ilm al-mu'āmala* and a science of unveiling or *'ilm al-mukāshafa*, rooted in the theory of eternal happiness (*sa'āda*) and encompassing also his major ethical-economic teachings.

Abū Ḥāmid al-Ghazālī, or simply Imām al-Ghazālī, was born in AD 1058 in the town of Tābarān in Khorāsān, Persia.[1] His father was a pious man who raised him and his brother, Aḥmad; however, it was al-Juwaynī (d. 1085), his teacher—a prominent poet who mastered rhetoric in Persian and Arabic, a Sunni Shāfi'ī jurist, and a theologian—who passed his acquired knowledge on to his disciple. Al-Juwaynī was a respected authority in Islamic jurisprudence and theology who had escaped persecution under the Ash'arīte Muslims, who were officially recognized and expanded under the Saljūq Empire (1037–1194). Al-Juwaynī received a teaching position at the Niẓāmiyya *madrasa* in Nīshāpūr, where he studied Greek philosophy and its epistemological significance in

[1] All dates in this book are written according to the Gregorian calendar, indicating the abbreviation of Anno Domini.

relation to Islamic theology. By that time, Aristotelian philosophy was well known to Muslim scholars, especially to al-Farābi (d. 951) and Ibn Sīnā (d. 1037), while al-Juwaynī was the first to seriously engage Ibn Sīnā's works on the great philosopher.[2]

Al-Ghazālī's *madrasa* studies infused in him a strong desire for knowledge, and he pursued studies in Islamic sciences, including Qur'ān, *Ḥadīth*, and Islamic jurisprudence. At an early age, al-Ghazālī went to Baghdād, where he was appointed lecturer at the Niẓāmiyya School (1091), established by Saljūq vizier Niẓām al-Mulk (d. 1092). During his lifetime, al-Ghazālī went through various stages of acquiring knowledge in Islamic law, theology and philosophy, and *taṣawwuf*. Despite being a renowned scholar, he gave up his position as a lecturer at the Baghdād college and embarked on a 10-year-long journey visiting Damascus, Jerusalem, Mecca, Medina, and other cities in order to perform the pilgrimage and to achieve the "inner truth" he himself was preaching about, or at least this is what he tells his readers in his intellectual autobiography. This journey was also politically motivated and at the same time was not simply a travel expedition, but rather a quest to encounter the true meaning of knowledge and to perfect the experience of inner-worldly existence. Acquiring knowledge from diverse sources meant also acting upon it—the more al-Ghazālī immersed himself in spiritual quest, the more apparent the flaws in his knowledge became.[3]

Frank Griffel, who has made a substantial contribution by investigating al-Ghazālī's life, his theory of cosmology, and the idea of occasionalism, holds that many personal accounts of al-Ghazālī are shrouded in mystery or misconstrued. For instance, according to his biographer A'bd al-Ghāfir al-Fārīsī (d. 1134), al-Ghazālī, during his 10 years as a wandering *ṣūfī*, gave "the impression that he stopped teaching and avoided all forms of public life."[4] This, however, is incorrect. Moreover, his year of birth too is disputed. It is generally believed that al-Ghazālī was born in 1058 or 1059. This date, which most of al-Ghazālī's biographers have accepted, first appears in Ibn al-Jawzī's (d. 1200) obituary of al-Ghazālī, composed at least 60 years after al-Ghazālī's death. Ibn al-Jawzī writes that "it is said (*dhukira*) he was born in 450 A.H."[5] However, in his letter to Sanjar, the vice-regent of Khorasan, he states that at the time of writing he was 35 years old; notwithstanding the

---

[2] See Dhia' al-Dīn 'Abd al-Malik ibn Yūsufī al-Juwayni, *A Guide to the Conclusive Proofs for the Principles of Belief*, trans. Paul E. Walker (Reading, UK: Garnet, 2001); Frank Griffel, *Al-Ghazālī's Philosophical Theology* (Oxford: Oxford University Press, 2009), 29.

[3] Eric L. Ormsby, *Ghazali: The Revival of Islam* (Oxford: Oneworld, 2007), 106.

[4] Griffel, *Al-Ghazālī's Philosophical Theology*, 20. For notes on al-Ghazālī's biography, see also page 22 in Griffel and al-Ghazālī, *al-Munqidh min al-Ḍalāl* (Beirut: Dār al-Mandas, 1967).

[5] Griffel, *Al-Ghazālī's Philosophical Theology*, 23.

difference in calculating his age according to either the solar or lunar calendar, he might have been born at least a year or two earlier—that is, between 1056 and 1057.[6] Al-Ghazālī's birthplace, Tābarān, was located in the district of Ṭūs. As there is a lack of biographical information about al-Ghazālī's early life, not much can be said about his background either, apart from the fact that he and his younger brother were given over to the foster care of a *ṣūfī* friend.[7]

Al-Ghazālī lived in a time not only of political unrest but also of the increasingly developed and structurally arranged educational system of *madrasas* (Islamic educational centers), which preferred a particular version of Sunni Islam. The Saljūq Empire, which ran from Anatolia to Central Asia, united the political landscape of the Muslim lands and promoted the Turko-Persian tradition. The Saljūqs also played an important role during the First and Second Crusades and were patrons of education and literature, as well as Arabic and Persian languages. Under the Saljūq Empire, Niẓām al-Mulk created intellectual centers where Sunni jurisprudence and Ash'arīte theological thought were studied. Niẓām al-Mulk, who also founded the Niẓāmiyya *madrasa* by advocating the theological jurisprudence of Sunni Islam, eventually invited al-Ghazālī to teach at the college in Baghdād. Al-Ghazālī arrived in Baghdād from Isfahān, where he was appointed a lecturer in 1091.[8] Before al-Ghazālī left Isfahān, vizier Niẓām al-Mulk bestowed upon him the honorary title "Proof of Islam" (*hujjat al-Islām*), which has been preserved. Al-Ghazālī wrote many books before he commenced teaching at the *madrasa* in Baghdād (one of the most important being the *Incoherence of the Philosophers*); these works were issued by the caliph's court and bore the name of one of the 'Abbāsid caliphs. The time al-Ghazālī spent in Baghdād, however, was as turbulent for the empire as it was for al-Ghazālī himself. In 1092, Niẓām al-Mulk was murdered while returning from Isfahān to Baghdād. Scholars believe an Ismā'īlī adherent assassinated him. Later on, Sulṭān Malikshāh appointed Tāj al-Mulk Niẓām's successor; he was also murdered a year later, and within less than two years, the whole political apparatus of the Saljūq Empire was put to an end, causing turmoil and devastation in the provinces and bringing the dominant political and religious leadership into question.[9] In *Counsel for Kings*, a book al-Ghazālī originally wrote in Persian, he critiqued and gave advice to rulers and caliphs, despite the fact that this book was the result of a request

---

[6] Al-Ghazālī, *Letters of al-Ghazali*, trans. Abdul Qayyum (New Delhi: Kitab Bhavan, 1992), 20–23; Griffel, *Al-Ghazālī's Philosophical Theology*, 23.

[7] See al-Subkī, *Ṭabaqāt* and al-Isnawī, *Tabaqāt*, in Griffel, *Al-Ghazālī's Philosophical Theology*, 26.

[8] Griffel, *Al-Ghazālī's Philosophical Theology*, 32.

[9] See Juwaynī, *Tarīkh Jahāngushāy* in Griffel, *Al-Ghazālī's Philosophical Theology*, 36.

made by Sanjar, the vice-regent of Khorāsān.[10] Griffel notes that even before the assassination of vizier Niẓām al-Mulk, the Ismāʿīlī Shiite movement had broken its political agreements with the Fāṭimid Empire, whose seat was in Cairo, and managed to seize control in Iran. In 1090, its stronghold moved to Alamūt in the northern province of Iran, which was led by famous chieftain Ḥasan ibn al-Sabbāh (d. 1124).[11]

Al-Ghazālī became acquainted with the teachings of al-Juwaynī and the refutation of the philosophers' claim that the world is eternal; yet despite his disputes with Ibn Sīnā about philosophy, he was to an extent influenced by Ibn Sīnā's notion of "necessary being" (*wājib al-wujūd*) and "dependent or contingent being" (*mumkin al-wujūd*).[12] After acquiring knowledge from various sciences, he asserted that divine truth can be obtained by following four paths: the tradition of theological discourse or *kalām*, rational inquiry or *falsafa*, the *imām* and the Ismāʿīlī doctrine, and the mystical path of the *ṣūfīs*.[13] Al-Ghazālī departed from all four pathways, but he resorted to many of their methodological and conceptual elements and gradually accepted the teachings of *taṣawwuf*.[14] This is narrated only in his intellectual autobiography. Al-Ghazālī studied not only the works of his teacher al-Juwaynī but also the writings of important *ṣūfīs* such as al-Ḥārith al-Muḥāsibi (d. 857), Abū Yazīd al-Bisṭāmī (d. 874), al-Junayd (d. 910), al-Shiblī (d. 946), Abū Ṭālib al-Makkī (d. 996), and al-Rāghib al-Iṣfahānī (d. 1109), learning about the tradition of *taṣawwuf* and the spiritual stations of *maqāmāt*. Even though he remained a firm believer in the Day of Judgment and engaged with various Islamic sciences, he also nurtured a desire for questioning those very sciences as part of his inner journey of leaving behind riches and attaining what he referred to as spiritual knowledge.[15] Many figures in human history have experienced a similar existential crisis; however, what sets al-Ghazālī apart is perhaps the outcome of his spiritual venture, due to which he not only became more involved in the tradition of *taṣawwuf* but also produced some of the greatest works in Islamic intellectual history.[16] The fact that al-Ghazālī was himself from Khorāsān by descent, came to teach at

---

[10] Griffel, *Al-Ghazālī's Philosophical Theology*, 39.

[11] On the historical accounts of the stronghold of Alamut and the development of the character of Ḥasan ibn al-Sabbāh, see also the novel *Alamut*, written by Slovene author Vladimir Bartol (d. 1967). Vladimir Bartol, *Alamut* (Ljubljana: Sanje, 2001).

[12] Griffel, *Al-Ghazālī's Philosophical Theology*, 32.

[13] See al-Ghazālī, *Munqidh*, 10–11; al-Ghazālī, *The Faith and Practice of al-Ghazālī* (*Deliverance from Error*), trans. Montgomery Watt (London: G. Allen and Unwin, 1967), 26.

[14] For more on al-Ghazālī's *ṣūfī* view, see, e.g., Margaret Smith, *Al-Ghazālī: The Mystic* (Lahore: Hijra International Publishers, 1983).

[15] Al-Ghazālī, *Munqidh*, 56.

[16] See al-Ghazālī's encyclopedic work *Iḥyā' Ulūm al-Dīn* (Beirut: Dār al-Maʿrifa, 1982). Griffel notes *tawba* or public repentance is one of the most important notions in *ṣūfī*

the famous Baghdād college under the Saljūq rulership, and was a recognized theologian who ultimately accepted the teachings of Sufism while resorting to philosophical methodology indicates how intertwined intellectual and political life were in the twelfth century and points to al-Ghazālī's quest to surpass religious affiliations in order to devote himself to the pursuit of eternal happiness based upon ethical psychology and the teachings of *taṣawwuf*. He confesses he was caught in the throes of worldly pleasures for not seeing the higher causes of the knowledge he acquired, and, as a consequence of that, for living behind the veil of such personal convictions. Thus, he sets about rectifying his own shortcomings:

> Next I considered the circumstances of my life, and realized that I was caught in a veritable thicket of attachments. I also considered my activities of which the best was my teaching and lecturing, and realized that in them I was dealing with sciences that were unimportant and contributed nothing to the attainment of eternal life. After that I examined my motive in my work of teaching, and realized that it was not pure desire for the things of God, but that the impulse moving me was the desire for an influential position and public recognition. I was for certain that I was on the brink of a crumbling bank of sand and in imminent danger of hell-fire unless I set about to mend my ways.[17]

For more than half a year in 1095, al-Ghazālī was perplexed about and struggled with the desires of the mundane while pondering the stipulations of the hereafter. Allegedly, he could not utter a single word and thus abstained from lecturing. This inner crisis led him to leave his prestigious position at the Niẓāmiyya *madrasa* in Baghdād, where he had taught for three consecutive years following his appointment by Niẓām al-Mulk. Amidst his spiritual crisis and the various rumors about his condition that were spreading in Baghdād, he managed to take upon himself a great task and embark on a journey that would transform his perception of the phenomenal world. He snuck out of Baghdād under the pretext of performing the Hajj pilgrimage, since this was the only way deemed justifiable by the political and religious authorities. What followed was a significant personal account of a mystical experience, which is why the style of *Munqidh*—which ought not to be perceived only as a personal narrative but also as al-Ghazālī's own intellectual and spiritual conviction—falls between health and malady, ignorance and knowledge, error and truth,

---

and theological literature, which made al-Ghazālī distance himself from the political authorities of the empire in 1095. See Griffel, *Al-Ghazālī's Philosophical Theology*, 43.

17 Al-Ghazālī, *Deliverance*, 56.

and above all, between skepticism and certainty, and this further led him to discoveries of the heart and emotional intelligence.[18] He dispersed the wealth he possessed and kept only the basic necessities for himself, despite the prominent position he used to occupy.[19] While Omid Safi claims al-Ghazālī's account about his spiritual voyage has to be read with great skepticism, he also suggests it was more about Niẓām al-Mulk's state apparatuses and the notion of surveillance that al-Ghazālī tried to escape rather than about strictly spiritual or political issues.[20] While all of these reasons are valid in justifying al-Ghazālī's journey, it seems they are interrelated and hence cannot be read completely separately. At the same time, whether al-Ghazālī's decision was first and foremost political or existential in nature, it was nonetheless a legitimate cause for him to depart from Baghdād because of his genuine dissatisfaction with both his personal involvement with the Saljūq administrators and the overall political atmosphere in the city, which went against his conviction about leading an ethically engaged life. Denying al-Ghazālī's account by disputing the length of his stay in Damascus or Jerusalem would also mean denying the thirst for knowledge that motivated him to examine various predicaments of the heart (*qalb*) as a path for achieving eternal happiness.

Contemporary Palestinian author A'bd al-Laṭīf Ṭībāwī believed al-Ghazālī traveled to Damascus since he was attracted to the ideas of famous *ṣūfī* and Shāfi'ī scholar Abū al-Fath Naṣr ibn Ibrāhīm al-Maqdisī.[21] After his inner crisis, al-Ghazālī entered Damascus, where he allegedly remained for nearly two years "with no other occupation than the cultivation of retirement and solitude, together with religious and ascetic exercises, as I busied myself purifying my soul, improving my character and cleansing my heart for the constant recollection of God most high, as I had learnt from my study of mysticism."[22]

Also in Damascus, in the Umayyad mosque, al-Ghazālī attracted many students to his lessons as he read from the *Iḥyā'*. He apparently resided in the room of the minaret, a dwelling place for *ṣūfīs* of the time, as reported by Ibn Jubayr (d. 1217).[23] After half a year, al-Ghazālī left Damascus for Jerusalem,

---

[18] Eric L. Ormsby, "The Taste of Truth: The Structure of Experience in al-Ghazali's Munqidh min al-dalal," in *Islamic Studies Presented to Charles J. Adams*, ed. Wael B. Hallaq and Donald P. Little (Leiden: Brill, 1991), 131–52 at 135; al-Ghazālī, *Munqidh*, 133.

[19] "Nowhere in the world have I seen better financial arrangements to assist a scholar to provide for his children [than in Baghdad]." Al-Ghazālī, *Deliverance*, 59.

[20] Omid Safi, *The Politics of Knowledge in Premodern Islam* (Chapel Hill: University of North Carolina Press, 2006), 107–10.

[21] See Ibn 'Asākir, *Tabyīn*; al-Subkī, *Ṭabaqāt*; and al-U'laymī, al-Uns al-Jalīl, in Griffel, *Al-Ghazālī's Philosophical Theology*, 43.

[22] Al-Ghazālī, *Deliverance*, 59.

[23] See reference 177 in Griffel, *Al-Ghazālī's Philosophical Theology*, 44.

arriving there in 1096, where he published a short excerpt, *Letter of Jerusalem* (*al-Risāla al-Qudsiyya*), that would later become part of the *Iḥyā'*, intended not only for scholars but also for laics.[24] The works he produced in this period were radically different from his earlier texts.[25] While his early works predominantly addressed theological and philosophical issues, his later oeuvre included *Iḥyā'*, one of his most important works, seen as an amalgamation of philosophical and *ṣūfī* teachings. This encyclopedic volume brought him the title *mujaddid al-dīn* ("renewer of faith"),[26] a title by which later generations called him.[27] Having acquired such a title does not mean that he debunked authoritative texts, as there is ample evidence of al-Ghazālī relying on many prevalent legal and theological postulates,[28] but rather that he aimed at questioning the very foundations of authority as such.

After a journey more than a decade long, during which he revamped *ṣūfī* teachings and also examined his inner doubts and beliefs, he finally came back to his birth town of Ṭūs, where his family was waiting for him. Whatever the political reason for his departure, partial seclusion and purification of the heart and body (*tazkiyya*) by means of the remembrance of God (*dhikr*) in order to disseminate acquired knowledge is the path al-Ghazālī chose out of his thirst for knowledge and dissatisfaction with the religious scholars of the day, who were supposed to guard it. During his partial seclusion, al-Ghazālī continued to teach and disseminate knowledge on what he called the science of the hereafter, in whose core was a transformational religious doctrine of ethical dimensions. He did not completely retreat from public life, but avoided consorting with public officials and rulers, as he noted in his correspondence with Sanjar in 1108.[29] Al-Ghazālī had a good reason for this: not only would he perhaps have been brought in for questioning for leaving his position in Baghdād but he also feared his views might be opposed and repudiated. In 1108, he was indeed accused of disbelief by the representatives of the Sunni jurists in Khorāsān, for he supposedly adhered to the teachings of philosophers and Zoroastrians.[30] He had also previously engaged with political disputes with the Ḥanafī school, despite the fact that Sanjar himself was a Ḥanafī.

---

[24] Al-Ghazālī, *Iḥyā'*, Vol. 2, book 3; Griffel, *Al-Ghazālī's Philosophical Theology*, 45.

[25] Ormsby, "The Taste of Truth," 134.

[26] Al-Ghazālī, *Deliverance*, 14–15; al-Ghazālī, *Munqidh*, 49.

[27] See Eric L. Ormsby, *Theodicy in Islamic Thought: The Dispute over Al-Ghazali's "Best of All Possible Worlds"* (Princeton, NJ: Princeton University Press, 1984).

[28] Ormsby, "The Taste of Truth," 136.

[29] For al-Ghazālī's *Faẓāil al-anām* and the translation of his correspondence, see al-Ghazālī, *Letters of al-Ghazali*; al-Ghazālī, *Briefe und Reden des Abu Hamid Muhammad al-Gazzali*, trans. Dorothea Krawulsky (Freiburg im Breisgau: K. Schwarz, 1971).

[30] Al-Ghazālī, *Faẓāil al-anām* in Griffel, *Al-Ghazālī's Philosophical Theology*, 54.

Sanjar nonetheless agreed to build a *madrasa* for al-Ghazālī and refused to strip him of his teaching position.

For some Muslim intellectuals, the Prophet Muḥammad was a spiritual figure and a social and political leader of the first Muslim community. His time in the Ḥirā' cave, where the first verses of the Qur'ān were allegedly revealed to him, including the Meccan life, constitute the so-called spiritual period, while his time in Medina, where a set of social and juridical rules were introduced, points to the social and political struggles in an urban setting.[31] The proponents of such views associate the Prophet Muḥammad's spiritual quest with the inwardness of Sufism. They also defend the idea that Sufism equally pertains to spiritual retreat and an engaged social life. Even though al-Ghazālī merged various teachings and methodologies into the theory of eternal happiness, a rather dynamic amalgamation of engagement in worldly affairs and an ascetic renunciation of mundane life is also evident in his economic writings, which advocate a righteous earning as part of one's devotional praxis. While al-Ghazālī was politically involved with Abbāsids and Saljūqs, as an adherent of *taṣawwuf*, he was also compelled to abstain from worldly endeavors in order to devote himself to religious knowledge. This, however, did not deter him from completely renouncing his teaching obligations and political involvement—rather the opposite. In order to "revive" the religious sciences of the past, he had no choice but to engage in intellectual and political life. Al-Ghazālī's decade-long spiritual journey influenced his understanding of various Islamic sciences, including *taṣawwuf*, which in turn became visible in his writings. The "early" al-Ghazālī aimed at mastering the knowledge of normative Sunni Islam. In *Al-Munqidh min al-Ḍalāl*, he explains four types of knowledge—namely philosophy, that is, ratio, utilized by scientists; theology, which is a combination of ratio and revelation; esotericism, the claim that special knowledge is reserved only for some individuals whom we have to follow; and *taṣawwuf*, that is, knowledge of experience where faith interacts with action.[32] After his spiritual voyage, however, al-Ghazālī experienced a resurgence that granted him the title *mujaddid* or *muḥyī al-dīn*.[33] Al-Ghazālī was not content with gaining knowledge for its own sake, but rather he envisioned knowledge in the service of spiritual devotion in order to revive the tradition, while he labeled ignorance a matter of spiritual deprivation or ailment.[34]

---

[31] Alija Izetbegović, *Moj bijeg u slobodu* (*My Escape into Freedom*) (Sarajevo: Izbrana djela, OKO, 2003), 236–37.

[32] See al-Ghazālī, *Munqidh*.

[33] Al-Ghazālī, *Munqidh*, 49; Griffel, *Al-Ghazālī's Philosophical Theology*, 25, 75.

[34] Al-Ghazālī, *Deliverance*, 6, 88, 89.

The time of al-Ghazālī witnessed the decline of the caliphate and Muslim scholars' growing preoccupation with philosophy, while economic thought was overshadowed by the study of other disciplines.[35] Although political and religious factions were to an extent linked to military power, they generated diverse cultural movements together with scientists and *'ulamā'*.[36] Economic concerns in the eleventh century often engaged social and political questions. Yet, the intellectual diversity of the time was also centered on the critique of Greek philosophy and the development of Islamic legal philosophy, despite the fact that the political decline of the caliphate had led to a limited attention and support of that critique.[37] Al-Ghazālī's writings on economic philosophy can also be perceived as presenting an ideal economic system and a subtle critique of religious and political authorities. Al-Ghazālī's contribution to the field of ethical economics is hence valuable and remains an impetus for further development of economic thought, not least because he challenged the environment of his time. His approach asserts that externalities or materiality in economics—transactions, commodities, barter exchange, and so forth—overlap not only with juridical and theological stipulations but also with ethical ones. The introduction of moral economic thought by classical Muslim scholars is a necessary mechanism for licit conduct in order to, at least in theory, avoid economic disturbances and social upheavals in the service of higher moral objectives.

Al-Ghazālī contested orthodox theology and those in favor of *taqlīd* (blindly following certain dogmas). By examining various branches of tradition, he detested the sectarian mind, for he was convinced sectarianism is based on a lack of understanding of the phenomenal world and the knowledge thereof, by examining various branches of tradition. A great deal of the knowledge he discussed in his works is based upon the outcomes of what he deems scientific observation embedded in virtuous traits of character and hence linked to what we would nowadays call spiritual or ethical psychology. According to al-Ghazālī, one needs a guide for a journey toward inwardness, and because he underwent a spiritual crisis, he set out on a quest to discern essential knowledge that would bring him closer to a higher or divine order. Such a path entails not only practical aspects of religious obligations but first and foremost a moral orientation that includes economic behavior as part of one's *'ibādāt*. He exhausted himself due to the belief that the knowledge he possessed was not genuine and thus void. The wisdom that the pen is mighty but the tongue is mightier led him to keep quiet and turn toward self-examination. This crisis

35 Ashker and Wilson, *Islamic Economics*, 222.
36 Ashker and Wilson, *Islamic Economics*, 230.
37 Ashker and Wilson, *Islamic Economics*, 231–32.

was his second after the long state of doubt in his youth. This uncertainty led al-Ghazālī to question the role of the senses, scrutinize the channels of knowledge, and track the revealed knowledge that sometimes ended up in "epistemological vertigo."[38] He challenged unreflective acceptance of the knowledge afforded by the senses, and immersed himself in retreat to reach beyond what is believed to be the certainty of knowledge. After years in partial seclusion, he returned to Khorāsān, rejecting state officials but continuing to teach in private schools.[39] Before his death, he quit teaching in Nīshāpūr and returned to his birth town of Ṭūs, where he passed away on December 18, 1111.

Al-Ghazālī's literary legacy covers the fields of theology, jurisprudence, logic, philosophy, and *taṣawwuf.* His more important works include *Iḥyā' 'Ulūm al-Dīn* (*The Revival of Religious Sciences*), which is regarded as his most revered book, and which also focuses on ethics and economic conduct. *Iḥyā'*, discussed in detail later, covers all aspects of human life within an ethical framework; *Al-Mustaṣfā fi 'Ilm al-Uṣūl* (On Legal theory of Muslim Jurisprudence), a text discussing Islamic jurisprudence and theology, written towards the end of his life; *Bidāyat al-hidāyah* (*The Beginning of Guidance*) serves as an introduction to *Iḥyā'*.[40] The text addresses the ways and means of the purification of the heart and directs the reader to the larger corpus of al-Ghazālī's works. His other major works include *Al-Iqtiṣād fi'l I'tiqād* (*Moderation in Belief*), a book on Islamic theology; *Mīzān al-'amal* (*The Criterion of Action*), a text on ethics; *Al-Munqidh min al-Ḍalāl* (*Deliverance from Error*), an intellectual autobiography explaining his personal account and religious thought; *Tahāfut al-falāsifa* (*The Incoherence of the Philosophers*), a book denouncing Muslim philosophers such as al-Fārābī and Ibn Sīnā, since in al-Ghazālī's view they followed Greek philosophy and at times contradicted basic Islam tenets; and *Kitāb Naṣīḥat al-Mulūk* (*Book of Counsel for Kings*), a manual for rulers outlining just political conduct, originally written in Persian, in which al-Ghazālī discusses recommendations for Islamic rulers on how to reign justly and treat subjects on a fair basis, including economic conduct. Examples addressing many different topics are culled from various historical sources—the Prophet of Islam, the Bible, and the Torah, as well as other Islamic and even Roman and Chinese sources.[41]

Numerous books of al-Ghazālī have been translated into Western languages and scholars have written many theses on his scholarship, yet researchers

---

[38] Ormsby, "The Taste of Truth," 135; al-Ghazālī, *Munqidh*, 13.

[39] Griffel, *Al-Ghazālī's Philosophical Theology*, 49.

[40] Ashker and Wilson, *Islamic Economics*, 246.

[41] See al-Ghazālī, *Counsel for Kings*, trans. F. R. C. Bagley (London: Oxford University Press, 1964); Mohammad Ghazanfar, *Medieval Islamic Thought: Filling the "Great Gap" in European Economics* (London: Routledge, 2003), 38.

have made very few inquiries into his ethical-economic thought and have not carried out thorough investigations into the interplay between his personal life and economic views.[42] Al-Ghazālī was already well known to medieval Christian scholars and highly regarded as a philosopher, theologian, and *ṣūfī*. He maneuvered between different realms and sought to master various disciplines, not only to prove their adherents wrong but also to elevate his own understanding of the external world and to exercise the wisdom he preached for the sake of attaining the divine truth. One of these accounts can be found in his intellectual autobiography.

1.2 *Munqidh min al-Ḍalāl* and the Critique of the Self

Munqidh min al-Ḍalāl is important for our discussion because it informs us about al-Ghazālī's inner crisis, his perspectives on philosophical thought, and why he accepted the teachings of Sufism, whose ethics had repercussions also for his burgeoning economic thought. *Munqidh*, which is al-Ghazālī's later work, discusses these and other topics in retrospect after al-Ghazālī came back to his birth town, pinpointing epistemological differences with his other works. Al-Ghazālī informs us that by confronting various religious sects and engaging in theological debates, he aimed to reach beyond the religious and political confinements of his time. In his autobiographical yet profoundly intellectual work, in which he explains his position on theological, philosophical, and mystical vistas, he writes:

> From my early youth, since I attained the age of puberty before I was twenty, until the present time when I am over fifty, I have ever recklessly launched out into the midst of these ocean depths, I have ever bravely embarked on this open sea, throwing aside all craven caution; I have poked into every dark recess, I have made an assault on every problem, I have plunged into every abyss, I have scrutinized the creed of every sect, I have tried to lay bare the inmost doctrines of every community. All this have I done that I might distinguish between true and false, between sound tradition and heretical innovation. Whenever I meet one

[42] For more on al-Ghazālī's biography and on his thought, see some of the selected works: Mustafa Abū-Sway, *Al-Ġazālī: A Study in Islamic Epistemology* (Kuala Lumpur: Dewan Bahasa dan Pustaka, 1996); Malik Badri, *Contemplation: An Islamic Psychospiritual Study* (London: Human Behaviour Academy, 2000); Griffel, *Al-Ghazālī's Philosophical Theology*; Ormsby, *Ghazali*, and so forth. On his economic thought, see, e.g., Ghazanfar and Islahi, *Economic Thought of al-Ghazali*; Setia, "Al-Ghazālī on the Proprieties of Earning and Living."

of the Bāṭinīyah, I like to study his creed; whenever I meet one of the Ẓāhirīyah, I want to know the essentials of his belief. If it is a philosopher, I try to become acquainted with the essence of his philosophy; if [it is] a scholastic theologian[,] I busy myself in examining his theological reasoning; if [it is] a Sufi, I yearn to fathom the secret of his mysticism; if [it is] an ascetic (*muta'abbid*), I investigate the basis of his ascetic practices; if [it is] one of the Zanādiqah or Mu'aṭṭilah, I look beneath the surface to discover the reasons for his bold adoption of such a creed.[43]

As al-Ghazālī observes in *Munqidh*, attaining justice in scholarly debates and also by leading life accordingly was becoming a rare endeavor during the tumultuous times in the empire. The inner necessity to advance the practical aspects of his ethics of happiness made al-Ghazālī embark on his journey toward personal revelation, aligned also with political developments in Baghdād, which became not only an indispensable tool for delving deeper into mystical exploration but also a virtuous ethic concerning one's character, deeds, and the very preservation of the self:

I therefore said within myself: "To begin with, what I am looking for is knowledge of what things really are, so I must undoubtedly try to find what knowledge really is." It was plain to me that sure and certain knowledge is that knowledge in which the object is disclosed in such a fashion that no doubt remains along with it, that no possibility of error or illusion accompanies it, and that the mind cannot even entertain such a supposition. Certain knowledge must also be infallible; and this infallibility or security from error is such that no attempt to show the falsity of the knowledge can occasion doubt or denial, even though the attempt is made by someone who turns stones into gold or a rod into a serpent. Thus, I know that ten is more than three.[44]

Al-Ghazālī's *Munqidh*, which is an account of his theological, philosophical, and *ṣūfī* beliefs, is also an important source of information about his private intellectual life. It is a rather unusual autobiographical text, since he discusses philosophical and theological disputations with some of the Islamic philosophers (*falāsifa*) and the reasons for his spiritual crisis. In *Munqidh*, al-Ghazālī presents the reasons for his intellectual and inner growth and his

[43] Al-Ghazālī, *Deliverance*, 20–21.
[44] Al-Ghazālī, *Deliverance*, 21–22.

argumentations for defending a spiritual practice in Islamic tradition, instead of a purely rational thought.

In this regard, it is important to note that al-Ghazālī based his worldview not exclusively on rational argumentation, since he rendered sensual perceptions inadequate.[45] His endeavors in the *ṣūfī* tradition shaped his scholarly path also in retrospect—that is, al-Ghazālī as a *ṣūfī* did not cease to be a jurist, a philosopher, or a theologian. Despite the admiration he had for Islamic theology, he found it void since it did not satisfy his inner need to observe a life of higher aims. As for philosophy, al-Ghazālī was mostly concerned with "theistic" philosophers such as al-Farābi and Ibn Sīnā (Avicenna).[46] These philosophers based their teachings on Neoplatonism and adapted them to the teachings of Islamic monotheism (*tawḥīd*). Many views were incorporated into the Islamic corpus; others, due to their contradiction of Islamic principles, were rejected. Al-Ghazālī's contribution to philosophy was mastering Aristotelian logic and incorporating it into Islamic theology in order to expose the logical inconsistencies of their philosophy.[47] Likewise, he opposed authorities or scholars who held fast to the idea that truth is to be attained by the infallibility of an *imām* or a spiritual leader.

The second theme of *Munqidh* is interrelated with the aforementioned quest for meaning and pertains to al-Ghazālī's analysis of knowledge, which, once attained in its final stage, does not differentiate *'ilm* from *'amal* (knowledge and deed).[48] Knowledge, however, was for al-Ghazālī easier to gain than to convert into practice. Ormsby notes that al-Ghazālī's second crisis, the one that made him depart from his position in Baghdād, was not due to doubt but rather truth,[49] for the knowledge he possessed thus far enabled him to relinquish the study of some sciences in order to reach for higher levels of attainment.[50] In other words, intellectual satisfaction, despite its importance, did not suffice for the goal he was determined to pursue, therefore concepts such as *tazkiyya* (purification of the heart), *zuhd* (renunciation of pleasures), *dhawq* (taste), and *tawakkul* (trust in God), are central terms in his *ṣūfī* epistemology, consolidating the faculty of reason with the mystical experience in an effort to elevate oneself above the confinements of the mundane world and develop an ethical

[45] See Timothy J. Gianotti, *Al-Ghazali's Unspeakable Doctrine of the Soul: Unveiling the Esoteric Psychology and Eschatology of the Ihya'* (Leiden: Brill's Studies in Intellectual History, Book 104, 2001).

[46] Al-Ghazālī, *Deliverance*, 32. For more on Islamic philosophy, see Majid Fakhry, *A History of Islamic Philosophy* (New York: Columbia University Press, 2004).

[47] Al-Ghazālī, *Deliverance*, 29–30.

[48] Ormsby, "The Taste of Truth," 138–39. See also al-Ghazālī, *Deliverance*, 45.

[49] Al-Ghazālī, *Deliverance*, 45.

[50] Al-Ghazālī, *Deliverance*, 45; al-Ghazālī, *Munqidh*, 35.

concept of infinity. Hence, *tasting* relates directly to weaving knowledge into practice.[51]

The autobiographical information in *Munqidh* is rather little in comparison to the more theoretical-spiritual development of al-Ghazālī's thought, which is the main theme of the book. Al-Ghazālī predominantly aimed to examine the principles of the a priori truths related to his inquiry into the power of doubt.[52] He pondered the nature of sensual comprehension, claiming that the perception of the intellect is also arbitrary and can thus be proven wrong through its own judgment. Since Islamic theology (*kalām*) could not provide all the answers to quench his thirst for truth, he believed, his own feelings of lassitude and mediocrity desperately needed to be revived.

Many works have been written on the contribution of al-Ghazālī's thoughts on and criticism of philosophy.[53] His *Tahāfut al-falāsifa* (*The Incoherence of the Philosophers*)—not *Incoherence of Philosophy*—presents a breaking point in classical Islamic philosophy, adding to the Neoplatonic comprehension of Aristotelian philosophy, as it was challenged only from the fourteenth century onward in a movement commonly known as nominalism.[54] In al-Ghazālī's other book, *Maqāṣid al-Falāsifa* (*Intentions of the Philosophers*), he tackles the notions of logic, metaphysics, and the natural sciences in Avicenna's works.[55] For al-Ghazālī, *The Incoherence* presented a way of refuting philosophers' ideas, insofar as they were misperceptions of the teachings of Aristotle. He aims at more than simply rejecting their ideas, as he simultaneously develops his own teachings and discusses them in detail. The gist of the critique, however, is disputing the philosophers' claims, not their findings.[56] Since human knowledge about God is limited, philosophers are in error when invoking His name, as their reasons for the existence of souls in the hereafter are not compatible with the teachings of Islamic tradition. An accompanying claim some philosophers put forward is their denial of the revelation; their method had never been thoroughly questioned, as the philosophers simply inherited their arguments

---

51 Al-Ghazālī, *Deliverance*, 55; al-Ghazālī, *Munqidh*, 36, 40–45; Ormsby, "The Taste of Truth," 140–41.

52 Ormsby, "The Taste of Truth," 135.

53 See, e.g., ʿAlī Muḥī al-Dīn al-Qaradaghi, "ʿAṣr al-Ghazālī," in *al-Waṣīt fī al-mathhab*, ed. Abū Ḥāmid al-Ghazālī, 21–293 (Cairo: Dār al-Anṣār, 1983); Montgomery Watt, *Muslim Intellectual: A Study of al-Ghazali* (Edinburgh: Edinburgh University Press, 1963).

54 "Nominalism is the position that abstract concepts and universals have no independent existence on their own." Griffel, *Al-Ghazālī's Philosophical Theology*, 97.

55 See al-Ghazālī, *Tahāfut al-Falāsifa*, ed. Sulyman Dunya (Cairo: Dār al-Marifa, n.d.).

56 See al-Ghazālī, *Munqidh*; Al-Ghazālī, *Maqāṣid al-Falāsifa*: *fī al-Manṭiq wa-al-Ḥikmah al-Ilahiyah wa-al-Ḥikmah al-Ṭabīʿiyah* (Cairo: al-Matbaʿah al-Mahmudiyah al-Tijariyah bi al-Azhar, 1936); Griffel, *Al-Ghazālī's Philosophical Theology*, 98.

from earlier thinkers. Al-Ghazālī accepts "the truth of the *falāsifa*'s teaching but rejects their claim to knowing it through demonstration," as proof of truth for him is obtained through revelation; however, the philosophers had simply excerpted some of their findings for the sake of their own argumentation.[57] In *Munqidh*, al-Ghazālī writes:

> They are unable to satisfy the conditions of proof they lay down in logic, and consequently differ much from one another here. The views of Aristotle, as expounded by al-Fārābī and Ibn Sinā, are close to those of the Islamic writers. All their errors are comprised under twenty heads, on three of which they must be reckoned infidels and on seventeen heretics. It was to show the falsity of their views on these twenty points that I composed *The Incoherence of the Philosophers*. The three points in which they differ from all the Muslims are as follows: a) They say that for bodies there is no resurrection; it is bare spirits which are rewarded or punished; and the rewards and punishments are spiritual, not bodily. They certainly speak truth in affirming the spiritual ones, since these do exist as well; but they speak falsely in denying the bodily ones and in their pronouncements disbelieve the Divine law. b) They say that God knows universals but not particulars. This too is plain unbelief. The truth is that "there does not escape Him the weight of an atom in the heavens or in the earth" (Q. 34:3). c) They say that the world is everlasting, without beginning or end. But no Muslim has adopted any such view on this question.[58]

Al-Ghazālī regarded some of the philosophers' positions as inadequate in that they omitted the theological significance of Islamic belief. In comparing the philosophers and the Mu'tazilites, al-Ghazālī concluded that the two bear resemblances. This, however, does not mean that both movements can be in Ghazālī's view deemed unbelievers, but rather that they resorted to some extent to innovation or *bida'*.[59] Al-Ghazālī aimed to be considerate in not accusing any group of disbelief, as long as it did not oppose or contradict the basic Islamic teachings and the scriptural sources.[60] In relation to the notion of the five stages of being, al-Ghazālī states as follows:

---

[57] Griffel, *Al-Ghazālī's Philosophical Theology*, 100.

[58] Al-Ghazālī, *Deliverance*, 37.

[59] Griffel, *Al-Ghazālī's Philosophical Theology*, 103.

[60] According to al-Ash'arī, a righteous Muslim, for instance, does not only believe in the divine law but also accepts the Prophet's Sunna. See Griffel, *Über Rechtgläubigkeit und religiöse Toleranz. Eine Übersetzung der Schrift Das Kriterium der Unterscheidung zwischen*

> The literal meaning (*ẓāhir*) that comes first is the true being (*al-wujūd al-dhātī*). Once confirmed, it includes all other beings. If, however, it is nullified, then the sensual being is enacted (*al-wujūd al-ḥissī*). If it is confirmed, it includes that which comes after it. If nullified, then the imaginative being (*al-wujūd al-khayālī*) is enacted, or the rational (*'aqlī*). If nullified, the similar being (*al-wujūd al-shibhī*) is enacted, which is metaphorical.[61]

The philosophers, in al-Ghazālī's view, aimed to undermine revelation by extrapolating their conviction about their own intelligence. Mu'tazilites, however, argued humans have free choice (*ikhtiyār*) and ought to utilize their own intellect in order to make theological decisions too.

Al-Ghazālī positioned the subjects of his critique into four categories: theologians or *mutakallimūn* follow intellectual speculation; *baṭinīyyah* follow "authoritative instruction" (*ta'lim*) and believe they derive truth from the *imām*'s infallibility; *philosophers* or Neoplatonists are the exponents of logical argumentation; and *ṣūfīs* claim that only they were part of God's presence and thus possess intuitive understanding.[62] Despite the fact that al-Ghazālī considered *kalām* or Islamic theology a science, it was nonetheless inadequate for him, since "its aim was merely to preserve the creed of orthodoxy and to defend it against the deviations of heretics. Theology was not adequate to my case and was unable to cure the malady of which I complained."[63] Al-Ghazālī turned to philosophy after he had acquired various trends within theology. Due to doubts in established systems of belief closely related to his existential crisis, he intended to scrutinize every norm of knowledge so that he would form an understanding of the issue at stake:

> I was convinced that a man cannot grasp what is defective in any of the sciences unless he has so complete a grasp of the science in question that he equals its most learned exponents in the appreciation of its fundamental principles, and even goes beyond and surpasses them, probing into some of the tangles and profundities which the very professors of the science have neglected. In their writings none of the theologians engaged in polemic against the philosophers. […] I realized that to

---

Islam und Gottlosigkeit (*Fayṣal at-tafriqa bayna l-Islam wa-z- zandaqa*), trans by Frank Griffel (Zurich: Spur Verlag, 1998)..

61 See al-Ghazālī, *Fayṣal al-Tafriqa*, ed. Maḥmūd Bījū (Damascus: Maḥmūd Bījū, 1993), 47.

62 Al-Ghazālī, *Deliverance*, 27.

63 Al-Ghazālī, *Deliverance*, 27.

> refute a system before understanding it and becoming acquainted with its depths is to act blindly.[64]

As for the schools of philosophers, al-Ghazālī divided them into three categories: the materialist or *dahriyūn* deny the Creator and the Day of Reckoning, since they consider the world everlasting on its own; the naturalists or *ṭabi'yūn* engage in research into nature, animals, and plants. They do affirm God's creation; however, to al-Ghazālī, these are irreligious people since they do not believe in the Last Day. The final group is the theists or *ilahiyūn*—that is, philosophers such as Socrates, Plato, Aristotle, and so on, who introduced logic into the field of philosophy, but their theory bears many flaws. Islamic philosophers such as Ibn Sīnā, al-Farābi, and others had followed their path or incorporated some of their ideas and teachings.[65]

Al-Ghazālī also considered six philosophical sciences—mathematics, logic, natural science, theology, politics, and ethics.[66] Despite his recognition of various and at times opposing philosophical and theological arguments on the existence of God and the divine law, he contested ignorance and blind imitation. The science of theology or metaphysics is the field that most of the philosophers comprehended incorrectly, since, according to al-Ghazālī, they were unable to reconcile their logic with Islamic theological teachings. This is indicated in three points; the philosophers' claim that bodies undergo no resurrection and that rewards and punishments are spiritual and not bodily; that God knows universals but not particularities; and that the world is eternal and not contingent.[67] Al-Ghazālī stated everyone who follows legal matters according to a certain authority belongs to the Ḥanafi or Shāfi'ī school of law. But even if legal certainty is provided, many questions on the nature of existence itself remain unanswered. Hence al-Ghazālī asks:

> "What does such a man do in the question of the *qiblah* where there is dubiety and the independently judging authorities differ?" My opponent will say: "The man must use his own judgement to decide which is the soundest authority and the most learned in the proofs of the *qiblah*, and then he *follows* his own decision." Exactly the same happens in deciding between religious systems (and so the principle of "authoritative instruction" is admitted to be inadequate).[68]

---

[64] Al-Ghazālī, *Deliverance*, 29.
[65] Al-Ghazālī, *Deliverance*, 32.
[66] Al-Ghazālī, *Deliverance*, 33–43.
[67] Compare with the Qur'ān 34:3.
[68] Al-Ghazālī, *Deliverance*, 48.

According to al-Ghazālī, who concerned himself with rational theology, the revelation is of high importance.[69] He believed whenever possible scholars should seek to understand its literal meaning. If unsuccessful, then one should resort to metaphorical meaning (*bāṭin*) or try to perceive it according to the teachings of the Prophet. The last resort would be imaginative perception.[70] On other occasions, he contended against the use of personal opinion (*ra'y*) and analogy in legal matters (*qiyās*) as elements of truth.[71] Since faith or personal belief surpasses pure knowledge, scholars also have to resort to their opinions and not only to *taqlīd*, because it cannot be verified or scrutinized easily. As a consequence of such reasoning, uncertainty might arise.[72]

Kojiro Nakamura examined al-Ghazālī's take on the famous Islamic theologian al-Ash'arī, to whom al-Ghazālī allegedly adhered, by addressing al-Ghazālī's juridical and theological affiliation.[73] Al-Ghazālī holds that those who regard disbelief as the denial of al-Ash'arī or any other sect and its teachings, such as Mu'tazilites or Ḥanbalites, can be designated as narrow-minded and bound by *taqlīd*, or blind imitation of tradition. His approach, however, does not mean that al-Ghazālī aimed at disproving some teachings of sects and upholding others, but rather that he aimed at analyzing the faultiness of particular groups when delineating Islamic theology and God's attributes as everlasting. This might explain why al-Ghazālī believed one should stop depending on the tradition of different schools of law, and instead focus on his own reasoning and way of demonstration (*naẓar*).[74] Al-Ghazālī clearly stated he differentiates between theoretical and legal matters: "With regard to theoretical matters (*ma'qūlāt*), there are [for me] the way (*madhhab*) of demonstration and what logical argument requires. As for legal matters (*shar'īyāt*), there is the way of the Qur'ān. I never follow (*taqlīd namī konam*) any one of

---

[69] See, Al-Ghazālī, *Al-Iqtisād fī al-I'tiqad* (Damascus: Dār Kutayba, 2003); Al-Ghazālī, *Al-Ghazali's Moderation in Belief*, trans. Aladdin M. Yaqub (Chicago: University of Chicago Press, 2013); Al-Ghazālī, *Uber Rechtgläubigkeit und religiose Toleranz. Eine Ubersetzung der Schrift Das Kriterium der Unterscheidung zwischen Islam und Gottlosigkeit*, trans. Frank Griffel (Zurich: Spur, 1998).

[70] Griffel, *Al-Ghazālī's Philosophical Theology*, 112.

[71] See al-Ghazālī, *Al-Mustasfā fi 'Ilm al-Usūl* (Medina: Intisharāt Dār al-Dhahā'ir, 1993).

[72] For al-Ghazālī, the Ismā'ilites are in error since their teachings depend on the knowledge of the *imām*, who was reportedly infallible in the realm of creation. As such, the words and deeds of the *imām* are to be taken for granted since he presented himself as an undisputable source of theology or law. Al-Ghazālī, *Munqidh*, 29.

[73] Kojiro Nakamura, "Was Al-Ghazali an Ash'arite?" Originally published as "Gazali and Ash'arite Theology," *Isuramu Sekai* (*The World of Islam*), Vol. 41, 1993.

[74] Al-Ghazālī, *Mīzān*, 409 in Nakamura, "Was Al-Ghazali an Ash'arite?" 3.

the Imāms. Neither Shāfiʿī has any claim upon me, nor Abū Ḥanīfah has any right upon me."[75]

This is only one of many statements depicting al-Ghazālī not only as a scholar who broke with traditionalism but also as someone who aimed at reconciling at times conflicting epistemologies in order to develop ethics of happiness in the context of the hereafter. Al-Ghazālī commenced the study of important *ṣūfīs* such as Abū Ṭālib al-Makki, al-Muḥāsibī, al-Junayd, al-Shiblī, and Abu Yazīd al-Bistāmī. Some of al-Ghazālī's most influential and prominent students were Abū Bakr ibn al-ʿArabī (d. 1148) from Seville al-Andalus, Ibn Tūmart (d. 1130), who founded the Almohad Empire in northern Africa and al-Andalus, and ʿAyn al-Quḍāt al-Hamadhānī (d. 1131).[76] Sufism or *taṣawwuf* played an important role also concerning the practice of *ijtihād*. For al-Ghazālī, *taṣawwuf* was the last step in his spiritual awakening, as it had the potential to direct his intellectual and metaphysical endeavors to a righteous confrontation within the mundane. After he finished examining the methods and trends within theology and philosophy, he turned toward Sufism. In experiencing the inward dimension of the phenomenal world, he writes:

> I knew that the complete mystic "way" includes both intellectual belief and practical activity; the latter consists in getting rid of the obstacles in the self and in stripping off its base characteristics and vicious morals, so that the heart may attain to freedom from what is not God and to constant recollection of Him. The intellectual belief was easier to me than the practical activity.[77]

Despite the fact that he was, according to some scholars, an adherent of the Shāfiʿī legal school and Ashʿarī theological belief that provided particular stipulations on religious matters, by studying the *ṣūfī* tradition and advancing his masters' teachings, al-Ghazālī developed his own ethical theory of salvation, which pertains also to economic deliberations, one that is embedded in the notion of hereafter and achieved by disciplining the soul and purifying the heart as well as by righteous participation in economic life. His position on ethics also characterizes his approach to the Muʿtazilites, albeit a great difference emerged between their strands. While the Muʿtazilites believe

---

[75] Al-Ghazālī, *Faḍā'il*, 12 in al-Ghazālī, *Briefe und Reden*, 79; Nakamura, "Was Al-Ghazali an Ashʿarite?" 6. See also *Letters of al-Ghazali*, trans. Abdul Qayyum (New Delhi: Kitab Bhavan, 1992).

[76] Al-Ghazālī, *Deliverance*, 54; see also chapter 2 in Griffel, *Al-Ghazālī's Philosophical Theology*, 61–95.

[77] Al-Ghazālī, *Deliverance*, 54.

every human being has a rational faculty, for al-Ghazālī, a human being is free, although predestination (*qadar*) does play a certain role, in that mystical union with the divine does not exclude the element of reason.[78] For both the Mu'tazilites and the Ash'arītes, Islamic theology is based upon the idea that any body or substance consists of atoms (atomism), while the human soul or *nafs* is a combination of atoms and accidents. According to Ibn Qayyim al-Jawzīyya (d. 1350), the disciple of Ibn Taymiyyah, the orthodox theologians, who attribute various bodily faculties to the soul, contradict the philosophers, who regard the soul as a simple being (*wujūd mujarrad*). Al-Ghazālī upheld the Ash'arīte idea of the soul, referring to the "heart" (*qalb*), which has at least two meanings in Arabic pertaining to both biological and metaphysical realms and which forms the gist of his *ṣūfī* epistemology.[79] *Qalb* is a subtle and divine substance related to the spirit (*rūḥ*), which renders the senses of secondary importance.

While al-Ghazālī believed in the redemptive qualities of the divine law, he also sought to examine the structures of *Sharī'a* through the lens of ethical stipulations. In *Munqidh*, he states he acquired the knowledge necessary for reaching eternal happiness, but not the practical aspects of it, which he deemed the most demanding:

> I apprehended clearly that the mystics were men who had real experiences, not men of words, and that I had already progressed as far as was possible by way of intellectual apprehension. What remained for me was not to be attained by oral instruction and study but only by immediate experience and by walking in the mystic way.[80]

He further explains the reasons for surpassing rigid patterns of orthodoxy, based on the imitative approach of obtaining transmitted knowledge. It is widely believed al-Ghazālī's intellectual thought, rooted in the Shāfi'ī legal school and Ash'arī theology, culminated in the *ṣūfī* tradition. For him, the *ṣūfī* path (*al-ṭarīqa al-ṣūfiyya*) commences with the purification of the heart as the first step toward attaining the hereafter, and ends with complete absorption of the self (*fanā'*) in the realm of the divine.[81] The three degrees of reaching for the divine are *'ilm* or knowledge, *dhawq* or tasting or immediate and direct experience, and, finally, *imān* or faith. On the heart or *qalb*, al-Ghazālī

---

[78] Nakamura, "Was Al-Ghazali an Ash'arite?" 11. For more, see chapter 4 of Griffel, *Al-Ghazālī's Philosophical Theology*, 111–22.

[79] See al-Ghazālī, *Iḥyā'*, book 3.

[80] Al-Ghazālī, *Deliverance*, 55.

[81] Al-Ghazālī, *Munqidh*, 100; Al-Ghazālī, *Deliverance*, 61.

states "it is which, if man knows, he indeed knows himself, he indeed knows his Lord,"[82] by driving one nearer to the divine presence, and "the real nature of his [heart's] spirit which is the seat of his knowledge of God, and not the flesh and blood which he shares with the corpse and the brute beast."[83] In attaining the divine, independent legal reasoning (*ijtihād*) also is indispensable since:

> Prophets and religious leaders of necessity made mankind to have recourse to independent judgement, even although they knew that they might fall into error. Indeed the Messenger of God (peace be upon him) said, "I judge by externals, but God administers the inmost hearts"; that is to say, "I judge by the more probable opinion, based on the account of the witnesses, but the witnesses may be mistaken." The prophets had no way to obviate error in the case of such matters of independent judgement. So how can we hope to attain that?[84]

Al-Ghazālī's vantage point can hence be perceived as one from which he merged different fields of inquiry within the Islamic tradition, by eventually committing himself also to *ṣūfī* teachings, yet in the name of developing his particular ethics of happiness, which permeates the entirety of his later thought, especially in *Iḥyā' 'Ulūm al-Dīn.* Given his religious, intellectual, and spiritual investment in attaining the ethics of happiness, it might be safe to state al-Ghazālī was in essence an ethicist more than a philosopher, a theologian, or a *ṣūfī*, or rather that his ethics is a result of a conjunction between and among those branches and traditions. Most of his ideas on the so-called ethical-economic thought, building upon both philosophical reasoning and teachings of *taṣawwuf*, as part of his overall attempt to purify the *qalb* and revive the lost religious science, are presented within his notion of the hereafter and corresponding ethical codes, and are found in his voluminous commentary on religious life—*Iḥyā' 'Ulūm al-Dīn.*

1.3 *Iḥyā' 'Ulūm al-Dīn* and the Quest for Eternal Happiness (*Sa'āda*)

Despite the fact that al-Ghazālī was involved in the Saljūq empire not just intellectually but also to an extent politically, he nonetheless resented many of the religious and political authorities because of their corruption and hypocrisy. Given that the political leadership at the time in Baghdād was crumbling,

---

[82] Al-Ghazālī, *Iḥyā'*, books 3 and 2 in Nakamura, "Was Al-Ghazali an Ash'arite?" 16.

[83] Al-Ghazālī, *Deliverance*, 69; Al-Ghazālī, *Munqidh*, 115.

[84] Al-Ghazālī, *Deliverance*, 48; see also Griffel, *Al-Ghazālī's Philosophical Theology*, 103.

al-Ghazālī chose to leave his teaching position and to devote himself more to the practical aspects of ethical teachings. *Iḥyā'* was hence in big part not only a product of his departure from Baghdād but primarily a channel through which he could revive the sciences of the past and introduce his theory of happiness to the masses.[85] At the very beginning of *Iḥyā'*, he writes, "The road to the next world is without guides or companions despite its many hazards."[86] The learned scholars of the time who should have acted as the role models for the masses were at times perceived with suspicion, and could not offer al-Ghazālī the wherewithal to quench his thirst for knowledge and certainty. During the years of partial self-imposed seclusion after his departure from Baghdād, al-Ghazālī composed his major work *Iḥyā' 'Ulūm al-Dīn*.

Before delving into the intricate relation between philosophical reasoning and intuitive knowledge on eternal happiness, directly linked also to al-Ghazālī's economic teachings, we take a brief look at the composition of *Iḥyā'*. In this book, al-Ghazālī writes about the various paths that lead toward achieving higher ends concerning both the mundane and the hereafter. *Iḥyā'* covers a plethora of theological, legal, philosophical, and *ṣūfī* ideas and considerations.[87] It addresses a wide range of topics, including economic analysis, regulations, and ethical-economic virtues in light of *tawḥīd*. It is divided into four volumes:

The Book of Worship (*Rubʿ al-ʿibādāt*) consists of 10 books: These include The Book of Knowledge, Foundations of Belief, Mysteries of Purity, Mysteries of Worship, Mysteries of Charity, Mysteries of Fasting, Mysteries of Pilgrimage, Manners of Qur'ānic Recitation, On Invocations and Supplications, and On the Arrangements of Litanies and Divisions of the Night Vigil.

The Book of Worldly Usage or Daily Life (*Rubʿ al-ʿādāt*) also comprises 10 books: Manners of Eating, Manners of Marriage, Manners of Earning a Livelihood, The Lawful and the Prohibited, Manners of Intimacy, Brotherhood, and Friendship, Manners of Seclusion, Manners of Traveling, Manners of Music and Singing, Commanding Right and Forbidding Wrong,

---

85 "Al-Ghazālī did not simply write this work as a guide available to those interested parties who might find some use in it; he wrote it as a broadside against the religious sciences as they were practiced in his day and it is a summons to all religious scholars to the pursuit of felicity." Kenneth Garden, *The First Islamic Reviver: Abū Ḥāmid al-Ghazālī and His Revival of the Religious Sciences* (New York: Oxford University Press, 2014), 68.

86 Al-Ghazālī in Ormsby, "The Taste of Truth," 138.

87 "Ghazālī, like a good bricoleur, employed the very materials used by his predecessors, such as verses of the Qur'ān; prophetic reports (aḥādīth); philosophical, legal, and theological discourses; and the narratives of mystics. But he did so with a crucial difference. He combined a variety of genres so that they constituted an organic unity. Not only was the whole of the new narrative very different from the sum of its parts, but the narrative also transformed the whole." Moosa, *Ghazālī and the Poetics of Imagination*, 38.

and Manners of Living and Prophetic Morals. In particular, Manners of Earning a Livelihood deals with economic conduct. Al-Ghazālī believed human beings are sleepwalking through life—that is, performing daily obligations and commitments without being completely aware of their actions and duties—hence his determination to address the subject of economic thought and its ethical aspects.

The Book of Destructive Evils (*Rub' al-muhlikāt*) likewise includes 10 books: Wonders of the Heart, Disciplining of the Soul, Refining Morals, and Treating Diseases of the Heart, Harms of Greed and Sexual Passion, Harms of the Tongue, Harms of Anger, Hatred, and Envy, Condemnation of the Mundane, Evils of Wealth and Miserliness, Condemnation of Vanity and Ostentation, Condemnation of Pride and Conceit, and Condemnation of Delusion. The third volume addresses the wonders of the heart or *muhlikāt*, vices that kill the heart. Notions like vanity, arrogance, illusion, persona (the term *shakhsiyya* is in modern Arabic translated as *personality*, but in essence refers to shadow, mask, or a disguise), and many others are discussed in this volume. The concepts of *tawakkul* (trust in God) and *tawḥīd* are also analyzed. For al-Ghazālī, *tawḥīd* is a constant and utterly conscious presence of God in every single endeavor, action, or deed. The message of the third volume, in brief, is that one should react to tribulations not with heedlessness but with patience and gratitude.

The Book of Constructive Virtues or Ways to Salvation (*Rub' al-munjiyāt*) contains 10 books: Repentance, Patience and Gratefulness, Fear and Hope, Poverty and Asceticism, *Tawḥīd* and *Tawakkul*, Love, Longing, Affection, and Contentment, Intention, Truthfulness, and Devotion, Self-Examination and Self-Reckoning, Contemplation, and Remembrance of Death and the Hereafter. The fourth volume examines humans' final destination—that is, death or eternal happiness. A prevalent aspect of the book is that all types of knowledge are closely associated. Hence, while *iḥsān* leads to a constructive life, human beings should achieve purity also as a means to an end, including through righteous economic endeavors.

Being that al-Ghazālī is a towering figure with a highly diverse opus, it is difficult to pin down his narrative or to confine him to only one particular field of inquiry. While *Munqidh* is often regarded as al-Ghazālī's work in Sufism, this cannot be said with complete certainty for *Iḥyā'*, even though in it one can find not only theological-philosophical but also *ṣūfī* currents, especially in the fourth volume.[88] *Iḥyā'* certainly presents an overture of orthodox Sunni belief and

[88] For more on al-Ghazālī, *kalām*, and the notion of God, see, e.g., Richard M. Frank, *Al-Ghazālī and the Ash'arite School* (Durham, NC: Duke University Press, 1994); Fadlou Shehadi, *Ghazali's Unique Unknowable God* (Leiden: Brill, 1964).

ṣūfī piety. For Kenneth Garden, *Iḥyā'* is not a work on Sufism, even though it makes references to earlier *ṣūfī* works.[89] Using conceptualizations from various traditions, *Iḥyā'* can perhaps be first and foremost positioned at the crossroad of both philosophical and *ṣūfī* epistemology, in whose essence is the science of the hereafter (*'ilm al-ākhira*), achieved through the ethics of happiness (*sa'āda*), covering theoretical and practical aspects as well as the sciences of praxis (*'ilm al-mu'āmala*) and unveiling (*'ilm al-mukāshafa*), believed to have *ṣūfī* origins.[90] *'Ilm al-mu'āmala* refers to both knowledge and conduct and includes *'ibādāt* or man's relation to God, *'ādāt* or man's social relation, and the very knowledge of the soul, such as *ṣabr* or patience, *shukr* or thankfulness, *khawf* or fear, *rajā* or hope, *zuhd* or renunciation, *ḥasad* or corruption, *kibr* or pride, and other concepts.[91] *'Ilm al-mukāshafa* is a confirmation and a certitude of a purified heart stemming from *'ilm al-mu'āmala*, serving as a basis for a direct vision of the divine.[92] The very science of unveiling—as the true knowledge of God's essence—is, for al-Ghazālī, constituted by philosophical and *ṣūfī* traditions, taking stock also in Ibn Sīnā's work.[93] By combining philosophical ethics with moral law, *Iḥyā'* is certainly rooted also in *ṣūfī* teachings of *ilhām* or inspiration. It coalesces various disciplines, teachings, and methodologies—despite al-Ghazālī's critique of different schools of thought—that distinguish his theory of eternal bliss and set his work apart from other similar literature, in whose core lies his theory of happiness—that is, ethical stipulations for achieving the hereafter. This narrative can be read also in *Mīzān al-'amal*, written before his departure from Baghdād. *Mīzān* is a rather short work of ethics that calls for the pursuit of happiness in the hereafter through acquired knowledge (*'ilm*) and ethical practice (*'amal*). While al-Ghazālī in *Mīzān* might be more concerned with theoretical accounts of the ethics of happiness, affirming both philosophy and

---

[89] Garden, *The First Islamic Reviver*, 10; Abū Ṭālib al-Makkī, *Qūt al-Qulūb* (Cairo: Maktaba Dār al-Thurāth, 2001).

[90] *Al-mu'āmala* is in my view more accurately translated as *praxis* rather than *practice*. While the latter denotes an immediate activity, the former implies an active and continuous process in which theory, teaching, or intuitive reasoning is enacted and realized.

[91] M. 'Umaruddin, *The Ethical Philosophy of al-Ghazzālī* (Delhi: Adam, 1996), 102.

[92] Purification of the heart has to be aligned with seeking the knowledge of the divine. See al-Ghazālī, *Iḥyā'*, Vol. 3, book 1.

[93] For more, see, e.g., Garden, *The First Islamic Reviver*, 73; Avner Gil'adi, "On the Origins of Two Key Terms in Al-Ġazzālī's Iḥyā' 'Ulūm al-Dīn," *Arabica*, Vol. 36, No. 1 (1989): 81–93; Alexander Treiger, "Al-Ghazālī's Classifications of the Sciences and Descriptions of the Highest Theoretical Science," *Divan*, Vol. 2011, No. 1 (2011): 1–32. According to Garden, "Gil'adi points out that the broader division of the Science of the Hereafter, into a Science of Unveiling and the Science of Praxis, is philosophical in origin, going back to Aristotle and reproduced in the writings of al-Fārābī and Ibn Sīnā."

Sufism as viable paths to achieve it, in *Iḥyā'*, he lays down complete guidance and practical advice on how one can fulfill salvation as part of revival.[94]

In al-Ghazālī's time, philosophy and Sufism were clearly distinguishable, yet in his own writings, he intertwines the two paths in his search for the divine, whereby rational discursive accounts of the former and the inner or intuitive of the latter are often blurred.[95] The disciplines also shared communalities, since they presented a path to cleanse the human soul in order to attain the divine, yet their methods differed substantially. While Garden claims Sufism was, unlike philosophy, primarily a practical science consisting of various spiritual stations or *maqāmāt*, Alexander Knysh asserts the *ṣūfī* science or *'ilm al-taṣawwuf* emerged already among the second and third generations of Muslims, pointing to the fact that the practical aspect of Sufism also contains a profound theoretical framework pertaining to scientific, psychological, spiritual, and ethical dispositions.[96] Al-Ghazālī took stock in *ṣūfī* scholarship, especially in the writings of al-Muḥāsibī[97] and al-Iṣfahānī.[98] It is true, however, that Sufism "as a homogenous and coherent movement originating in the first century of the Muslim era and resting on a common set of ideals and practices was largely a creation of later Sufi historiography."[99]

On happiness, a core concept in his ethical worldview, al-Ghazālī states "the source of *sa'āda* in this world and the hereafter is science (*'ilm*)"[100] and *sa'āda* can be "obtained only by those who know God."[101] In volume four of *Iḥyā'*, specifically in The Book on Patience and Gratefulness, we read that the very knowledge of God is rooted in the notion of happiness.

> The highest aim of the science of unveiling (*'ilm al-mukāshafa*) is the knowledge (*ma'rifa*) of God. This is the aim that is sought as an end in itself, for it is through it that happiness is achieved. Or rather it [knowledge of

---

[94] In *Iḥyā'*, al-Ghazālī never explicitly states he is a *ṣūfī*—this is rather indicated in *Munqidh* a decade after he finished his voluminous work. Generally, however, *ṣūfīs* rarely used the term to describe their own affiliation to the tradition.

[95] Garden, *The First Islamic Reviver*, 32, 37.

[96] Alexander Knysh, *Islamic Mysticism: A Short History* (Leiden: Brill, 2000), 10.

[97] Al-Hārith al-Muḥāsibī, *Al-Makāsib wa al-Wara'* (Beirut: Mu'ssasa al-Kutub al-Thaqāfiyya, 1987); Al-Hārith al-Muḥāsibī, *al-Ri'āya li-ḥuqūq Allāh*, ed. 'Abd al-Ḥalīm Maḥmūd and 'Abd al-Qādir 'Aṭā (Cairo: Dār al-Kutub al-Ḥadītha, 1970).

[98] Abu al-Ḳāsim al-Ḥusayn b. Muḥammad b. al-Mufaḍḍal al-Rāghib al-Iṣfahānī, *The Path of Virtue*, trans. Yasien Mohamed (Kuala Lumpur: International Institute for Islamic Thought and Civilization, 2006).

[99] Knysh, *Islamic Mysticism*, 47.

[100] Al-Ghazālī, *Iḥyā'*, Vol. 1, 6.

[101] Al-Ghazālī, *Iḥyā'*, Vol. 1, 54.

God] is itself happiness, even though in this world the heart may not feel so but will only feel this in the hereafter.[102]

This implies eternal happiness on the path to salvation is the highest aim of the science of the hereafter. All human activities, including economic engagements, are geared toward an end. Human efforts and moral ends constitute the theory of happiness as the highest principle of the science of the hereafter, and are not imposed from outside but have to come from within as inner development of the self. In other words, knowledge of the self is the key to knowing God. The ultimate end or *sa'āda* can also be a means and it is a cherished endeavor in itself. For 'Umaruddin, al-Ghazālī distinguishes two types of happiness—the means toward the ultimate end or *sa'āda al-ukhrawiyya* and the ultimate end itself or *sa'āda al-ḥaqiqiyya.*[103] The end itself is the realization of the divine, achieved through one's knowledge of God and His attributes as a path toward that perfection. In *Mishkāt al-Anwār*, which comes chronologically after *Iḥyā'*, al-Ghazālī reveals his intimate knowledge of esoterism and mystical union with the divine by analyzing the notion of light in the Qur'ān, as well as Neoplatonic emanation and gnosticism.[104] The theme of the divine also permeates *Iḥyā'* and its ethical concerns.

Iḥyā' primarily deals with ethical manners of conduct, and it can be regarded as al-Ghazālī's effort to devise a comprehensive moral epistemology and as an outcome of his own striving to attain atonement with God. Since acquiring knowledge is inextricably related to its practice, *Iḥyā'* can also be depicted as a referential book on how to perform obtained knowledge or demonstrative proof (*burhān*) in day-to-day life, addressing the topic of various human actions.[105] *Burhān* is the "type of knowledge that prompts humans to act rightfully, staying clear of knowledge that has no consequences for human actions."[106] As a guide on how to achieve the afterlife (*'ilm ṭarīq al-ākhira*), *Iḥyā'* is about practical aspects, as it is about ethical-psychological components for obtaining the goal of moral convalescence as part of the overall revival of Islamic sciences.[107] In al-Ghazālī's words, the book is about human actions (*'ilm al-mu'āmala*), yet throughout the book al-Ghazālī also introduces numerous

---

[102] Al-Ghazālī, *Iḥyā'*, Vol. 4, 137.

[103] Means are further classified according to their usefulness and their impact in relation to good or bad deeds in both worlds. 'Umaruddin, *Ethical Philosophy of al-Ghazzālī*, 123; see al-Ghazālī, *Iḥyā'*, Vol. 4.

[104] Knysh, *Islamic Mysticism*, 147; Al-Ghazālī, *Mishkāt al-Anwār*, ed. 'Abd al-'Azīz al-Sīrawān (Beirut: 'Ālam al-kutub, 1986).

[105] Al-Ghazālī, *Iḥyā'*, 71.

[106] Griffel, *Al-Ghazālī's Philosophical Theology*, 48.

[107] Al-Ghazālī, *Iḥyā'*, Vol. 1, 19.

accounts of *ʿilm al-mukāshafa*.[108] Along these lines, *Iḥyā'* aims to reexamine the spiritual laws of the otherworldly realm by combing the guidelines of *Sharīʿa*'s moral law with earlier *ṣūfī* and philosophical contemplations.[109] Often regarded as the source or encyclopedia of knowledge, *Iḥyā'* deals with the intimate relationship between deeds and the disposition of the soul, the outer and inner worlds, as well as with their regulations and values. From his own sources, we know al-Ghazālī was not in complete solitude during his travels, as he describes it in *Munqidh*. Nonetheless, during his journey, in Damascus, he committed himself to solitary contemplation and devoted himself to writing *Iḥyā'*. He stated that one has to realize the tribulations of this world and that the love for this world diminishes the knowledge of the divine from the heart. Divine experience is never gained without renouncing the world first.[110]

Al-Ghazālī discussed the notions of divine and acquired knowledge, rational discourse, and intuitive disposition. While knowledge means understanding the intelligible forms of life (*al-ʿaqliyāt*), ethical practice entails curtailing lust and purifying the soul (*nafs*). After that stage comes the pursuit of theoretical science or *al-ʿilm al-naẓarī*, which is knowledge of the divine or eternal happiness.[111] A virtuous or purified soul follows both the revealed moral law and philosophical ethical postulates. Eternal happiness (as infinite pleasure) can be hence attained by combining *ʿilm* and *ʿamal*, especially in the field of economic thought, which constitutes an important component of al-Ghazālī's theory of eternal happiness. Al-Ghazālī reminded his readers that mundane affairs have to be tackled with ethical considerations and that the human life is only a path toward redemption, which cannot be achieved without a certain degree of service to the community. Since all deeds to which humans bear witness in their day-to-day lives are rooted in other causes, trying to abstain

---

108 See al-Ghazālī, *Iḥyā'*, Vol. 1, 19. *ʿIlm al-muʿāmala* also relates to "the science of states of the heart" (*ʿilm aḥwāl al-qalb*) as pertaining to the study of inner dispositions and virtues that underlines the very prescriptions of the divine law. See Hourani, "Ghazālī on the Ethics of Action," 70.

109 For ethical thought in Sufism, see, e.g., Ibn Miskawayh, *Refinement of Character* (*Tahdhīb al-akhlāq*), trans. Constantine Zuryak (Chicago: Kazi, 2002); Mohammed Arkoun, "Deux epitres de Miskawqyh," *Bulletin d'Etudes Orientales* (Institute Français de Damas), Vol. 17 (1961–62), 7–74; Al-Makkī, *Qūt al-Qulūb*; Saeko Yazaki, *Islamic Mysticism and Abū Ṭālib al-Makkī: The Role of The Heart* (London: Routledge, 2013); al-Iṣfahānī, *The Path of Virtue*.

110 Al-Ghazali, *The Revival of Religious Sciences*, trans. Behari Bankery (Vrindaban: Mata Krishna Satsang, 1964), 7–8, 97–98.

111 See al-Ghazālī, *Mīzān al-ʿAmal*, ed. S. Dunyā (Cairo: Dār al-Maʿārif, 1964) and al-Ghazālī's *Iḥyā'*. For the German translation, see al-Ghazālī, *Das Kriterium des Handelns*, trans. Abd-Elsamad Abd-Elhamid Elschazli (Darmstadt: WBG, Wissenschaftliche Buchgesellschaft, 2006).

from void discussions that bear no direct significance or consequences for human behavior is deemed a prerogative.[112] This has relevance for all activities that rest upon individuals' decisions and responsibilities, including economic and financial undertakings. Al-Ghazālī does not distinguish between voluntary and involuntary actions, for an action is nothing more than a human faculty that appears as a link in the chain of all causes.[113] Knowledge and learning were virtues for al-Ghazālī, compulsory for every Muslim. Invoking the Prophet's cousin and son-in-law 'Ali bin 'Abī Ṭālib, al-Ghazālī warns as follows:

> Knowledge is superior to wealth. Knowledge guards you, and you have to guard wealth. Knowledge is [an] arbiter [of justice], but wealth is judged upon. Wealth decreases with expenditure (*nafaqa*), whilst knowledge expands with expenditure. [...] If the heart is not given wisdom (*hikma*) and knowledge (*'ilm*) for three consecutive days, it dies. Indeed, the food for the heart is wisdom and knowledge which sustains him, as does food keep the body alive. One who does not have knowledge, his heart goes through a disease, and death is inevitable. Yet, he might not feel such because of his joy for and preoccupation with this world, since he loses his senses for it, just as excessive fear prevents one from feeling the pain of the existing wound.[114]

Learning is hence not simply acquiring knowledge in the field of religion, but is also linked to the mundane world in that it stipulates how one should lead life in the *dunyā* (worldly life). Knowledge can be sought either as a means or as an end in itself. When it is sought as an end in itself, then it is absolutely good, whereas if it is sought as a means toward an end, it can be either good or bad—good when conducive to the individual and the general welfare in society, and bad when harmful. Arguably, for al-Ghazālī, knowledge must be associated with human activities, and the very process of acquisition of knowledge itself underlies the Qur'ānic worldview of the importance of human labor and the nurturing of well-being within society.[115] In al-Ghazālī's view, spiritual devotion means maintaining a balance between desire and abstinence from the material world in order to reach inner contentment with *tawḥīd*. This presupposes that one does not need to sacrifice all the pleasures of *dunyā*

---

112 See al-Ghazālī's, *Iḥyā'* Vol. 1; Griffel, *Al-Ghazālī's Philosophical Theology*, 216.

113 Griffel, *Al-Ghazālī's Philosophical Theology*, 217.

114 Al- Ghazālī, *Iḥyā'*, Vol. 1, 7–8; see also al-Ghazali, *Revival of Religious Learning*, trans. Fazl-ul-Karim (Karachi: Darul-ishaat, 1993), 21–22.

115 See the fourth book of the fourth volume in al-Ghazālī's *Iḥyā'*.

for the sake of *ākhira*, but rather to constantly nurture the intricate balance between the two. The understanding of the metaphysical dimensions of the hereafter is thus entangled with worldly endeavors in society. Even if economic and material lives appear planked down, the change of social adjustments and one's implementation of ethical variables require constant consideration and active participation. The transmission of knowledge is not carried out only by imitating the tradition; its essence stretches beyond simple imitation of tradition, which functions solely as a mediator. For al-Ghazālī, knowledge cannot be transmitted if "the heart is deprived of faith"; only the form of words in which wisdom was originally expressed can be handed down. If the ideation of oral and, later, written knowledge provides the very basis of attaining salvation in Islamic tradition, then al-Ghazālī's attempt to translate words into ethical praxis is vital for understanding the very foundations of its potency.[116]

One of al-Ghazālī's first fields of inquiry was *kalām*, the field in which he defended orthodoxy.[117] Al-Ghazālī discloses his urgent desire for truth while openly detesting the passivity of the religious and laymen of his era. These views, informed by his insight into the matters of faith, intellect, and spirituality, brought him to the verge of collapse, hence his decision to seek out "true knowledge" that would serve as the highest cause of piety.[118] Al-Ghazālī, who once agreed with more orthodox views on *kalām*, felt one has to have a complete grasp of the science in question before discarding what appears to be defective in any of the sciences.[119] In this context, he is labeled the first Muslim theologian to prompt the naturalization of philosophical science into the realm of the Islamic tradition of *kalām*.[120] Rationalism as "the eclipse of theology" was influenced by Greek thought and incorporated in Islamic intellectual history by classical Muslim scholars, who saw it as congruent with Qur'ānic metaphysics. Despite (or rather because of) the rational component, various theologians or *mutakallīmūn* developed a distinct concept of "epistemological functionality," contrary to the Greek model. While in *Munqidh*, al-Ghazālī favors Sufism as the soundest and most apt way of religious life, he nonetheless never parts from rational argumentation when devising an epistemology of happiness, especially in *Iḥyā'*. Al-Ghazālī simultaneously upheld reason as a possibility of obtaining knowledge and undermined the very nature of what defines reason and its scope. As a skeptic, he did not reject reason—quite the opposite—his approach to the very foundations of

---

116 Watt, *Muslim Intellectual*, 158.
117 Fakhry, *A History of Islamic Philosophy*, 247.
118 Al-Ghazālī, *Munqidh*, 29; Fakhry, *A History of Islamic Philosophy*, 11.
119 Al-Ghazālī, *Munqidh*, 29.
120 Griffel, *Al-Ghazālī's Philosophical Theology*, 7.

religious sciences were rational and yet also grounded in the science and ethos of *taṣawwuf*. Al-Ghazālī's meticulous study of Islamic philosophy, *kalām*, legal theory, and *taṣawwuf* not only indicates how versatile a scholar he was in aiming to revive the underlying ethics of reciprocity but, more importantly, also points to his multifaceted study of the phenomenal world (including economic behavior) through ethical psychology. Instead of demarcating Sufism as a branch of Islam that represents (only) inner-worldly mysticism, al-Ghazālī (and many other classical Muslim scholars) substantiated that *zuhd* as renunciation is inextricably linked to *kasb* as an active engagement with the world, including economic provision. Al-Ghazālī's take on philosophical reasoning and ethical psychology appears as a dynamic engagement in order to purify the ego or self (*nafs*) of its whims and is based on logical reasoning and spiritual retreat that also puts forward an idea for an active participation in economic life. Even though reason must constantly be employed when pondering legal and theological questions, it is not the final arbiter of *truth*, for reason alone might be misguided by the senses.[121] Therefore, al-Ghazālī's system of ethics of the hereafter is not based on extreme religious piety as some believe to be encapsulated in the tradition of *taṣawwuf*, but on logical composition imbued with spiritual qualities, which he employs in framing his ethical-economic teachings.[122]

Devotional intelligence is upheld in society and private life and extends to economic conduct, which is seen as a component of overall human activity pertaining to worldly inquiries, permeated with spiritual qualities. Economic behavior, for al-Ghazālī, signifies a strong correlation between mental efforts and ethical principles of beneficence, non-maleficence, and justice on one side, and engaged social practice on the other. Such behavior entails partaking in specific economic undertakings such as purchasing licit goods in the market, nurturing a frugal attitude in dealing with personal wealth, and securing healthy trade through the governmental authority as part of his theory of the science of the hereafter.

Considering al-Ghazālī's analysis of economic life, as we see in Chapter 3, it is also appurtenant to touch upon his critique of *'ulamā'* or Muslim scholars who formed a part of religious and political life in the caliphate. In the first book of *Iḥyā'*, al-Ghazālī lays the groundwork for the concept of knowledge (*'ilm*) and tackles the role of the official *'ulamā'*. Criticism of Muslim

---

[121] For more on the position of reason in human life and on the relation between reason and revelation, see Griffel, *Al-Ghazālī's Theological Philosophy*, 71, 79, 100, 115, 116, 119, 121, as well as al-Ghazālī's *Munqidh*.

[122] In relation to the intellect, al-Ghazālī states it is "the arbiter who neither withdraws nor alters" (Al-Ghazālī, *Al-Mustasfā fi 'Ilm al-Usūl*, 1:3, in Ormsby, *Ghazali*).

scholars is no novelty, since rulers and their mundane affairs have been vigorously disapproved and heavily criticized since the establishment of caliphates. The 'Abbāsid caliphate expanded the Umayyad phenomenon of religious intellectuals, to whom it gave official stipends, and so-called scholar-jurists, appointed as judges, worked on behalf of the caliph.[123] The new educational system also developed the study of religious sciences, including Islamic law.[124] In his critique of the jurist-scholars of the day, al-Ghazālī holds honest scholars will engage neither in legal and formal opinion giving with political leaders nor in business activities, due to the formers' calculative nature and their political engagement that has repercussions also for social values. This view emerged during his appointment at the Baghdād Niẓāmiyya school from 1091 to 1095, during which he was involved in the intellectual and political life of the Saljūq regime.

The intellectual class in society plays a certain role pertaining to public activism, since "the intellectuals are the bearers of the ideas through which a society directs its activity."[125] Even before the time of al-Ghazālī, the role of an intellectual was introduced through the concept of *'ilm*, while *'ālim* came to designate a knowledgeable, learned individual. In this regard, al-Ghazālī's concept of "revival," especially in respect to *Iḥyā'*, also means reviving the intellectual spirit of governmental officials and learned individuals, since their contribution to the well-being of society and a human being's general spiritual provision had become negligent. It seems al-Ghazālī attempted to rescue the (religious) sciences and to reestablish the tenets of Islamic ethical jurisprudence in relation to economic thought, not only as preparation for the hereafter as a supreme end (*'ilm tarīq al-ākhira*) but also to manage worldly affairs.

---

123 On the development of the judiciary system in Islamic tradition, see, e.g., Wael Hallaq, *The Origins and Evolution of Islamic Law* (Cambridge: Cambridge University Press, 2005).

124 See, e.g., Watt, *Muslim Intellectual*, 109.

125 Watt, *Muslim Intellectual*, 156.

Chapter 2

HISTORY OF ISLAMIC ECONOMIC THOUGHT

Chapter 2 begins with an overview of the great gap theory in economic history—believed to have existed from the time of the ancient Greeks to the European Renaissance—and surveys some of the major economic ideas in European scholasticism that are closely associated with al-Ghazālī's economic philosophy. This brief survey is crucial for understanding the position of power when it comes to affirming economic (and various other) fields within Islamic intellectual tradition that contemporary scholarship has often undervalued. Classical Muslim scholars, who have historically been underrepresented but have, in detail, analyzed economic thought from legal, theological, and ethical perspectives, not only devised a new genre and field of inquiry but also impacted the very understanding of the burgeoning economic science in the following centuries and influenced major trends in European scholasticism. This chapter then continues with the history of economic thought in Islamic tradition, explicating its key elements and propositions as an ethical human endeavor. The final section of this chapter addresses contemporary Islamic economics as a modern field that breaks apart from the classical economic scholarship in Islamic tradition in how it utilizes and defines economic subjectivity by in part following the modern division of sciences.

2.1 On Economic Gaps, Exchanges, and Scholasticism

Economic ideas predated Islam, especially those of the Greeks, who are considered the forefathers of what is today known as Western economic thought. In its early phase, according to Islahi, Islamic economic thought was not influenced by external elements, but primarily rested upon the teachings of the Qur'ān and Sunna.[1] While this proposition can be taken with a grain of

---

[1] Abdul Azim Islahi, *Contribution of Muslim Scholars to Economic Thought and Analysis, AH 11–905/AD 632–1500* (Jeddah: Islamic Economics Research Centre, King Abdulaziz University, 1425/2004), 12.

salt, simply because of various external factors and channels of influence from the ancient Near East on the Qur'ān that have also penetrated other fields such as Islamic philosophy, Islamic law, and even political thought, classical Muslim scholars devised a fully-fledged and detailed economic philosophy based on *Sharī'a*'s moral law, which was nonetheless often explicitly based on historical and social precedent. While the pre-Islamic era was known for its trade routes and economic relations and activities with other communities, a systematic theoretical and intellectual economic account did not exist; according to Islahi, scholars have found no evidence of foreign texts being translated into Arabic in that period, or of the application of foreign ideas as far as economic development is concerned. While this claim might be a stretch in that not only economic ideas per se, but also other philosophical-theological sources contributed to the flourishing of economic ideas, the bulk of works were indeed translated in the following periods. The Qur'ānic economic teachings are few in number, since the Qur'ān chiefly set up principles underlying ethics and morals.[2] Derived rules became the fundamentals of jurisprudence (*usūl al-fiqh*), applicable to diverse social and economic patterns and referring to the scriptural sources of Islam. Muslim scholars applied analogy (*qiyās*) as well as other rules deduced from *Sharī'a* injunctions in order to face new challenges. This is how Sunni Islamic juridical schools of thought emerged[3] during the centuries after the death of the Prophet Muḥammad.[4] Economic questions comprised only one component of ethical jurisprudence, which aimed to provide guidance in pursuing economic endeavors. Even though the history of economic thought in Islamic tradition is grounded in the very first scriptural sources of Islam—namely, the Qur'ān and Sunna—they contain a rather small number of economic teachings. Nonetheless, classical Muslim scholars utilized these two sources to explain various conditions for what the tradition holds to be fair economic conduct. The Qur'ān deemed teachings ahistorical, surpassing time and space, whereby human beings must resort to critical interpretation and understanding, and apply them accordingly.[5] Muslim scholars accepted the economic teachings of these two sources as the basic starting point for further investigation and elaboration, in combination with the

---

2 See, e.g., Muhammad Akram Khan, *An Introduction to Islamic Economics* (Islamabad: International Institute of Islamic Thought and Institute of Policy Studies, 1994).

3 For more, see, e.g., Ashker and Wilson, *Islamic Economics*; Hallaq, *Origins and Evolution of Islamic Law*.

4 The schools were eventually named after their leading figures or eponyms—namely, Abū Ḥanīfa, Mālik ibn Anas, Ibn Idrīs al-Shāfi'ī, and Aḥmad bin Ḥanbal. For more on the formations of the major Sunni schools, see Hallaq, *Sharī'a*, 60–70.

5 Hallaq, *Sharī'a*, 11.

independent legal reasoning (*ijtihād*) of learned men or *'ulamā'* in solving the emerging difficulties in communities. The process of also extracting teachings from other religious and philosophical systems (e.g., Greek ideas) has always been continuous in Islamic intellectual history.

In relation to this twofold aim, scholars such as Helmut Ritter[6] claim classical Muslim economic thought can be traced to Bryson's *Oikonomikos*, from which Muslim scholars devised their philosophies of ethics (*akhlāq*), household management (*oikonomia*; *tadbīr al-manzil*),[7] and political science (*'ilm al-madani*),[8] making economics a more "practical science" by addressing notions of market, price, monetary exchange, and supply and demand, and thus extending it to a macroeconomic level. However, classical economic thought in Islamic tradition was mostly preoccupied with issues like taxation, property, inheritance, usury, market flow, exchange of goods, and charity, not only in the realm of Islamic jurisprudence but also in the area of virtue ethics, which eventually led to the proliferation of *ḥisba* handbooks.[9] By monitoring the flow of products sold at the market and seller–buyer relationality, unlike their European successors in the modern period, classical Muslim scholars did not differentiate ethics from economic thought as a separate entity. Al-Ghazālī and many other classical scholars maintained Islamic tradition intertwines material life with the ultimate objectives of the hereafter, linking ethical ideals (*akhlāq*, which ought not to be disassociated from morals) with daily activities. Classical Muslim scholars' economic ideas influenced their European counterparts and scholasticism in turn.

The term *scholasticism* relates to the Christian philosophical approach that aimed to reconcile theology with philosophy, commencing with thinkers such as Thomas Aquinas (d. 1274).[10] Western Christian intellectual history is in this context described as a gradual process of secularization springing from the traditions of the Renaissance and the Reformation, which later had an impact on the

---

6 Helmut Ritter, "Ein Arabiches Handbuch Der Handelswissenshaf," *Der Islam*, No. 7 (1917): 1–91.

7 "To pay attention to where things lead" ("*an tazzura ilā mā ta'ūlu ilayhi 'āqibatuhu*"). Ibn Manẓūr, *Lisān al-'Arab*, 1979.

8 F. E. Peters, *Allah's Commonwealth* (New York: Simon and Schuster, 1973).

9 The institution of *ḥisba* played a different role under various rulers in the classical Islamic milieu. See Ameer Ali and Herb Thompson, "The Schumpeterian Gap and Muslim Economic Thought," *Journal of Interdisciplinary Economics*, Vol. 10 (1999): 31–49, available at www1.aucegypt.edu/faculty/thompson/herbtea/articles/jie3.html.

10 St. Thomas Aquinas, *Summa Theologica*, trans. Fathers of the English Dominican Province (Perrysburg, OH: Benziger Bros. edition, 1947); S. M. Ghazanfar and Abdul Azim Islahi, "Economic Thought of an Arab Scholastic: Abu Hamid Al-Ghazali," *History of Political Economy*, Vol. 22, No. 2 (1990): 381–403 at 381.

French Revolution too, while for some scholars, the Islamic world remained tied to its "religious corpus" and hence never parted from its reasoning.[11] This claim can be rather easily debunked, for social, political, and economic percepts were for many classical Muslim scholars interwoven with ethical ones despite that *Sharīʿa's* moral law undergirded much of their deliberations.

Furthermore, Islamic tradition has established a multiplicity of views and approaches within its own history, at times pertaining to opposing methods and traditions.[12] Yet for many Western scholars economic accounts often omitted the moral law and the writings of classical Muslim scholars, generating the so-called great gap in world economic history. When medieval Europe became interested in science and philosophy between the tenth and fifteenth centuries, classical Muslim scholars had already developed disciplines founded on rational predicaments and religious scriptures. The channels of influence from which texts and ideas flowed from Muslim societies to medieval Europe included scholars who traveled the lands, students who studied in Italy, Spain, and southern France, translations of Arabic texts into Latin, oral transmission, and trade and commerce. Al-Ghazālī's influence on scholastic writers, especially St. Thomas Aquinas, was significant in constructing an economic doctrine in Europe grounded on religious ethic. His approach to merge rational thinking with systematic theology and philosophy with science is evidenced in scholastic writings, also in the context of economic thought. Al-Ghazālī's *Iḥyāʾ* became available in Latin translation before 1150. Aquinas, who studied at the University of Naples, was influenced also by Arab literature. In 1224, Frederik II (d. 1250) established a center for learning in Naples, chiefly to introduce Islamic philosophy and science in Europe, where Arabic works were translated into Latin. In *Summa Theologica*, Aquinas tried to reconcile Aristotelian philosophy with Christian theology, while also making references to Muslim philosophers. Against this backdrop, by harmonizing faith and reason—despite fundamental differences on economic ethics with al-Ghazālī and his classical counterparts—Aquinas holds that cheating in the market is prohibited and is an unlawful trading practice. Aquinas affirms the prohibition (or condemnation) of usury, which dates back to the ancient Greeks, including specific usurious practices such as fixing a price for the use of money, because money was meant to be used only as a medium of exchange.[13] Generally, classical Muslim scholars held that the value of a

---

[11] See Ali and Thompson, "The Schumpeterian Gap and Muslim Economic Thought," 31–49.

[12] For more, see, e.g., Thomas Bauer, *Die Kultur der Ambiguität. Eine andere Geschichte des Islams* (Berlin: Verlag der Weltreligionen, 2011).

[13] Aquinas, *Summa Theologica*.

good or commodity is independent of the lapse of time, and hence did not believe in what is nowadays called the time value of money. According to al-Ghazālī, however, usury can occur with differences in quantity or at the time of delivery. Hence, exchange should be equal in quantity, and the transfer of a good should occur simultaneously. A somewhat similar account is presented by Aquinas, who stated that one cannot sell a good (as a deferred payment) for more than what is its just price.[14]

The medieval scholastics perceived economic activities as an integral part of theological reasoning pertaining to the common good and social justice. Al-Ghazālī is quoted by Thomas Aquinas (as well as other scholastic writers), as his *Summa Theologica* aimed to "harmonize Christianity with Aristotelian philosophy by a Thomistic synthesis."[15] Ghazanfar states that two centuries earlier, al-Ghazālī's *Iḥyā'* had aimed to reconcile "Islamic ethos with Aristotelian rationalism," which can be interpreted as an attempt to inquire into Hellenism from an Islamic perspective.[16] Both figures shared certain religious and philosophical predispositions, one of them being that faith and reason must be reconciled, which was one of the main premises of al-Ghazālī's philosophical theology. Both thinkers held that "there is a certain region lying outside the scope of reason into which philosophy cannot venture. Thus, whatever lies outside the scope of human cognition, it is necessary to resort to scriptures."[17]

Joseph Schumpeter discussed the notion of the great gap in the evolution and history of economic thought in his famous *History of Economic Analysis.*[18] Various scholars have commented on Schumpeter's book, in which he presented the early, classical, and modern history of economics in an elaborate fashion.[19] Despite the importance of Schumpeter's analysis of the development of economic history, he left out an important part of this history—namely, the contribution of Muslim scholars to the field. Schumpeter's account is not an exception, but rather a common approach to economic history, indicating a

---

[14] Aquinas, *Summa Theologica.*

[15] Eugene A. Myers, *Arabic Thought and the Western World* (New York: Fredrick Unger, 1964), 16; Philip Newman, Arthur Gayer, and Milton Spencer, eds., *Source Readings in Economic Thought* (New York: W. W. Norton, 1954), 16.

[16] Mohammad S. Ghazanfar, "The Economic Thought of Abu Hamid Al-Ghazali and St. Thomas Aquinas: Some Comparative Parallels and Links," *History of Political Economy*, Vol. 32, No. 4 (2000): 857–88 at 867.

[17] Fakhry, *A History of Islamic Philosophy*, 88.

[18] Joseph Schumpeter, *History of Economic Analysis* (New York: Oxford University Press, 1997), 73–74.

[19] For the expanded theory on the great gap, see the works by Ghazanfar and Islahi.

paradigmatic flaw in dealing with non-Western and in particular Muslim economic thought from a position of epistemic power. Even though Schumpeter's primary aim was the analysis, not the theory, of economic thought,[20] the Schumpeterian great gap has been questioned by scholars such as Ghazanfar, Islahi, Siddiqi, and Mirakhor[21] due to the omission of Islamic economic history and the influence it had upon the ideas of medieval European scholars. The study of classical Islamic economic thought and Arab scholastics indicates Muslim contribution to the subject bears a profound relevance for the overall development of scholastic and modern economic thought. The great gap in economic history and specifically the omission of al-Ghazālī—considered one of the forerunners of Islamic economics—sheds light on how neglected the writings of Muslim contributors to economic philosophy have been in the modern era. But it is not only negligence or omission at stake here but rather the systemic understanding that classical Muslim economic ideas are unworthy of being analyzed scientifically and epistemologically. Yet economic philosophy by classical scholars in general, and al-Ghazālī in particular, provides a sophisticated account of pervasive theoretical postulates and ethical considerations, highly applicable in scholastic economic ideas, yet often disjointed from the entanglements with the modern division of sciences in early modern Europe.

The great gap can be divided into several periods. Islahi proposes three phases: the formation, translation, and transmission periods.[22] The formation period spanned from the commencement of the Qur'ānic revelation to the end of the era of Companions—that is, *ṣaḥāba* (AD 632–718). The translation period marked the influx of foreign intellectual ideas into the Arab-Muslim cultural milieu (eighth–eleventh centuries). The transmission period witnessed the dissemination of translated texts from the hands of Muslim scholars when Greco-Islamic ideas reached Europe (twelfth–fifteenth centuries). This is the era during which foreign ideas and works of foreign authors—for example, the Greeks—were translated into Arabic, bearing a certain relevance for the further development of classical Islamic economic science by introducing foreign sources to the Islamic heritage. The three phases can instead be divided according to the contents of scholars' writings, such as ethical-economic

---

20 See Ali and Thompson, "The Schumpeterian Gap and Muslim Economic Thought."

21 For more, see Mohammad Nejatullah Siddiqi, *Muslim Economic Thinking: A Survey of Contemporary Literature* (Jeddah: International Center for Research in Islamic Economics and Leicester, Islamic Foundation, 1981); Abbas Mirakhor, "Muslim Scholars and the History of Economics: A Need for Consideration," *American Journal of Islamic Social Sciences*, Vol. 4, No. 2 (December 1987): 245–76 at 249.

22 Islahi, *Contribution of Muslim Scholars to Economic Thought and Analysis*, 11–18.

writings versus technical-legal economic accounts.[23] Scholars who wrote on policy ordinances sometimes framed them as part of Islamic governance based on *Sharīʿa*, and these include Abū Yūsuf,[24] Kinānī,[25] al-Farra,[26] al-Sarakhsī,[27] al-Māwardī,[28] Ibn Taymiyya,[29] and others. Other scholars such as Muḥammad bin Ḥasan al-Shaybānī, Ibn Abī al-Dunyā, al-Muḥāsibī, and al-Ghazālī addressed legal-mystical principles by invoking both *kasb* as acquisition of wealth and *zuhd* as renunciation of worldly gains in economic thought, while still others wrote on economic thought in a more systematic fashion, and these include Ibn Taymiyya, Ibn Qayyim al-Jawziyya,[30] Ibn Khaldūn,[31] and al-Maqrīzī.[32] Other Muslim philosophers or *falāsifa* who touched upon economic ideas and also employed Greek philosophy include Fakhr al-Dīn al-Rāzī,[33] Ibn Rushd,[34] Ibn Ṭufayl,[35] and others.

2.2 Major Ideas in Classical Economic Thought

Historically, Islamic civilization came to be affiliated with trade and familiarity with market functioning as well as with the difficulties related to it. The

---

[23] For more on the historical overview, see the table in Appendix 1.

[24] Abū Yūsuf (d. 798) is perceived as one of the earliest jurists who wrote on land tax (*kharaj*) in Islamic tradition.

[25] Abū Bakr Yahya b. ʿUmar al-Kināni (d. 901) was a Mālikite jurist whose work *Kitāb Aḥkām al-Sūq* deals with economic issues in the market.

[26] See Abū Yala Muḥammad bin al-Husain al-Farra's (d. 1066) "al-Aḥkām al-Sulṭāniyya."

[27] Abū Bakr al-Sarakhsī (d. 1090) was a Hanafi jurist who lived and worked in Transoxania.

[28] Abū al-Ḥasan ʿAlī Ibn Muḥammad Ibn Ḥabīb al-Māwardī (d. 1058) was an Islamic jurist famous for his *al-Aḥkām al-Sulṭāniyya*. See al-Māwardī, *al-Aḥkām al-Sulṭāniyya* (Misr: al-Babi al-Ḥalabi, 1973).

[29] Ibn Taymiyya (d. 1328) was a member of the Ḥanbali legal school famous for works on legal theory including work on *ḥisba*, and he is nowadays regarded as a source of inspiration for current orthodox Salafism.

[30] Ibn al-Qayyim (d. 1350) was a pupil of Ibn Taymiyya who furthered Taymiyya's legal, theological, and economic ideas and developed his own economic theory in *Ẓad al-Maʿad*.

[31] Ibn Khaldūn (d. 1406) is best known for his book *Muqaddimah* or *Prolegomena* in which he discusses the cycles and life spans of empires as well as economic development. In his writings, Ibn Khaldūn also discussed Sufism and urged that it be based in *ʿumrān* as a dynamic social process.

[32] Al-Maqrīzī (d. 1441) was a scholar from Egypt who provided official advice to the Fatimid government.

[33] Fakhr al-Dīn al-Rāzī (d. 1209) was a famous jurist and theologian.

[34] Ibn Rushd (d. 1098) wrote on laws of purchases and sales in *Bidāyat al-Mujtahid*. For the English translation, see Ibn Rushd, *The Distinguished Jurist's Primer*. Translated by Imran Ahsan Khan Nyazee. Reading: Centre for Muslim Contribution to Civilization, 1996.

[35] Ibn Ṭufayl (d. 1182) wrote a famous philosophical novel, *Ḥayy ibn Yaqẓān*, in which he presented Islamic philosophical and mystical elements.

notion of administrative fixation of price was already known during the time of the Prophet Muḥammad, who did not support it, since he favored the determination of price by market forces—that is, according to supply and demand.[36] Islamic civilization contributed immensely to economic thought amid Islamic expansion of knowledge during what is in the West known as the Middle Ages. "Arab Scholastics were about as 'European' as any scholarship at the time," and for centuries much intellectual development and exchange of knowledge took place in the Mediterranean.[37] Since the whole pleiad of classical Islamic scholars cannot be introduced in one chapter, the following scholars, perceived as representatives of the Islamic economic tradition who wrote on the *kasb-zuhd* perspective by merging legal theory with *ṣūfī* and ethical conceptualizations, are briefly examined. In addition to al-Ghazālī, who was a member of the Shāfi'ī school as much as an adherent of the *ṣūfī* tradition, these are the aforementioned Muḥammad bin Ḥasan al-Shaybānī (d. 805), who treated earning as an wholesome subject in *Kitāb al-kasb*;[38] al-Hārith al-Muḥāsibī (d. 857), a famous ninth-century mystic;[39] Ibn Abī al-Dunyā (d. 894), a prominent scholar of Islam who wrote on economic behavior in *Iṣlāḥ al-māl*;[40] al-Dimashqī, a twelfth-century merchant from Damascus who defined an early form of price theory and expressed support for acquiring wealth in *Kitāb al-Isharāh ila Maḥāsin at-Tijārah*;[41] Ibn Taymiyya (1263–1328), who belonged to the Ḥanbali school and who was a source of inspiration for current orthodox Salafism;[42] and Ibn Khaldūn (1332–1406), who belonged to the Māliki school and contributed to the tradition, which in nineteenth-century Europe became known as the social sciences.[43]

Al-Shaybānī, al-Muḥāsibī, Ibn Abī al-Dunyā, and al-Ghazālī's writings espouse ethical views on economy by examining the moral and spiritual

---

[36] Islahi, *Contribution of Muslim Scholars to Economic Thought and Analysis*, 25. One of the earliest accounts of price variation came as a result of good or bad harvests or an increase or decrease in the supply of agricultural goods, as stated by Ibn Muqaffa'.

[37] Ghazanfar, *Medieval Islamic Thought*, 49.

[38] Muḥammad bin Ḥasan al-Shaybānī, *Al-Iktisāb fī al-Rizq al-Mustaṭāb* (Beirut: Dār al-Kutub al-Ilmiyyah, 1986).

[39] al-Muḥāsibī, *al-Makāsib wa al-Wara'.*

[40] Ibn Abī al-Dunyā, *Iṣlāḥ al-Māl* (Beirut: Mu'assasa al-Kutub al-Thaqāfiyya, 1993).

[41] Abū al-Fadl Ja'far al-Dimashqī, *Al-Ishāra ilā Maḥāsin al-Tijāra* (Cairo: Maktabah al-Kulliyyat al-Azhariyyah, 1977).

[42] Ibn Taymiyya, *Al-Ḥisbah fī al-Islām* (Cairo: Dār al-Sha'b, 1976); English translation by Muhtar Holland, *Public Duties in Islam: The Institution of the Hisbah* (Leicester: Islamic Foundation, 1982); Ibn Taymiyya, *Majmū' Fatāwa Shaykh al-Islām Aḥmad Ibn Taymiyya*, ed. al-Najdi, 'Abd al-Raḥmān b. Muḥammad (Al-Riyāḍ: Matabi' al-Riyāḍ, 1963).

[43] Ibn Khaldūn, *Muqaddimah* (Beirut: Dār al-Fikr, n.d.).

components of economic life.[44] Their economic philosophy addresses the function of money, the role of *ḥisba*, price control, the value of goods, barter exchange, and the role of Islamic governance. The main concepts of their economic philosophy, despite their different accounts of particular economic elements, center on *Sharī'a* as moral law, *akhlāq* (ethical conduct), *tas'īr* (price control), *zuhd* (renunciation), *kasb* (earning or economic provision), *iḥsān* (benevolence), and *maṣlaḥa* (public or common good). Since *zuhd* does not presuppose an absolute negation of worldly affairs, *kasb* has to be maintained as part of one's spiritual quest. *Zuhd* and *wara'* (prudence) are the subject of al-Shaybānī's economic analysis of safeguarding one's behavior and wealth from corruption while maintaining an honest livelihood.[45] *Kasb* is, despite its association with wealth and material provision, a necessary endeavor, since it concerns the righteous provision of basic necessities, having the capacity to levitate one's spiritual life.[46] The values of money and of trading activities are analyzed in the context of piety and asceticism. Al-Muḥāsibī's book *al-Makāsib wa al-Wara'* elucidates human economic behavior and its link to the spiritual world by stipulating lawful and conscientious economic activities through acts of mindfulness, remembrance (*dhikr*), and the purification of the heart (*ṭahārat al-qulūb*).[47] Ibn Abī al-Dunyā's *Iṣlāḥ al-Māl* (*The Emendation of Wealth*) analyzes earning and wealth through material and moral realms by delving into the spiritual reverberations of just economic conduct.[48] Al-Dimashqī claims all wealth is beneficial,[49] yet it can be acquired through certain means in order to not deprive others.[50] He advocated a communal life and cooperation between industries. Ibn Taymiyya, a Muslim scholar who is better known nowadays in the West as the initiator of puritan reforms in Islam and is believed to have

---

44 See Adi Setia, "Imam Muḥammad Ibn al-Ḥasan al-Shaybāni on Earning a Livelihood: Seven Excerpts from His Kitāb al-Kasb," *Islam & Science*, Vol. 10, No. 2 (2012): 99–116; Adi Setia, "The Restoration of Wealth: Introducing Ibn Abī al-Dunyā's *Iṣlāḥ al-Māl*," *Islamic Sciences*, Vol. 13, No. 2 (2015): 77–94; Adi Setia, "Al-Muḥāsibī: On Scrupulousness and the Pursuit of Livelihoods: Two Excerpts from His al-Makāsib wa al-Wara'," *Islamic Sciences*, Vol. 14, No. 1 (2016): 67–90.

45 Setia, "Imam Muḥammad Ibn al-Ḥasan al-Shaybāni on Earning a Livelihood," 105. See also Hallaq, *The Impossible State*, 114–16.

46 Al-Shaybānī, *Al-Iktisāb fī al-Rizq al-Mustaṭāb*, 71.

47 For the English translation, see Adi Setia, *Kitāb al-Makāsib (The Book of Earnings) by al-Ḥārith al-Muḥāsibī (751–857 C.E.)* (Kuala Lumpur: IBFIM, 2016).

48 For the purposes of this research, by enumerating those (and other) scholars and their relation between mystical concepts and economic ideas, I do not intend to position Sufism or *ṣūfī* literature on a pedestal, but rather to expound dynamic and nuanced correlations between mystical, theological, legal, and economic ideas.

49 Al-Dimashqī, *Al-Ishāra ilā Maḥāsin al-Tijāra*, 69.

50 Al-Dimashqī, *Al-Ishāra ilā Maḥāsin al-Tijāra*, 69, 85.

inspired Wahhabism in nineteenth-century Saudi Arabia, also made seminal contributions to economic thought. He spent most of his life in Damascus, an important center of trade between China, India, and Asia Minor. The term *just/fair price* became the focal point of his economic thinking. Even though Islamic jurisprudence does not specifically mention just price, al-Ghazālī and especially Ibn Taymiyya paid attention to it in shaping social boundaries along the lines of the common good. Ibn Taymiyya holds that value is an increment obtained from both labor and capital.[51] He considers value creation attributable to all factors, including land, water, air, raw materials, labor, and capital.[52] Ibn Taymiyya aimed to analyze the cost of production as well as the theory of value. Nasr al-Dīn al-Ṭūsi (d. 1274) too developed a holistic approach to economic ethics, focusing on the individual level of human behavior in relation to economic activities, aiming to analyze human goals and achievements that would lead to overall satisfaction, while also describing the role of money as a medium of exchange.[53]

Classical Islamic scholars, including Ibn Taymiyya and Ibn Khaldūn, discussed labor and just earnings in their works. According to Ibn Taymiyya, a fair amount of the profit should be distributed between workers and employers and the rate of *zakāt* plays a certain role therein, for it is measured according to a worker's labor input and his income—the lower the income, the lower the *zakāt*.[54] Since exploitation of labor might occur through unlawful earnings such as gambling and speculations, the majority of classical scholars regarded such earnings as prohibited. Commerce and labor therefore have to be connected to socially beneficial activities. For Ibn Taymiyya, labor and capital are inextricably related: "Profit is an increment gained from the use of one man's labour and another man's capital. So it should be divided among them as any increment resulting from two factors."[55]

Ibn Khaldūn, who is known as a historian and is often called the father of modern sociology, provided a more rational approach to economic reasoning, yet his thought has close ties to ethical and spiritual convictions.[56] In his opus *Muqaddimah* (*Prolegomena*), which many sociologists describe as one of "the

---

[51] Ibn Taymiyya, *Majmūʿ Fatāwa Shaykh al-Islām Aḥmad Ibn Taymiyya*, Vol. 30, 87.

[52] Ibn Taymiyya, *Majmūʿ Fatāwa Shaykh al-Islām Aḥmad Ibn Taymiyya*, Vol. 29, 103.

[53] See Abū Naṣr al-Sarrāj al-Tūsi, *Kitāb al-Lumaʿ fī al-Taṣawwuf*, ed. Reynold Alleyne Nicholson (Leyden: Brill, 1914).

[54] Toseef Azid, "The Concept and Nature of Labour in Islam: A Survey," *Review of Islamic Economics*, Vol. 9, No. 2 (2005): 93–122 at 99.

[55] Ibn Taymiyya in Toseef Azid, "The Concept and Nature of Labour in Islam," 103.

[56] See Robert Irwin, *Ibn Khaldun: An Intellectual Biography* (Princeton, NJ: Princeton University Press, 2018).

greatest work[s] of its kind,"[57] Ibn Khaldūn attempted to detect the natural laws present in the development of societies: "We must study human society and distinguish its essential features from its accidental ones and trace the social laws that are at work within it and use them as criteria as to the value of historical assertions."[58] One of Ibn Khaldūn's most important contributions was that economic development appears in his theory of cycles to correlate with the expansion of urban areas and empires. Once an empire reaches its highest point in development, a decline commences, also in strictly economic terms.[59]

As far as the labor theory of value goes, Ibn Khaldūn, similar to other classical scholars, insists profit is the value realized from man's labor.[60] On another occasion he states, "When [a person] does not use [his income] for any of his interests and needs, it is not called 'sustenance,'"[61] and "it should be further known that profit results from the effort to acquire [things] and the intention to obtain [them]."[62] According to Ibn Khaldūn, it is the duty of everyone who is capable to contribute to the labor force: "But human labor is necessary for every profit and capital accumulation. [...] If the profit results from something other than a craft, the value of the resulting profit and acquired [capital] must [also] include the value of the labor by which it was obtained. Without labor, it would not have been acquired."[63]

---

[57] Joseph J. Spengler, "Economic Thought of Islam: Ibn Khaldun," *Comparative Studies in Society and History*, Vol. 6 (1964): 268–306.

[58] Ibn Khaldūn cited in M. A. Nashat, *Ibn Khaldun: Pioneer Economist* (Le Caire: Imprimerie Nationale Boulac, 1945), 380–81.

[59] "The assessments increase beyond the limits of equity. The result is that the interest of the subjects in cultural enterprises disappears, since when they compare expenditures and taxes with their income and gain and see the little profit they make, they lose all hope. Therefore, many of them refrain from all cultural activity. The result is that the total tax revenue goes down, as (the number of) the individual assessments goes down. Often, when the decrease is noticed, the amounts of individual imposts are increased. This is considered a means of compensating for the decrease. Finally, individual imposts and assessments reach their limit. It would be of no avail to increase them further. The costs of all cultural enterprise are now too high, the taxes are too heavy, and the profits anticipated fail to materialize. Thus, the total revenue continues to decrease, while the amounts of individual imposts and assessments continue to increase, because it is believed that such an increase will compensate (for the drop in revenue) in the end. Finally, civilization is destroyed, because the incentive for cultural activity is gone. It is the dynasty that suffers from the situation, because it (is the dynasty that) profits from cultural activity." Ibn Khaldūn, *The Muqaddimah*, 3 vols., trans. Franz Rosenthal (London: Routledge and Kegan Paul, 1958), Vol. 1, 89–90.

[60] Khaldūn, *Muqaddimah*, Vol. 2, 310–11.

[61] Khaldūn, *Muqaddimah*, Vol. 2, 312.

[62] Khaldūn, *Muqaddimah*, Vol. 2, 312.

[63] Khaldūn, *Muqaddimah*, Vol. 2, 313.

While the aforementioned scholars had diverse academic backgrounds and lived in different eras, sociopolitical and cultural contexts, they often invoked both material and ethical ideas when explicating the complexity of economic history in their works. Focusing on the intertwinement of ethical and economic presuppositions of classical Islamic discourses bears importance also for the development of epistemology in modern Islamic economic thought, which in my view differ in their epistemological reasoning.

2.3 An Overview of Modern Islamic Economics

Religious scholars and Muslim economists established Islamic economics as an independent study in the twentieth century entailing the religious teachings of Islam and economic science, advocating for a new paradigm that is distinguishable from both socialism and mainstream capitalism.[64] For some scholars, Islamic economics has been prompted by the necessity to overcome the devastating effects of the global economy and by the lack of theoretical considerations enhancing ethical stipulations.[65] Opponents of the Islamic economic project claim, however, that Islamic economics does not provide for the benefit of the people and has been established on dubious grounds.[66]

Qur'ānic epistemology is considered the origin of the economic underpinnings within Islamic intellectual history and by classical thinkers or *mutakallimūn*.[67] While the Qur'ān comprises a moral epistemology that encompasses also commerical activites, the bulk of contemporary Muslim economists established a direct link between human development, social interactions, and economic stipulations within the institution of *Sharī'a* as a legal institution. This moral-economic worldview is for contemporary Muslim

---

64 For more, see, e.g., Abul 'Ala al-Mawdudi, *The Economic Problem of Man and Its Islamic Solution* (Lahore: Islamic Publications, 1947); Muḥammad Bāqir al-Ṣadr, *Iqtiṣāduna*, 3. vols. (Beirut: Dār al-Ta'ārif, 1987); Umer Muhammad Chapra, "Islamic Economics: What It Is and How It Developed." Paper written for EH. NET's Online Encyclopedia of Economic and Business History, http://eh.net/encyclopedia/article/chapra.islamic (accessed April 17, 2013); Masudul Alam Choudhury, *The Principles of Islamic Political Economy: A Methodological Enquiry* (New York: Macmillan, 1992); Masudul Alam Choudhury, *The Islamic World-System: A Study in Polity–Market Interaction* (New York: Routledge, 2004); Syed Nawab Haider Naqvi, *Islam, Economics, and Society* (London: Kegan Paul International, 1994); Siddiqi, *Muslim Economic Thinking*.

65 See the proponents of Islamic economics in the previous reference.

66 See, e.g., the writings of Timur Kuran and the later writings of Ahmed Muhammad Khan.

67 Masudul Alam Choudhury, "Towards Islamic Political Economy at the Turn of the Century," *American Journal of Islamic Social Sciences*, Vol. 13, No. 3 (1996): 366–81 at 367.

economists based on the principle of *tawḥīd*, but presents a rather cyclic understanding of the universe.[68]

Engaging in some type of commerce is an integral part of society and therefore indispensable to other dimensions of human life in how it shapes the very understanding of one's economic role in community in relation to broader psychological and ethical concerns.[69] Every economic system rests upon certain philosophical worldviews, and the same holds for modern Islamic economics. Islamic tradition has encouraged trading activities and the purchases of licit economic commodities.[70] At least four different dimensions of economic analysis can be identified: studies that relate to economic issues within the discipline of *tafsīr* (exegesis) as a hermeneutics of the Qur'ān, such as prohibition of usury; economic matters within the discipline of *fiqh* (Islamic jurisprudence), such as the contemporary and more technical aspects of Islamic economics and its lawful and unlawful categorization; elaboration upon economic questions from the perspective of Islamic ethics by *ṣūfīs*, philosophers, and other scholars; and numerous works on economic science written by contemporary Muslim scholars as a response to the growing need of the time.[71] Al-Ghazālī's economic ideas relate to the third stage, addressing economic conduct through ethical norms.

Contemporay Islamic economics has been variously defined by different scholars and Muslim economists pinpointing to confusion in the field. Muhammad Akram Khan proposes the following definition, linking the notions of common and individual undertakings: "Islamic economics aims at the study of human *falāḥ* (derives from the Arabic verb *aflah*, *yuflihu*—to thrive, achieve happiness, success, etc.) achieved by organizing the resources of the earth on the basis of cooperation and participation."[72] The Qur'ān emphasizes that *falāḥ* (individual and common success or good) has to be achieved in worldly life, although the ultimate goal is *falāḥ* in the hereafter. The notion of *falāḥ* has to be categorized into spiritual, economic, cultural, and political domains, and it can be differentiated on the basis of survival

---

68 See, e.g., Masudul Alam Choudhury, "A Critique of Modernist Synthesis in Islamic Thought: Special Reference to Political Economy," *American Journal of Islamic Social Sciences*, Vol. 11, No. 4 (1994): 475–506.

69 Aidit Ghazali and Abul Hasan Muhammad Sadeq, eds., *Pregled islamske ekonomske misli* (*An Overview of Islamic Economic Thought*) (Sarajevo: El-Kalem, 1996), 12.

70 Abul Hasan Muhammad Sadeq, "Al-Ghazalijevi pogledi na ekonomske probleme i neka etičko-pravna pitanja značajna za ekonomsko ponašanje," in Ghazali and Sadeq, *Pregled islamske ekonomske misli*, 159–62 at 148.

71 Sadeq, "Al-Ghazalijevi pogledi na ekonomske probleme i neka etičko-pravna pitanja značajna za ekonomsko ponašanje."

72 Khan, *An Introduction to Islamic Economics*, 33.

(physical health, economic base, social brotherhood, political participation, etc.) and freedom (self-reliance, respect, civil liberties, etc.). These two categories exist on the personal (micro) as well as at the state (macro) level.[73]

A vast legal literature reserved for economics deals with the verses and injunctions from the Qur'ān and Sunna regarding economic questions and conduct, financial management, interests, heritage, economic ethics, and other juridical issues. Due to human self-interest, material progress, and the inherent tendency to maximize material welfare, Muslims scholars deal with fairness and equity in the field of economics too.[74] Material welfare is not considered the supreme force that empowers Muslim societies; classical scholars upheld the virtues of modesty and piety. Muhammad Akram Khan contends that Islamic economics is about *falāḥ*—achieving individual or common good. If one elaborates on the economic domain of *falāḥ*, one notices that spending on others (those who need economic support) is both a social and spiritual necessity according to the Qur'ān.

This twofold perspective can also be found in other economic mechanisms, such as *zakāt* and *ribā*. The institution of *zakāt* (an Islamic wealth tax levied on savings and assets) has been reserved precisely for the weak in order to balance wealth and increase social welfare among the population.[75] *Zakāt* has not only a religious-moral but also a socioeconomic character. The Qur'ān mentions *zakāt* 82 times in combination with Islamic prayer (*ṣalāt*), which shows its importance and the interrelation between tax charity and spiritual uplift. Mechanisms such as *zakāt* combine religious imprint with social tendencies, since poverty is as much a social as a spiritual matter.[76] Despite various definitions of and approaches to *ribā*,[77] the prohibition of it[78] was believed to be based on the Qur'ān. *Ribā* was common among pre-Islamic Arabs. Classical Muslim scholars distinguish making profit in commercial activities from charging interest in light of the prohibition of *ribā*.[79] The main reason *ribā* was put into force was to prevent the accumulation of wealth and to diminish the economic differences between different layers of society. There are, however, many misperceptions about contemporary Islamic economics and its relation to conventional economics.

---

[73] Khan, *An Introduction to Islamic Economics*, 35–36.

[74] Khan, *An Introduction to Islamic Economics*, 59.

[75] Qur'ān 4:28, 100:8.

[76] Such a view has also been preserved among some of the contemporary Muslim politicians. "*Zakāt* tackles the misery of the poor and the equanimity of the rich. It alleviates the material differences between people and it binds them spiritually." Alija Izetbegović, *Islam između istoka i zapada* (*Islam between East and West*) (Novi Pazar: El Kelimeh, 1996), 198.

[77] See Rauf Azhar, *Economy of Islamic Economics* (Leiden: Brill, 2010).

[78] Interest on capital loan. Khan, *An Introduction to Islamic Economics*, 25.

[79] Qur'ān 2:275.

Conventional economic systems, discussed in detail in Chapter 5, presuppose that human beings are intrinsically selfish and that they strive to increase their satisfaction (income) and to maximize their profit. The result is an interest-based system built upon a deeply individual-oriented behavior within society. Contemporary mainstream economic thought assumes material satisfaction means the minimization of pain,[80] inflicted by a thirst for consumption, whereas the proponents of Islamic economics recognize the dual nature of humankind as both selfish and altruistic.[81] This understanding seeks to control the negative pole in order to regulate both the private and public domains or humanitarian charity endowment (*waqf*), an Islamic institution that stresses an individual's role in active assistance and the promotion of the common good within society. Thus, from such a perspective, material culture is an "embellishment of life" and is therefore secondary in importance to moral injunctions.

Yet, despite the fact that contemporary Muslim economists base their argument in the fundamental sources of Islam, they do not develop their epistemology from the classical scholarship, but rather from their vision of Islamic economics as a social science within the current division of knowledge, or by referring to the Islamization of knowledge project that commenced in the 1970s as a reconciliation effort between Islamic teachings and modernity, which brings about numerous epistemological and methodological inconsistencies.[82] Contemporary Muslim economists argue the Islamic worldview builds upon the fundamental premise of *tawḥīd* or the divine unity of God (or pure monotheism), which encompasses the moral, aesthetic, scientific, economic, and sociopolitical domains.[83] Classical Muslim scholars, whether philosophers, rationalists, or traditionalists, also inquired into the material and phenomenal world from the *tawḥīd* perspective, yet contemporary Muslim economists' reasoning subsumes all fields of knowledge under the premise of *tawḥīd* while resorting to economic and other social sciences and their methodologies.[84] The importance of *tawḥīd* epistemology is certainly visible in the scholarly literature, but for the majority of contemporary Muslim economists, it presents nothing more than a point of venture for their scholarly argument.

---

[80] Nomani and Rahnema, *Islamski ekonomski sistemi*, 555.

[81] Khan, *An Introduction to Islamic Economics*, 5.

[82] For a detailed account of the hybrid reality of contemporary Islamic economics and its epistemological differences with the classical economic ethics in Islamic tradition, see Al-Daghistani, "The Making of Islamic Economics."

[83] Choudhury, *The Islamic World-System*, 8.

[84] Rationalism was in classical Islamic philosophy championed by *muʿtazila*, whilst the traditionalist movement designated as *mutakallimūn* engaged with Islamic scholasticism. See, e.g., Fakhry, *A History of Islamic Philosophy*.

Contrarily, many classical scholars interrogated various economic aspects within the fields of *fiqh*, *falsafa*, *kalām*, and *taṣawwuf* as ethical categories. The classical scholars' standpoint on economic engagements was deeply influenced by the sciences of nature as ethical axioms and thus provided a different epistemological understanding of the relations between the social and metaphysical worlds. Such an understanding covers issues in both the mundane and the superlunary realms, exhibiting a form of epistemological multiplicity.[85]

Another reservation for contemporary Islamic economics is its economic mechanisms. While nowadays *ribā* is an essential factor in the Islamic economic and banking system, current trends within Islamic economics generally encourage a market economy, albeit through the imposition of ethically driven regulations and government intervention to disable the exploitation of power and the accumulation of wealth. Even if for many Muslim economists, "Islam envisages a world in which everyone with authority is accountable for his actions," aiming at establishing an economic order based upon the ethical regulations of *Sharī'a*, contemporary Islamic economics neither altered the existing economic worldview nor impinged its ethical regulations on the wealthy segment of the population.[86] It seems rather that those mechanisms operate within the prevalent neoliberal structures, obtaining not to the masses but to a particular clientele from which they receive support.

Only a few contemporary Muslim scholars such as Adi Setia,[87] Muhammad Ghazanfar,[88] and Abdul Azim Islahi[89] have engaged with al-Ghazālī's economic philosophy. While Adi Setia, is interested in *ṣūfī* economic thought, Ghazanfar

---

[85] In distinguishing cultural patterns from religious ones, some contemporary scholars differentiate between *Islamic* and *Islamicate*: the first pertains to Islam in the proper, religious sense, while the latter encompasses "the social and cultural complex historically associated with Islam and Muslims." If one affirms this somewhat problematic distinction, since al-Ghazālī's religious thought cannot be disassociated from his ethical stipulations, then by economic thought in Islamic tradition, in the first case we mean the theological backdrop of economic ideas, while in the second we mean the corpus of Islamic law and its practice. Excluded from this theoretical compilation are, however, the cultural practices of Muslims in premodern Islamic era. See Hodgson in A. K. Reinhart, "Islamic Law as Islamic Ethics," *Journal of Religious Ethics*, Vol. 11, No. 2 (1983): 186. For a critique of Hodgson's reasoning and the Islamic/Islamicate distinction, see Shahab Ahmed, *What Is Islam?* (Princeton, NJ: Princeton University Press, 2016), chapter 2.

[86] Khan, *An Introduction to Islamic Economics*, 4.

[87] E.g., Setia, "Al-Ghazālī on the Proprieties of Earning and Living."

[88] Ghazanfar, "The Economic Thought of Abu Hamid Al-Ghazali and St. Thomas Aquinas"; Ghazanfar, *Medieval Islamic Thought*.

[89] E.g., Ghazanfar and Islahi. *Economic Thought of al-Ghazali*; Ghazanfar and Islahi, "Economic Thought of an Arab Scholastic."

and Islahi approach the subject from a more analytical-technical standpoint, discerning al-Ghazālī's economic philosophy, policies, and juridical-economic statements. Regardless of these contributions, the majority of contemporary Muslim economists do not delve into Islamic economic history and consequently omit a large chunk of the discussions on ethical-economic teachings and moral law. This is where al-Ghazālī's contribution is crucial both for understanding the complexity of the classical economic thought in Islamic tradition and for providing an epistemological critique of the contemporary Islamic economics as a hybrid system of conventional economics and basic Islamic tenets.

Chapter 3

AL-GHAZĀLĪ'S ECONOMIC TEACHINGS AND THE SCIENCE OF THE HEREAFTER (*'ILM AL-ĀKHIRA*)

Al-Ghazālī's writings on economic thought are generally regarded as technical and highly structured yet, overall, his work on economic philosophy is closely associated with the place of the human in the universe and hence with ethical cosmology ground in concepts such as *kasb*, *faqr*, and *zuhd*. This chapter weaves through some of the technical aspects of his argument, starting with an analysis of al-Ghazālī's approach to *Sharī'a* through the mechanism of *maṣlaḥa* and his understanding of *fiqh* as an ethical category. He views *Sharī'a* as a moral system related to a particular conceptualization of economic thought, which he links to an ethics of happiness. Next, this chapter segues into a discussion of how al-Ghazālī's economic thought was part of the science of the hereafter, one imbued with a moral understanding of the universe. For him, exercising righteous economic engagements would lead to eternal happiness and divine truth, and would encompass both reason and knowledge, the outer (*ẓāhir*) and the inner (*bāṭin*), actions of the body (*'amal*) and knowledge (*'ilm*). The latter sections of this chapter—namely the third, fourth, and fifth sections—interrogate major postulates, divisions, and definitions of economic mechanisms such as just conduct, the division of labor and development of markets, and the role of wealth, respectively. Finally, this chapter concludes with an introduction to al-Ghazālī's take on governmental authority and the institution of *ḥisba* as a moral institution.

Al-Ghazālī believed ethics advocate a balanced approach to one's life—fluctuating between the *here* and the *hereafter*—in managing worldly affluences and aiming for spiritual uplift. In the context of ethical-economic literature, he presented the culmination of the *kasb-zuhd* amalgam. Ethical principles are attained not only by learning (rational discourse) but also by introspection and training of the heart (intuition) to be applied in everyday life. This approach hence resorts to both *ṣūfī* and philosophical traditions, and forms the gist of the science of the hereafter in *Iḥyā'*. In delineating economic propositions, al-Ghazālī's economic teachings refer to and build upon the science of the hereafter as a virtue ethics to attain eternal happiness. Since it is impossible to discern al-Ghazālī's economic thought from his *ṣūfī*, philosophical, or more jurisprudential writings, in the next section, I take a closer look at *Sharīʿa* as an ethical system and a moral law, as well as his stance toward it. Al-Ghazālī's account of legal ethics also entails analyzing the concepts of *tawḥīd* or the unity of God and *maṣlaḥa* as social welfare or common good, due to the role they play in preserving economic stability.

3.1 *Sharīʿa* and *Maṣlaḥa* in Economic Activities

In the modern period, *Sharīʿa* as Islamic law has been often perceived as the "immutable law," a subsystem of modern Islamic economics. In the classical period, however, economic thought was rather one component of *Sharīʿa*'s moral law, often problematized within the framework of *tawḥīd* or the unity of God that stretched beyond the legal confinements of Islamic law.[1] For the majority of classical Muslim scholars who wrote on economic thought, *Sharīʿa* prioritized moral endeavors over purely legal obligations and rights. Classical Muslim scholars made contributions to (the theory of) knowledge within the framework of Islamic theological, philosophical, and legal discourses, covering different branches and fields of study, from Islamic philosophy to astronomy. Their writings, which merged various strands of intellectual thought, were eminent for the understanding of concepts such as *Sharīʿa*, ethics, and economic thought in Islamic tradition. In light of the theory of cultural ambiguity within Islamic tradition, they vigorously examined, compared, and even merged apparently opposing or ambivalent subfields within a particular discourse, especially the study of Islam's moral law.[2] For al-Shaybānī, al-Muḥāsibī, and al-Ghazālī, for instance, *Sharīʿa* presents the core of economic principles and offers a holistic worldview of reality, often expressed through the notion of *faqr* or poverty. The Qur'ān, through *Sharīʿa*'s moral law, provides a cosmology, a metaphysic, and a world system carved into the epistemological structures of theological thought.[3] Moreover, it provides a conceptual backdrop for developing an economic philosophy based on such a worldview, advocating for the unification of knowledge. In this context, *tawḥīd* rests upon the rules (*aḥkām*) derived from the Qur'ān and the deeds of the Prophet Muḥammad (Sunna), which can be seen as an interpretation of social reality. The fundamental concepts of ethical-economic teachings, such as the Unity

---

1 For more on *tawḥīd*, see, e.g., *The Encyclopaedia of Islam*, s.v. "*Tawḥīd*" (Brill: Leiden, 2010), Volume 10, 389.

2 See Bauer, *Die Kultur der Ambiguität*.

3 See Hallaq, "Groundwork of the Moral Law"; Hallaq, *Sharīʿa*.

of God (*tawḥīd*), justice (*'adl*), moderation (*iqtiṣād*), and benevolence (*iḥsān*), are its constitutive parts found in major texts on economic thought in Islamic tradition. Ethical-economic teachings tend to confirm the idea of *tawḥīd* and do not praise the importance of what is nowadays called the market economy; they however stipulate the market only as a means to achieve a higher end, as al-Ghazālī also asserted. Such teachings, often seen as an ideal and normative, can nonetheless contribute to establishing an interactive social system by providing basic necessities to the members of society.

Throughout history, economic teachings in Islamic tradition have been regarded as an integral part of religious norms, yet not always as a product of legal tradition, but rather as ethically driven knowledge. Many of the abovementioned classical Muslim scholars and legal specialists, including al-Ghazālī, were often trained as theologians and/or *ṣūfīs*.[4] On the contrary, in the contemporary era, the majority of contributions to Islamic economics view the subject matter as a by-product of Islamic legal norms, principles, and prescriptions derived from the Qur'ān and the Prophetic tradition upheld by contemporary Muslim economists. They are predominantly perceived through the *Sharī'a* legislative regulations, aiming to square economic and financial propositions within legal theory.[5]

The very science of *Sharī'a* is called *fiqh*, and *fuqahā'* are specialists in legal matters. The four basic Sunni Islamic schools of law—Ḥanafī, Mālikī, Shāfi'ī, and Ḥanbalī—agree upon the four fundamental sources of *Sharī'a*—the Qur'ān, Sunna, *ijmā'* (consensus), and *qijās* (analogy). While economic thought is derived indirectly from the Qur'ān and the Sunna, these texts are the basis of legal literature. However, the third element, the *fuqahā'*, mainly established the judicial system; they reflected on the ethical teachings of what is, according to Islamic law, regarded as lawful or licit conduct. In addition to the *fuqahā'*, various Muslim scholars who also wrote on ethical economic thought in Islamic tradition claim that *Sharī'a* covers all aspects of human behavior. In the 'Abbāsid era, Islamic economic jurisprudence took a specialized path with the writing of economic literature.[6] In addition to the four fundamental Sunni schools of law established exactly at that time, their exercising *ijtihād* in the field of human thought and in economic and legal writings contributed not

---

[4] See, e.g., Hallaq, *The Impossible State*.

[5] On the subject of modern Islamic economic thought, see the writings of, e.g., Chapra, Choudhury, Naqvi, and Siddiqi. On the critique of the subject, despite its shortcomings, see, e.g., Timur Kuran, *Islam and Mammon* (Princeton, NJ: Princeton University Press, 2005); Muhammad Ahmad Khan, *What Is Wrong with Islamic Economics? Analysing the Present State and Future Agenda* (Cheltenham: Edward Elgar, 2015).

[6] Ashker and Wilson, *Islamic Economics*, 155–57.

only to trade and economic management but also to the flourishing of a specific *ṣūfī* and ethical-economic genre.[7]

Every legal system is bound to various levels of rigidity and flexibility. Islamic law, despite being regarded as a divine law, stimulated various economic developments, even if certain practices in Muslim societies might have been rendered unfavorable. In the premodern period, lawmaking was an organic endeavor practiced by learned men who were themselves part of the social fabric. Similarly, in an economic context, *dīn* (religion) consists of *imān*, whereas *Sharīʿa* is perceived as the divine code of conduct.[8] An extension of this view relates to modern Islamic economics, erroneously presupposing that economic thought stems from *fiqh* literature, and that Islamic law was always historically centered only on legal-technical matters. While economic activities in Islamic tradition might be perceived as religiously stipulated according to *Sharīʿa*, they are not necessarily regarded as legal per se.[9] As such, one would think Islamic economic doctrine falls under the corpus of the Islamic legal system; however, this view can be contested since the economic thought classical Muslim scholars procured shows a great deal of ethical and cosmological deliberations, whereas the legal realm constituted only a part. Such reasoning advocates the idea that the discrepancy between *Sharīʿa* as the immutable divine law and *fiqh* or Islamic law as a manifestation or attempt to apply the divine law through a humanly maintained judicial system is apparent on an epistemological level, which mirrors socioeconomic teachings in the classical period. Thomas Bauer claims Islamic law has always been perceived as

---

[7] According to Wael Hallaq, *ijtihād* has been designated as an independent legal reasoning and has been practiced throughout the history of Islam, since it was utilized as a mental tool and emphasized by the Prophet of Islam himself. Hallaq claims that *ijtihād* as a mental effort that presupposes extracting passages from legal sources and exercising legal opinions has never ceased, since *mujtahids* (those equipped with knowledge who practiced *ijtihād*) have existed throughout history. On the notion of *ijtihād* in Islamic thought, see Wael B. Hallaq, "Was the Gate of Ijtihad Closed?" *International Journal of Middle East Studies*, Vol. 16 (1984): 3–41; Hallaq, "On the Origins of the Controversy about the Existence of Mujtahids and the Gate of Ijtihad," *Studia Islamica*, Vol. 63 (1986): 129–41; Shista P. Ali-Karamali and Fiona Dunne, "The Ijtihad Controversy," *Arab Law Quarterly*, Vol. 9 (1994): 238–57; Imaran Ahsan Khan Nyazee, *Theories of Islamic Law: The Methodology of Ijtihad* (Kuala Lumpur: Other Press, 1994), 269–301.

[8] Nomani and Rahnema, *Islamski ekonomski sistemi*, 14–15.

[9] The following paragraphs are based on an article I wrote in 2016 that explores this idea further. See Sami Al-Daghistani, "Semiotics of Islamic Law, Maṣlaḥa, and Islamic Economic Thought," *International Journal for the Semiotics of Law—Revue internationale de Sémiotique juridique*, Vol. 29, No. 2 (June 2016): 389–404. Accessible at doi.org/10.1007/s11196-016-9457-x.

religious law with a divine character, which became overarching.[10] Such a view can also be reformulated in regard to economic thought, if one follows the distinction between *Sharī'a* as God's law, Islamic law as *fiqh*, and legal stipulations as *aḥkām*. While classical legal works offer detailed discussions of legal stipulations, they are nonetheless framed and theorized as part of *Sharī'a*'s moral law. In line with Bauer's proposition and Nasr Abu Zayd's theory of God's speech, *Sharī'a* pertains to *ḥukm* not as legal stipulations or injunctions per se, but in terms of assessing overall human conduct. In this context, a rule or *ḥukm* is how divine speech (*kalām*) relates to human beings and their position in this world.[11] The methodology of Islamic law or *usūl al-fiqh* explains the process of deducting legal injunctions or *aḥkām* from the Qur'ān and the Sunna, which is in essence an *ijtihād*—a legal scholar's thorough exertion to understand and interpret the sources of law.[12]

Not all economic-related teachings and activities can be thus studied only within the legal body and its proceedings. Theoretically, certain activities within contemporary Islamic economics fall under the category of law, yet economic knowledge established by both the *fuqahā'* and classical Muslim scholars was premised upon *Sharī'a* ethical norms. They differ from the legal norms that constitute the sum of contemporary Islamic economic science. *Sharī'a* as a moral law (stemming from Qur'ānic normative teachings) and ethical-*ṣūfī* considerations constitute the core of classical economic thought in Islamic tradition, in that they extend to the questions of purchases, sales, commodities, obtaining food and shelter, utilization of money, and other activities as part of the ethical self-accountability.[13] Economic ideas hence do not rest only upon legal precepts, since economic problems presented by scholars like al-Ghazālī bear distinct ethical and broader metaphysical connotations, and cannot be conceptualized only as legal rulings.[14] The moral core of *Sharī'a* does not provide insights into how to manage the institutions of *zakāt*, *ribā*,

---

[10] On Islam as the culture of ambiguity (including the realm of Islamic law), see Bauer, *Die Kultur der Ambiguität.*

[11] Bauer, *Die Kultur der Ambiguität*, 158, and Abu Zayd's theory of divine speech and human hermeneutics.

[12] See, e.g., Wael B. Hallaq, "From Fatwās to Furū': Growth and Change in Islamic Substantive Law," *Islamic Law and Society*, Vol. 1, No. 1 (1994): 29–65.

[13] Qur'ān 25:67: "A true believer would not be extravagant nor miserly"; Qur'ān 2:275: "But Allah has permitted trade and forbidden usury"; Qur'ān 100:8: "Man is violent in the love of wealth."

[14] See, e.g., Abdel Rahman Yousri Ahmed, "The Scientific Approach to Islamic Economics: Philosophy, Theoretical Construction and Applicability," in *Theoretical Foundation of Islamic Economics*, ed. Habib Ahmed (Jeddah: Islamic Development Bank, Islamic Research and Training Institute, No. 3, 2002), 19–58.

and other conceptualities in light of legal-technical understanding, but primarily as a socioeconomic-ethical consideration.

Economic practices, although sometimes applied to the substantive law (*fiqh*) as the result of the process of deduction, do not automatically propose a legal character of economic teachings.[15] Classical legal scholar and eponym Abu Hanīfah (d. 767), in his work *al-Fiqh al-Akbar*, pointed out that *fiqh* pertains to one's comprehension and understanding of religious matters and scriptural sources of law.[16] In this context, *fiqh* can be understood as a process of delineating not only that which is legislated but also that which is formulated and produced via the scholarly community. Studying *fiqh* means delving into other Islamic sciences, such as systematic theology and mysticism, for it has to be analyzed in tandem with its ethical considerations. While *Sharī'a*'s moral law remains the imperative put forward by the Qur'ān, *fiqh* provides a legal substratum to tackle and solve more practical dilemmas within the Muslim community. Islamic law hence does not only pertain to statutes (*ḥudūd*) but also, as understanding (*fiqh*), imparts a metaphysical quality to Islamic legal doctrine. This also includes dealing with wealth and other economic activities, which are for the majority of classical Muslim scholars embedded in the idea of righteous living, organized between managing the mundane and seeking eternal happiness in the hereafter.

Research into the process of deducting the legal stipulations from the Qur'ān and tradition within Islamic intellectual history reveals economic ideas were seldom regarded as legally binding, but being a direct manifestation of the divine law, they were ethical interpretations by *'ulamā'*.[17] In modern times, one tends to associate the term *morality* with classical Islamic (Qur'ānic) exegeses, whereas law (practice) is considered exogenous, as if belonging to two different narratives. Yet this distinction did not flourish in classical economic philosophy, and was not enhanced by al-Ghazālī and his ilk.[18] Scholars like

---

[15] According to Toshihiko Izutsu, the moral code is one component of the overall ideology, embedded into the linguistic system, and therefore represents a certain worldview (*Weltanschauung*) and interprets it accordingly. See Mohamed Aslam Haneef and Hafas Furqani, "Developing the Ethical Foundations of Islamic Economics: Benefitting from Toshihiko Izutsu," *Intellectual Discourse*, Vol. 17, No. 2 (2009): 176.

[16] Abu Hanifa, *Imām Abū Ḥanifa's al-Fiqh al-Akbar*, trans. Abdur-Rahman ibn Yusuf (Santa Barbara, CA: White Thread Press, 2007); Abu Hanifa, *Al-Fiqh al-Akbar. Die Fundamente des Glaubens vom Imam Abu Hanifa*, trans. Ali Ghandour (Istanbul: Kalbi Kapital, 2009).

[17] According to Hallaq, Islamic law was not parted from the conception of Qur'ānic morality in the premodern era, which means the two fields were meshed together. See Hallaq, *Sharī'a*.

[18] Two ethical concepts that are crucial for the study of economic activities are *khalīfa* (vicegerent) and *'abd* (servant). The word *khalīfa* translates to *successor* or *vicegerent* and it has been bestowed to humankind according to the Qur'ān. Sura *al-Baqara* (see Qur'ān 2:30)

al-Ghazālī grounded economic behavioral patterns in the science of the hereafter as part of their overall ethics of happiness, which also entails al-Ghazālī's account of the objectives of *Sharī'a* and *maṣlaḥa.*

The objectives of *Sharī'a* or *maqāṣid al-Sharī'a* are crucial to the development of Islamic law. Even though *maqāṣid* have been less theorized in the field of economic thought, they can present important mechanisms for safeguarding economic provisions. Many authors from the classical and contemporary period, including al-Ghazālī, wrote on the objectives of the law.[19] *Maqāṣid al-Sharī'a* provide wisdom for legal rulings and can be seen as an ethical concept dealing with social welfare, human dignity, and economic preservation.[20] While *maqāṣid al-Sharī'a* were developed by classical scholars,[21] contemporary scholarship on *maqāṣid* introduced more detailed, universal percepts in comparison to *fiqh* literature.[22] For some scholars, *maqāṣid* represent legal change and reform.[23] *Maqāṣid* evolved after the Companion era, yet the objectives as we know them today were introduced much later, during the formative period. With the emergence of the philosophy of Islamic law, al-Jawaynī in the eleventh century utilized *maqāṣid* for his theory on necessities and needs. He coined the term by proposing five levels of *maqāṣid*: necessities (*ḍarūrāt*), public needs (*al-hāja al-'amah*), moral behavior (*al-makrumāt*), recommendations (*al-mandūbāt*), and specifics.[24] Al-Ghazālī elaborated them further in order to provide provision

mentions that human beings are created as *khalīfa* on Earth to ordain divine patterns through which they are granted free will to apply or reject ethically driven stipulations. Classical scholars regarded this role as based on trust through which human beings could establish a virtuous life. Such a role gives them a capacity to act accordingly in the domain of economics activities. As such, human beings are considered physical-intellectual-spiritual beings (Qur'ān 32:6–9). The role of *khalīfa* cannot be perceived as merely a personal obligation but rather a collective one. In this respect, the Qur'ānic worldview is essentially "theocentric," which further presupposes that major concepts are interrelated with the very metaphysics of the Qur'ān.

19 See al-Ghazālī, *Al-Mustaṣfā fi 'Ilm al-Uṣūl*; Jasser Ouda, *Maqāṣid al-Sharī'a* (Herndon, VA: Al-M'had al-'ālami lil fikr al-Islāmī, 2012); Muḥammad al-Ṭāhir ibn Muḥammad ibn 'Āshūr, *Treatise on Maqāṣid al-Sharī'a*, trans. Muḥammad al-Ṭāhir al-Masāwī (London: International Institute of Islamic Thought, 2006); Ibn 'Āshūr, *Maqāṣid al-Sharī'ah al-Islāmiyyah*, ed. Muḥammad al-Ṭāhir al-Masāwī (Amman: Dār al-Nafā'is, 2001).

20 See Ibn 'Āshūr, *Treatise on Maqāṣid al-Sharī'a.*

21 According to Jasser Ouda, traditionally, *maqāṣid* did not include the notion of justice and were extracted from *fiqh* literature and not by studying the original sources. Ouda, *Maqāṣid al-Sharī'a*, 4.

22 See Ibn 'Āshūr, *Treatise on Maqāṣid al-Sharī'a.*

23 Felicitas Opwis, *Maṣlaḥa and the Purpose of the Law: Islamic Discourse on Legal Change from the 4th/10th to the 8th/14th Century* (Leiden: Brill, 2010).

24 Ouda, *Maqāṣid al-Sharī'a*, 17.

for the well-being of humankind by safeguarding the categories of faith (*dīn*), human self (*nafs*), intellect (*'aql*), offspring (*nasl*), and wealth (*māl*).[25]

One of the main themes of al-Ghazālī's economic writings was the concept of *maṣlaḥa*, meaning the common good or social welfare, which pertains to the individual and society. The notion of *maṣlaḥa* has been predominantly discussed within the parameters of Islamic legal discourse. It also appears relevant for economic thought, since it includes the notion of economic preservation through ethical conduct. According to Muhammad Fahim Khan, many economic agents can be derived from the objectives of Islamic law as it was explored by al-Shāṭibī and al-Ghazālī. While all human conduct is framed in terms of social benefit and disutility (*maṣāliḥ-mafāsid*), it is subsumed by the moral law.[26] The function of the social welfare addresses human needs in relation to basic needs, such as food, clothing, shelter, secondary necessities, and luxuries. Economic development is in this light a requisite activity. Al-Ghazālī provided a thorough analysis of the role of voluntary trade, the evolution of markets, and means of accumulation, as well as the role of ethical conduct, whereas the role of the governmental authority is "to be limited to the provision of infrastructure and police powers."[27] His norms of economic behavior can be described as the achievement of the "middle path," the golden mean between material hedonism and spiritual understanding, emphasizing the cultivation of reason and righteous behavior before engaging in any (economic) activity. *Maṣlaḥa* would hence determine whether an economic activity should be pursued, promoting social welfare in a community.[28] This promotes the idea that economic behavior is considered within the scope of the higher objectives of *Sharī'a*, whereby an economic agent will try to seek *maṣlaḥa* instead of utility in a conventional sense.[29] Purely individual-based interests and endeavors are perceived as undesirable, unless fostering the concept of *maṣlaḥa*. Such an ethical perception advocates the idea of curtailing the wants as "*maṣlaḥa* lead to the concept of fulfilling needs."[30] All matters and activities have to be seen as a means to achieve goals toward increasing the social welfare. According to al-Ghazālī, there are the abovementioned five compulsory *Sharī'a*-based foundations or components for a proper and

---

25 Al-Ghazālī, *Mustasfā*, Vol. 1, 286–87.

26 Ghazanfar and Islahi, "Economic Thought of an Arab Scholastic," 383.

27 Ali and Thompson, "The Schumpeterian Gap and Muslim Economic Thought."

28 Al-Ghazālī, *Iḥyā'*, Vol. 2, 109.

29 Utility relates to the conceptualization deriving from individual endeavors, whereas *maṣlaḥa* "is amenable to objective verification." Muhammad Fahim Khan, "Theorizing Islamic Economics: Search for a Framework for Islamic Economic Analysis," *Islamic Economics*, Vol. 26, No. 1 (2013): 209–42 at 231.

30 Khan, "Theorizing Islamic Economics," 232.

just individual and social life: *dīn* (religion), *nafs* (life of soul), *naṣl* (family), *māl* (wealth), and *'aql* (intellect, reason).[31] *Maṣlaḥa* as a public good are inextricably related to *Sharī'a*, whose key objective is advocating what, according to the Qur'ān, is perceived as desirable in the mundane and in the hereafter (*maṣlaḥa al-dīn wa al-dunyā*). Hence, the noblest deed in the eyes of God is the promotion of the common (public) good in the community as an indispensable benefit for society. Al-Ghazālī discusses three aspects of *maṣlaḥa* in a hierarchical form: necessities (*ḍarurāt*), conveniences or comforts (*ḥajāt*), and refinements or luxuries (*taḥsināt*).[32] The members of the community have to constantly revise these aspects. The second element comprises "all activities and things that are not vital to the preservation of the five foundations, but, rather, are needed to relieve or remove impediments and difficulties in life," whereas the third element includes activities perceived as a surplus or additional to the basic necessities.[33]

3.1.1 Fiqh as an ethical category

Al-Ghazālī was believed to be the first Muslim scholar who introduced the study of Aristotelian logic into the discourse of Islamic jurisprudence and further developed al-Juwaynī's contributions in this field.[34] He based his legal arguments upon the Shāfi'ī tradition of Islamic law, composing new terminology and shaping a new discourse on legal matters.[35] His roles as a jurist by training,[36] a theologian by tradition, and a *ṣūfī* by conviction and devotion, which often incorporated philosophical reasoning, allowed al-Ghazālī to deftly intertwine different segments of intellectual tradition with the capacity to question the establishment and to initiate new channels of acquiring knowledge, all the while preserving ethical teachings he believed to be rooted in the tradition of *Sharī'a*.[37] His approach to Islamic tradition hence involves moral philosophy when addressing legal issues, a method he also implemented

---

[31] See al-Ghazālī, *Mustasfā*, Vol. 1, 286–87.

[32] For more, see Al-Ghazālī, *Mustasfā*, Vol. 1.

[33] Anas Zarqa, "Islamic Economics: An Approach to Human Welfare," in *Studies in Islamic Studies*, ed. Khurshid Ahmed (Markfield: Islamic Foundation, 1980), 3–118 at 13.

[34] Ormsby, *Ghazali*, 36.

[35] Muḥammad b. Idrīs al-Shāfi'ī (d. 820), was the author of the famous *Kitāb al-Umm* and is believed to have systematized Islamic law.

[36] As a jurist, al-Ghazālī's most influential book after the *Iḥyā'* is believed to be *Mustasfā*, a book on Islamic law and jurisprudence.

[37] He was labeled an adherent of *taṣawwuf* not because of the amount of knowledge he acquired but because of his contribution to the science of *taṣawwuf* as a spiritual and systematic field of inquiry that also included other epistemologies.

when analyzing economic ideas, indicating that human virtues and psychological sensitivities are indispensable components of other social, political, and even religious endeavors. Since the Shāfi'ī school of law also bases its legal reasoning on the method of analogy (*qiyās*), as indicated in the Qur'ān and the Prophetic tradition, al-Ghazālī utilized this approach to tackle various legal questions. "The use of analogy characterizes his *ṣūfī* writings, where it crops up repeatedly as a form of analogical intuition."[38] In al-Ghazālī's view, the jurist must engage directly with legal, social, ethical, and also economic affairs, and this has practical implications.

The law (*furū' al-fiqh*), or, rather, legal ethics, is something al-Ghazālī points out throughout *Iḥyā'*, in that following it constitutes part of the very science of the hereafter. Al-Ghazālī ushers us into the moral side of the law by saying *fiqh* used to be part of the sciences of the hereafter as an ethical category. Only later in Islamic history did it became associated with jurisprudence.[39] The very term *fiqh* as part of religious sciences (*'ulūm al-dīn*) was initially used to refer to "the path of the science of the hereafter that can be perceived through maturity of the intellect (*kamāl al-'aql*) and the clarity of the mind (*ṣafā' al-dhakā'*), while the intellect is the most honorable human characteristic,"[40] and "if we attach *fiqh* to the path of the science of the hereafter, it becomes honorable."[41] He further states *fiqh*

> has become a specialized branch of *fatwas* and *waqfs*, on small details about them, and excessive debates surrounding them. [...] The meaning of *fiqh* in the first period was, however, undisputedly linked to the science of the path of the hereafter, knowledge of the details of harmful matters of the self, that which corrupts human action, understanding of indulging in the wickedness of the world, perseverance for reaching the grace of the hereafter, and [God's] fear's domination over the heart.[42]

---

38 Ormsby, *Ghazali*, 38.

39 Garden, *The First Islamic Reviver*, 110; al-Ghazālī, *Iḥyā'*, Vol. 1, 32, 33. See also Moosa, *Ghazālī and the Poetics of Imagination*, 31–32. "Ghazālī reconstructed fiqh, normally described as positive law, to mean the discovery of knowledge that identifies the path to salvation in the afterlife. In other words, fiqh constitutes certain ethical practices that are preceded by the inculcation of virtues and character traits (ādāb and akhlāq). Once these virtues and traits are internalized, or traced onto the habitus of the ethical subject, one ceases to think of fiqh as positive law and begins to think of its function as a juridical ethics."

40 Al-Ghazālī, *Iḥyā'*, Vol. 1, 12.

41 Al-Ghazālī, *Iḥyā'*, Vol. 1, 17.

42 Al-Ghazālī, *Iḥyā'*, Vol. 1, 32.

The very engagement with law necessitates an ethical subjectivity.[43] Al-Ghazālī labeled the legal specialists or *fuqahā'* as the scholars of the world—*'ulamā' al-dunyā*—and posited law in the service of the science of the hereafter.[44] Apropos the four eponyms and founders of the Sunni legal schools of law, al-Ghazālī maintains they were all operating first and foremost in the service of the science of the hereafter and not out of any necessity to deal with technical aspects of the law.[45] Law is also inextricably related to philosophical and *ṣūfī* teachings, and hence never should be perceived as a separate entity from ethical considerations and higher ends.[46] George Hourani points out that *fiqh* as the ethics of action and *akhlāq* as the ethics of character correspond to the two human means to happiness.[47] While righteous (just) trading activities fall under the rubric of law, they are meant to be executed out of one's good deeds or *iḥsān* and moral deliberations. *Iḥsān* is crucial for carrying out righteous economic activities and for al-Ghazālī leads to salvation and eternal happiness. It is part of one's faith (*imān*) that one is encouraged to pursue. *Iḥsān* is closely associated with the practical stipulations of material life, indicating that the realm of *'ibādāt* is inseparable from the regulations of *mu'āmalāt*. According to al-Ghazālī's science of the hereafter, an ethical worldview consists of a total approach to the phenomenal world, whereby he attempts to coherently unify various fields under its principle while delineating economic activities. This worldview encompasses both material and nonmaterial realms. The eminent or intrinsic experience of the spiritual and that of the material world is referred to as *fiṭra*[48] in the Qur'ān, which mobilizes knowledge in the lived environment. For al-Ghazālī, ethical behavior concerning economic conduct is one constituent of the totality of his ethical theory of happiness.

Throughout *Iḥyā'*, one notices that the underlying notion of authority on how to deal with economic behavior in the mundane and the hereafter is the category of *Sharī'a* and the concept of fidelity. Law is thus never a plain

---

43 For more on the foundation of *fiqh* in ethical reasoning in al-Ghazālī, see, e.g., Yūsuf al-Qaraḍāwī, *Al-Imām Ghazālī bayna Mādiḥī wa-Nāqidhī* (Beirut: Mū'assat al-risāla, 1994); Moosa, *Ghazālī and the Poetics of Imagination*, 241.

44 Al-Ghazālī, *Iḥyā'*, Vol. 1, 19.

45 See the description of the four eponyms in al-Ghazālī, *Iḥyā'*, Vol. 1.

46 In Disciplining of the Soul, al-Ghazālī writes that religious and social rituals also have an impact on the heart. See al-Ghazālī, *Iḥyā'*, Vol. 3.

47 Hourani, "Ghazālī on the Ethics of Action," 77.

48 The term *fiṭra* designates the intrinsic purity or primary nature of man: an ability to comprehend the existence of God and His unity. According to the Qur'ān, the religion of Islam is often regarded as *dīn al-fiṭra*, implying its suitableness to the character of human spirit. See, e.g., Qur'ān 30:30, 7:172, 139.

regulator of licit or illicit conduct, but is a cosmological faculty, a spiritual call aiming to supply human actions with morally driven endeavors.[49] The strong connection between the notion of the hereafter and economic ethics for al-Ghazālī constitutes a dynamic relationship manifested in society, linking mundane activities with rewards in the afterlife. Even if *ākhira* (the hereafter) ought to be the ultimate aim, pursuing economic gains is not rejected, but rather desirable, if handled correctly.[50] The main concepts of al-Ghazālī's economic teachings that include the utilization of money, sales, and purchases have a direct cosmological correlation to a human being as a finite entity that is nonetheless geared toward higher ends.[51] An "economic agent" in light of his theory is thus one whose behavior is prompted by the norms of economic engagement, encapsulated in the values of the science of the hereafter by merging *Sharīʿa* law with metaphysical qualities. One's actions, including economic behavior, are seen as part of the commitment to follow that which is prescribed (*Sharīʿa*), not as a legal regulation, but rather as an ethical category. Al-Ghazālī's *Iḥyāʾ* informs us to conceive of economic thought as embedded in the science of the hereafter, in whose core is the ethics of happiness, rooted in philosophical discourse, the tradition of *taṣawwuf*, and legal culture of cosmological proportions. Since ethics also presupposes praxis, al-Ghazālī advocates an idea that ethical standards and norms do not only present legal stipulations but also entail moral patterns of socioeconomic behavior. In what follows, I turn to al-Ghazālī's economic teachings and its main postulates, divisions, and entanglements with legal and ethical reasoning.

3.2 Economics Fostered by Ethics of Happiness

Since al-Ghazālī positions economic activities within the parameters of his theory of happiness, the hereafter is seen as the ultimate goal of every

---

[49] See, e.g., al-Ghazālī, *Iḥyāʾ*, Vol. 3, 65.

[50] Al-Ghazālī, *Iḥyāʾ*, Vol. 2, 60.

[51] *The khalīfa* as a vicegerent on earth is an agent, a mediator through which the divine will is manifested. Applying the *khalīfa* concept in economic teachings would mean placing the divine will in the center of all matters. In this regard, the role of the *khalīfa* is a part of a grand raison d'être of creation—namely, to serve higher ends. The *dunyā* is through the role of *khalīfa* related to the *ākhira*, and economic activities rely on and are interdependent with the factor of time. The notion of time plays a significant role not only within the philosophical and theological tradition but also specifically in relation to ethical conduct and economic pursuits, in that it manages theories of production, capital, money, deferred payments, and labor. For more on the *khalīfa* in Islamic tradition, see, e.g., Muhammad Attas, *Prolegomena to the Metaphysics of Islam* (Kuala Lumpur: Dar al-Risala, 2001).

endeavor. All acts, pursuits, behaviors, predispositions, and imaginations deemed economically stipulated—in that they foster economic subjectivity—merge the material with the metaphysical. He teaches us that in economic subjectivity, the outer (*ẓāhir*) concurs with the inner (*bāṭin*) by incubating an ethical realization of the self. Rules of the legal, cultivation of the pedagogical self (*adab*), the argumentation of the philosophical, and the uplifting of the psychological realms all find their place in his virtuous economics. The technical is subsumed by the ethical, and the legal by the moral. These realms are often manifested by ascetic practice.

The Qur'ānic verse "*Lā tansa naṣībaka min al-dunyā*" ("Do not forget your share in this world") can be understood as not neglecting one's economic share or contribution in this world.[52] *Dunyā* or the mundane is not seen primarily as a place of dissolution, but rather as a path toward salvation realized through human endeavors and affairs, including economic pursuits. In this respect, (licit) economic activity is a prerequisite for salvation, since the real gain lies in the hereafter.[53]

Al-Ghazālī did not produce a specific book completely dedicated to economics, rather his economic ideas on *zakāt*, ethics, the role of governmental authority, and other related tools and concepts can be found throughout his works, especially in *Iḥyā'*, in addition to *Mīzān* and *Naṣīḥat*. His economic thought is a product of a specific era and culture—namely, that of the twelfth-century political-intellectual reality of the Saljūq empire. One cannot expect to find an elaborate theoretical system of economics similar to those in the modern period. Nonetheless, he ought to be considered as a thinker whose writings on economic thought present an important component of his overall ethical scholarship within Islamic sciences. Even if at times his economic account is highly normative and, in many regards, presents an ideal set of norms, his writings simultaneously suggest an implicit critique of government officials, a genuine dissatisfaction with the sociopolitical landscape of his time, and a fervent quest to revive the ethical teachings of religious life.

In *Mīzān*, al-Ghazālī positions economics between ethics and politics as part of practical science or *al-'ilm al-'amalī* to attain individual felicity.[54] Practical science encompasses various subdisciplines, including ethics, earning a living or *ma'īsha*, and other social or practical engagements and transactions or *mu'āmala*.[55] According to Ghazanfar and Islahi, his contribution to economic thought can be divided into four topics, systematically covering a

---

[52] Qur'ān 28:77.

[53] Al-Ghazālī, *Iḥyā'*, Vol. 2, 82.

[54] Al-Ghazālī, *Mīzān al-'Amal* (Cairo: Dār al-Ma'ārif, 1964), 50.

[55] Al-Ghazālī, *Mīzān*, 120.

variety of economic activities with ethical applications: voluntary exchange and evolution of markets, production activities and their hierarchy and stages, the barter system and the evolution of money, and the role of governmental authority and public finances.[56] This division can be, however, systematized in light of al-Ghazālī's ethical teachings, covering all subjects of economic thought as part of his overall attempt to revive the human soul, and can be divided into themes such as ethical jurisprudence and *maṣlaḥa*, a more spiritual take on economic gains in light of the hereafter, division of labor and development of markets, the function of money, and the role of *ḥisba* and governmental authority. These five components encompass his economic philosophy of eternal happiness rooted in both philosophical and mystical teachings. One component of this analysis of economic activities relates to engagements that (in)directly harm society as a whole. Several requirements can be deduced from al-Ghazālī's writings that a human being must meet for the overall preservation of the *dīn* while practicing economic activities.[57] First is a good intention (*niyya*) at the very beginning of any economic endeavor or activity as a moral reasoning, in order to free oneself from envy of and dependence on others, as well as to provide for one's own household. Intention is a prerequisite for the realization of action of the ethical self.[58] In this respect, one must bear in mind the economic state of others while exercising *'adl* (equity), *iḥsān* (benevolence), and *'amr bi al-ma'rūf wa nahy 'an al-munkar* (leading the path of rightness) by upholding the licit and preventing illicit acts or purchases.[59] Second, since economic activity is one of the basic human social needs, one fulfills the requirement of social utility in trade and commerce. Third, economic activities should not exempt one from following basic Islamic principles; therefore, the pursuit of the "mundane market" should be sought in correlation to the values of the hereafter. Fourth, the remembrance of God should be present in the market or in trading processes; further, the purchase of trading goods should not be based on greed and lust, although economic engagement is permitted and even encouraged in the Qur'ān, but rather on moderation and the conscious exercise of licit conduct along with sharing.[60] Apart from following

---

[56] Ghazanfar and Islahi, *Economic Thought of al-Ghazali*, 17.

[57] Ghazali and Sadeq, "Ghazalijevi pogledi na ekonomske probleme i neka etičko-pravna pitanja značajna za ekonomsko ponašanje," 159–62.

[58] Intention is inextricably linked to action. It is, however, action that drives the ethical self. "Thus, the self is an ethical subject related to actions rather than to pure intentions, even though intention is a crucial preliminary to action." Moosa, *Ghazālī and the Poetics of Imagination*, 229.

[59] For more on the definition of what is good and harmful, see al-Ghazālī, *Iḥyā'*, Vol. 2, 306, 307.

[60] Qur'ān 62:10.

legal opinions (*fatwā*), one should employ independent legal reasoning (*ijtihād*) in order to conduct trade according to Islamic principles and to uphold fair trade and behavior.[61]

Al-Ghazālī framed his economic ethics within the notion of the hereafter not as a goal of fatalistic proportions, but as a supreme end that awaits everyone. He mostly considered the consequences deeds have on the soul and therefore generated an ethics of happiness.[62] His economic ethics is closely related to the notion of *kasb* or wealth acquisition and *zuhd* that pertains to renouncing illicit (economic) behavior. By eternal happiness (*sa'āda*), al-Ghazālī means "everlasting without demise, pleasure without effort, felicity without tragedy, prosperity without poverty, perfection without defect, and esteem without humiliation."[63] Ultimate happiness is to be achieved through self-examination and self-knowledge by recognizing that one's heart is pure and that it becomes tainted by the pursuit of desires. Happiness hence depends on the usage of our faculties such as reason, imagination, and belief by emulating the most profound examples of human history (prophets) and their essential spirituality, and it is rooted in the recognition that the human soul carries a knowledge of pain. This recognition sets one on the path to happiness, which for al-Ghazālī encompasses all aspects of human life, including one's economic behavior. A state of discontent is created by enslavement of desire and the belief that one should satisfy only one's own desires. Acts are hence considered good or bad according to the nature of the effect they have on the soul in being conducive to the divine end, which further indicates that actions as such have no intrinsic meaning. Actions of an economic nature understandably intersect with ethical and jurisprudential teachings. If a comprehensive ethics of al-Ghazālī does exist, then it can be called the ethics of the soul, for he places all his efforts on the disengagement of one's soul in the worldly life. Since the soul (*nafs*) has access to the human senses, both the soul and the consciousness can consequently become affected by the physical senses. Because man is, in his consciousness, in a state of awakeness, one bears (personal and social) responsibilities when dealing with economic postulates. Since "rational sciences are insufficient for the health of the soul although it is in need of them, in the same way as reason is insufficient in continuance of the means of health of the body, but needs to know the properties of medicines and drugs by learning

---

61 Ghazali and Sadeq, "Ghazalijevi pogledi na ekonomske probleme i neka etičko-pravna pitanja značajna za ekonomsko ponašanje," 154.

62 Muhammad Abdul Quasem, *The Ethics of al-Ghazali* (Petaling Jaya: Quasem, 1975), 25.

63 Al-Ghazālī, *Criterion of Action*, trans. Muhammad Hozien, ed. S. Dunyā (Cairo: Dār al-Ma'ārif, 1964), 180; Al-Ghazālī, *Mīzān*.

from physicians; for mere reason cannot guide these, but their understanding after hearing is not possible except by reason,"[64] al-Ghazālī recognizes the categories of reason, revelation, and mystical experience that constitute his ethical system.[65]

Al-Ghazālī discusses economic issues predominantly in the third book of the second volume of *Iḥyā'*, entitled "Manners of Earning a Livelihood," although his economic ideas are also found in the fourth volume. Four chapters in this book are specifically intended to address economic theory and financial issues: the nature of work and various means of earning a livelihood; lawful means of earning concerning business, trade, and exchange; justice, equity, and fairness in gaining a livelihood, for example, cheating, counterfeiting, hoarding, over-praising commodities or wealth, exploiting costumers, and so forth; and benevolence and piety in trading and economic activities.[66] In *Kīmiyā-yi Sa'ādat* (*The Alchemy of Eternal Bliss*), which is often regarded as the concise summary of *Iḥyā'*, al-Ghazālī lays down his ethical principles of trade activities. The trader should be honest in his deeds and a man should earn his living by real work as a sign of his piety, therefore incentives to earn a licit livelihood are regarded as rewarding. Proper work is perceived as *tawakkul* or trust in God, while blindly following the patterns of one's predecessors without pondering issues (*taqlīd*) of trading activity goes against *Sharī'a*.[67] In accordance with *fiqh*, al-Ghazālī analyzed three elements of trade: agreements between buyer and seller, commodities of the transaction, and the content of the agreement.[68] The seller should not sell a commodity to a person who is a minor, mentally ill, a slave, or blind, or to someone who makes illicit gains, for this clearly undermines the ethical rulings of fair economic conduct due to the exploitation of the involved patrons on the basis of illicit appropriation.[69] Similarly, one should not perform trade activities with the following individuals for obvious reasons pertaining to their lack of ethical predisposition, unless dealings with them would avoid violating licit means of obtaining

---

[64] Al-Ghazālī in Quasem, *The Ethics of al-Ghazali*, 27. According to Quasem, ethics is included in religious sciences; however, reason in ethics is also recognized as a valuable source of knowledge.

[65] For more, see al-Ghazālī, *Munqidh*, 68–71.

[66] On the rules of earnings, trade and commerce, lawful and unlawful issues, rules of companionship and brotherhood, and rules of enjoining good and forbidding evil, see al-Ghazālī, *Iḥyā'*, Vol. 2.

[67] Al-Ghazālī, *Iḥyā'*, Vol. 4, 265.

[68] Ghazali and Sadeq, "Ghazalijevi pogledi na ekonomske probleme i neka etičko-pravna pitanja značajna za ekonomsko ponašanje," 150.

[69] Al-Ghazālī, *Iḥyā'*, Vol. 2, 64–65; Al-Ghazālī, *Kīmiyā-yi Sa'ādat*, trans. Muhammad Asim Bilal (Lahore: Kazi, 2001), 471.

goods: a tyrant, a usurer, a person who provides false accounts/statements, a thief, a person who indulges in bribery and corruption, or a person of doubtful character.[70] For al-Ghazālī, there should be no fraud in weights or quantities in determining the price of a commodity, since complete decency and honesty are to be expected.[71] Even though one is predisposed to temptation and illicit activities, no fraud should take place in the pricing of commodities and the correct price ought to be disclosed.[72] The principle of justice must be facilitated; therefore, if a buyer offers a higher price than the price on the market, the seller ought not to accept it, since an excess of profit might occur, even though the excessive price in itself is not considered unjust.[73] Al-Ghazālī upholds that *iḥsān* has to be practiced in the market and is labeled as doing something additional for another person, not out of fear or for material gain, "but merely as an act of generosity."[74]

According to Quasem, al-Ghazālī separates politics from the realm of ethics, following Avicenna's and al-Farābī's accounts.[75] For Quasem, ethical study can be divided into three parts: ethics as a theoretical study of the human nature of morality without influencing human conduct, the study of ethics as influencing actual conduct, and ethics as a criticism of standards of morality.[76] Yet it seems that al-Ghazālī would not only oppose the second approach, since moral principles have no value if not applied in practice, claiming that knowledge without practice is like ignorance, but also that he would not distinguish ethics from other fields of inquiry in the first place. His apparent separation of politics from ethics rests upon the recognition of the individual nature of moral conduct. The development of spiritual qualities emphasizes both the communal and individual outlook of the world, paying attention to the inner self, since an individual system of ethics relates to personal interest and good conduct, as well as to society at large.

3.3 Extravagance and Just Conduct

In *Iḥyā'*, in particular in Book 19, al-Ghazālī puts forward the idea that the very foundation of a just society is predicated upon the pious individual and one's own moral compass in dealing with matters of the household, not necessarily

70 Al-Ghazālī, *Iḥyā'* and *Kīmiyā-yi Sa'ādat*, 472.
71 Al-Ghazālī, *Kīmiyā-yi Sa'ādat*, 464.
72 Al-Ghazālī, *Kīmiyā-yi Sa'ādat*, 356.
73 Al-Ghazālī, *Iḥyā'*, Vol. 2, 79.
74 Al-Ghazālī, *Iḥyā'*, Vol. 2, 79.
75 Quasem, *The Ethics of al-Ghazali*, 23.
76 Quasem, *The Ethics of al-Ghazali*, 24.

the virtuous ruler. Yet he does affirm that the very objective of trade and commerce is twofold—to gain either subsistence or immense wealth.[77] The latter indicates an attachment to this world. Al-Ghazālī classifies people into three types: those who forget their contribution in the world and whose main objective is earning, those who do remember the hereafter yet because of it devote themselves to economic pursuits, and those who believe in the next world but also participate in trade and commerce for livelihood.[78] Al-Ghazālī heavily criticizes those who believe economic activities are related only to the substance of survival or living.[79] He cautions one should take only as many goods from the world as are absolutely necessary for one's earthly sojourn.[80] The level of consumption thus has to range between necessity and extravagance,[81] and while making profits is allowed, to take less profit of a commodity is an act of *iḥsān*.[82] Necessity has to be fulfilled by the consumer, for it is perceived as a religious obligation and extravagance is regarded as *ḥarām*. Indeed, all economic activities have to provide basic human needs such as food, clothing, and shelter.[83] They are consistent with *Sharīʿa* and are meant to improve the human social condition. In *Mīzān al-ʿamal*, al-Ghazālī mentions three levels of consumption: the lowest, the middle, and the highest, and each basic need can be applied to each of the three levels—as a necessity, convenience, or luxury (his discussion of the need and surplus of material life is linked with the relation between wealth and poverty, discussed in a separate subchapter).[84] Acquiring wealth is intrinsic to human nature as a means of fostering social well-being. Al-Ghazālī recognizes that "one loves to accumulate wealth and increases one's possessions of all types of property."[85] The reasons behind this, in his view, are the high aspirations of men and the illusion that wealth is everlasting. For such reasons, commodities should never be praised.[86] Al-Ghazālī is also critical of the disproportionate income levels in society, and he maintains that the *umma* (or community) ought to participate in humanitarian charity endowment (*waqf*). In addition, when

---

77 Al-Ghazālī, *Iḥyāʾ*, Vol. 2, 63.
78 Al-Ghazālī, *Iḥyāʾ*, Vol. 2, 60–61.
79 Al-Ghazālī, *Iḥyāʾ*, Vol. 2, 108.
80 Al-Ghazali, *The Revival of Religious Sciences*, 100; see also al-Ghazālī, *Iḥyāʾ*, Vol. 2.
81 Al-Ghazālī, *Iḥyāʾ*, Vol. 2, 1.
82 Al-Ghazālī, *Iḥyāʾ*, Vol. 2, 68.
83 Al-Ghazālī, *Mīzān*, 377.
84 Al-Ghazālī, *Mīzān*, 377.
85 Al-Ghazālī, *Iḥyāʾ*, Vol. 3, 290; see also Ghazanfar and Islahi, *Economic Thought of al-Ghazali*, 11.
86 Al-Ghazālī, *Iḥyāʾ*, Vol. 2, 74.

one earns, one must share, which is comprised of three stages: a lower level in which a person sacrifices for his brother without expecting anything in return, a higher level that presupposes that a person considers his brother as himself and spends upon him as if he would spend on himself, and the highest level, which indicates that another person's needs are to be preferred over one's own.

If voluntary participation is not an intrinsic constituent of one's moral system meant to benefit those who are in material or financial need, two problematic consequences are likely to emerge in a society—namely, extravagance and miserliness or avariciousness.[87] Both are clearly opposed to *Sharī'a*'s moral law, for excessive wasting or spending goes against the imperative of what is licit.[88] Hence, money or wealth (*māl*), a concept discussed in detail in the following chapter, has been created for the specific purpose of fulfilling one's needs. Miserliness means that where money should be spent is restricted, while extravagance suggests the opposite: instead of saving money, there is an excessive expenditure.[89] Utilization of wealth must therefore be seen in accordance with ethical jurisprudence, which would not only secure one's welfare but also extend to the very means of obtaining and spending goods in what al-Ghazālī deems a lawful way. By following these ethical principles, one's misuse of money would be minimized in light of *Sharī'a*'s ethical regulations, since, for instance, hoarding food supplies increases prices.[90] The ultimate goal, however, is not economic engagement as a goal to gain profits, but the remembrance of the hereafter. While the Qur'ān encourages the acquisition of wealth, it does not advocate lusting for money or spending beyond one's needs. By fostering ethical reasoning in economic subjectivity, al-Ghazālī warns individuals should pursue the objectives of wealth by following a righteous means to acquire income—they should earn and spend no more than needed and not neglect the truthful intentions behind their economic activities. All stages, including carrying out trading and commercial activities, have to be realized not for the sake of acquiring wealth but in the name of higher spiritual goals of *tawakkul*, and have to be embraced by the very idea of piousness (*taqwā*).

---

87 Al-Ghazālī, *Iḥyā'*, Vol. 2, 341; see also Ghazanfar and Islahi, *Economic Thought of al-Ghazali*, 12.

88 See, e.g., Qur'ān 17:29, 25:67. Licit and illicit are for al-Ghazālī primarily ethical categories of righteous conduct.

89 See, e.g., al-Ghazālī, *Mīzān*, 284.

90 Al-Ghazālī, *Iḥyā'*, Vol. 2, 73.

3.4 Division of Labor and the Development of Markets

The ethical-economic thought puts forward the idea that the physical materiality (and practicality) of work is bound to a metaphysical understanding of work as a vocation and the very production processes as being tied to higher orders of knowledge. Islamic sciences of nature are forged and predicated upon a cosmological understanding of the universe, whereby the aims of work integrate ethical-economic measures. In view of al-Ghazālī's theory of happiness, economists of the modern era cannot fully understand, analyze, and assess these complex realities of an economic life of means and ends. They have to address them in tandem with a moral philosopher, a theologian, and, after all, a scholar of polymathic proportions. Instead of replacing basic needs and desires, al-Ghazālī's philosophy proposes a multiple and broad-gauged use of economic values toward a spiritual end, and hence perceives (minimum) division of work as an inevitable process, while it rejects any form of hierarchy in such a division. The minimal division of labor was understood in the context of his ethical theory not as an obstacle to equality, but rather as a necessary mechanism in achieving equilibrium. Instead of capitalizing on wants, such a perspective draws on the concept of welfare, which guilds also practiced in the classical Islamic milieu. Guilds in Muslim society did not acquire (excessive) wealth and were not affluent. One of the reasons for this might lie in the fact that they were an organic part of the market society that was often run by a *muḥtasib* under the auspices of *Sharīʿa*'s moral law. Prior to the onslaught of European colonialism in the nineteenth century in the Middle East, which altered legal, educational, political, and economic systems, various divisions of guilds existed; their work relied on traditional doctrines and practices, highlighting their religious imprint.[91] El-Ansary states as follows:

> To avoid over- or under-supply of the market at a particular time, for example, a master craftsman could postpone or accelerate taking on extra apprentices while another qualified craftsman had insufficient or excess work, respectively. Equilibrium therefore occurred by design based on spiritual principles rather than as an unintended consequence of greed.[92]

---

[91] Aria Nakissa, "An Epistemic Shift in Islamic Law: Educational Reform at al-Azhar and Dār al-ʿUlūm," *Islamic Law and Society*, Vol. 21 (2014): 209–51; Aharon Layish, "Islamic Law in the Modern World: Nationalization, Islamization, Reinstatement," *Islamic Law and Society*, Vol. 21 (2014): 276–307; Iza Hussin, *The Politics of Islamic Law* (Chicago: Chicago University Press, 2016).

[92] Waleed El-Ansary, "Linking Ethics and Economics for Integral Development: The Need for a New Economic Paradigm and the Three Dimensions of Islam," Al-Alwani

Instead of wants, the motivation for production, sales, and purchases, as indicated in the scholarly literature, was not only self-interest but also an overarching idea to provide for other members of society and fostering social cooperation based on religious beliefs while minimizing competition. This is also evident in other economic mechanisms, such as *sadāqa* (voluntary provision), *zakāt* (obligatory poll tax), and various inheritance laws. *Sadāqa* has to be spent for the benefit of people and invested in the welfare of the community. The Qur'ān specifies that *zakāt* should be given to the needy, the poor, those in debt, travelers, and those in captivity (slaves). In the early period of Islamic history, *zakāt* was collected and distributed by governmental officials, part of which was allocated to decrease poverty. However, despite *zakāt* being the fifth pillar of Islam, its economic significance has diminished in modern times since it has been neither sufficiently implemented nor institutionalized in Muslim countries. Moreover, it alone cannot change economic outcomes in society. In addition to *sadāqa* and *zakāt*, which are directed toward the needy and poor, *waqf* (Islamic religious endowment)—which played an important economic role throughout Islamic history—is a voluntary institution that can enhance society's productive capacity by providing for social welfare, including educational institutions, schools, hospitals, and other public services.[93]

Since many verses from the Qur'ān and Sunna emphasize the importance of production and the role of human labor, increasing *maṣlaḥa* is highly valued and viewed as an obligation. Clearly the value of human labor should not rest on the idea of gaining profit alone. The production of basic necessities for the public good is perceived as a social and individual obligation (*farḍ kifāya*). In the writings of classical Muslim scholars, one might not find descriptive "efficiency-oriented" texts on laws of production, or the theoretical analysis thereof; however, classical scholars, especially al-Ghazālī, nurtured the continuation and optimization of production, such as division and specialization of labor, the role of human capital, and production activities.

Al-Ghazālī and his kind believe all labor is spiritual in essence and that production efforts of a person stem from *'ibāda*, whereby it does not only mean a physical-material engagement when producing a good, but first and foremost relates to its usefulness in order to improve economic conditions in society. The production of basic needs is hence seen as a social obligation. While Karl Marx argues the desire for private property inevitably leads to the division of

---

Lectures 202, Washington Theological Consortium. Accessible at https://washtheocon.org/wp-content/uploads/2012/11/Ansary-2012-Lecture.pdf.

93 For more on *waqf*, see, e.g., Muhammad Tariq Khan, "Historical Role of Islamic Waqf in Poverty Reduction in Muslim Society," *Pakistan Development Review*, Vol. 54, No. 4, (2015): 979–96.

labor, which he saw as the root of a capitalist economy and the subjugation of the proletariat by forcing them into cooperation with the general character of the bourgeois economy, Adam Smith is somewhat indecisive about the position of the division of labor and shares few ethical views with al-Ghazālī. [94] For Adam Smith,[95] introduced in more detail in Chapter 4, the division of human labor is the result of the immense potentiality and infinity of labor. According to al-Ghazālī, however, the inclination to barter exchange ought to be managed in accordance with ethical principles and legal stipulations of the moral law. If for Smith, the motive behind engagement with exchange is egoism, for al-Ghazālī, the minimal division of labor stems from the necessity to facilitate diverse commodity production and labor specialization.[96] In this respect, al-Ghazālī's notion of the division of labor differs from Smith's, and can thus be regarded as contrary to the view of Marx, who deemed it the reason of turmoil for the unprivileged.[97]

In al-Ghazālī's worldview, since the self-motivated human desire to satisfy economic needs exists, markets evolve naturally in their initial stage. This desire, however, is accompanied by man's intrinsic moral orientation to curtail certain character traits and excessive behavior. On the development of marketplaces, al-Ghazālī explains how people from different walks of life come together in order to conduct an exchange of goods:

> It occurs that [sometimes] farmers live where tools are not available, and that blacksmiths and carpenters live where farming does not take place. Hence, the farmer needs blacksmiths and carpenters, and they are also in a need of farmers. By nature, each of them strives toward satisfying his own needs by giving away a certain amount of his possessions. However, it can also occur that when the carpenter needs food in exchange for tools, the farmer is not in need of the [offered] tools, or when the farmer

---

[94] See Karl Marx, *Kapital und Politik* (Deutschland: Zweitausendeins, 2009).

[95] For detailed discussion of Smith's ideas and ethical stance on economics, see Chapter 4.

[96] Al-Ghazālī, *Iḥyā'*, Vol. 3, 227.

[97] "This division of labour [...] is not originally the effect of any human wisdom. [...] It is the necessary, [...] slow and gradual consequence of [...] the propensity to truck, barter, and exchange one thing for another. [...] Man has almost constant occasion for the help of others, and it is in vain for him to expect it from their benevolence only. He will be more likely to prevail if he can appeal to their personal interest, and show them that it is for their own advantage to do for him what he requires of them. [...] We address ourselves, not to their humanity but to their self-love, and never talk to them of our own necessities but of their advantages." Karl Marx, *Economic and Philosophical Manuscripts of 1844:* Translated by Martin Milligan. Moscow: Foreign Languages Publishing House, 1959.

> needs tools from the carpenter, the carpenter is not in need of food. Since these kinds of occurrences create difficulties, this generates the creation of trading spaces where different kinds of tools are exchanged and of warehouses where farmers' products are stored. Customers can come to collect goods and [as a consequence] both markets and storehouses emerge. Farmers bring their products to the markets and in case they cannot sell or exchange it, they can sell them at a lower price to the merchants who in turn store the products and try to sell them to the buyers with a profit. This goes for all types of goods and services. [...] People's needs and their interests generate the need for collaboration and transfer of goods. After that stage, a group of professional traders who transport goods from place to place comes into play. The reason for these activities is without a doubt the accumulation of profits.[98]

While al-Ghazālī affirms the need for profits, he also admits that the specialization of labor would be beneficial for the mutual exchange of goods in order to satisfy various needs in a society. This development in mutual cooperation also results in the creation of villages and urban centers and forms a new social order. If everyone would perform labor in only one particular field or industry, the livelihood and the diversification of goods would vanish. Consequently economic activities would cease; that is why multiplicity, also in socioeconomic terms, is seen as a blessing for society (*ikhtilāf raḥma*).

The linking and interdependence of industries inevitably lead to cooperation and division of labor, in which the interdependence of economic activities is emphasized:

> While the farmer produces grains, the miller then converts grains into flour, and the baker prepares bread from that flour. [...] The blacksmith produces the tools, so that the farmer can cultivate [grains] and the carpenter makes the tools that are needed by the blacksmith. [A] similar

[98] Al-Ghazālī, *Iḥyā'*, Vol. 3, 227. Note that al-Ghazali's insightful analysis of the markets precedes what many European classical economists, especially Adam Smith, asserted in their writings during the seventeenth to nineteenth centuries. It is especially interesting that the "farmer-carpenter" example here is analogous to Adam Smith's famous "butcher-baker" illustration. Ghazanfar and Islahi point out, while discussing "self-interest motivated behavior," Smith says, "It is not from the benevolence of the butcher, the brewer, or the baker, that we expect our dinner, but from their regard to their own self-interest." Nonetheless, Ghazanfar and Islahi do not recognize Smith's ethical approach toward human cognition and greed, especially noticeable in *Moral Sentiments*. For Smith's account of economic thought, see Chapter 4 of this book and Ghazanfar and Islahi, *Economic Thought of al-Ghazali*, 18 and 54 in references.

> process applies for those who partake in the production of other tools and equipment, necessary for securing food supplies.[99]

Here al-Ghazālī stresses that (minimal) specialization of labor is mandatory, which does not presuppose that individuals are being ranked according to a social strata, since classical scholars did not invoke a class system. Rather he pinpoints the significance of labor specialization in tandem with the concepts of equity and vocation. The necessity of the division and specialization of labor is seen as covering all aspects of human (economic) occupations and providing different ways of trading with respect to the diversification of work. The mutuality and interexchange of economic operations necessitates this division, resting upon specific trade ethics.[100] His account hence describes the various functions of workers in the production of daily foodstuffs, underlining the importance of each profession within the labor system.[101]

If exchange between people grows, then markets grow as well, and society's economic potential evolves as an indispensable element of social life. However, the production of materials and commercialization of society cannot occur without the regulation of the market and the empowerment of an individual through ethical predispositions. So what constitutes "the market" in al-Ghazālī's view, and how does capital manage it?

It is crucial to understand that the market in the classical period differed from the market forces prevalent in the modern era, which emphasize individual gains. The so-called free market as an economic system based on supply and demand with little government control and a spontaneous order may be efficient in providing services and goods on an individual level; however, it is less efficient when it comes to social planning and allocating services for the community as a whole. Classical Muslim scholars believed capital can never be an end in itself, but rather a means toward a higher goal—a tool to achieve and improve both individual and communal quality of life. Discussing market and capital, however, is also germane to the notion of fair or just price of goods in markets. For al-Ghazālī, fairness and equity have to be carried out in the market in order to attain price equilibrium. In other words, the just price of goods is the prevailing price in the market. Notwithstanding, if the prevailing price appears to violate basic standards of social justice or common good, and if sellers establish a monopoly in the market, the governmental authority has to intervene, since such development can lead to unlawful deeds such as

---

99 Al-Ghazālī, *Iḥyā'*, Vol. 4, 12; see also Ghazanfar and Islahi, *Economic Thought of al-Ghazali*, 25.

100 Ghazanfar, *Medieval Islamic Thought*, 29.

101 Al-Ghazālī, *Iḥyā'*, Vol. 4, 118, 119.

excessive gains or hoarding of goods and wealth. While al-Ghazālī recognized impersonal market forces, the governmental authority has to intervene if needed and provide basic necessities for the needy. Al-Ghazālī also affirmed the utility of a product and its value in cases of exchange. For instance, one has to exchange the same types of goods, such as gold for gold or silver for silver.[102] If, however, one exchanges different types of goods, the different value of commodities has to be acknowledged. In order for the market to function well, silver *dirhams* and gold *dīnārs* are used not for their own sake, but to establish fair rules for exchange in light of social justice: "*Dirhams* and *dīnārs* are not created for any specific person. They are without value in themselves, and are like stones. Rather, they are created for circulation [from person to person], in order to promote transactions."[103]

Al-Ghazālī provided a more thorough analysis of the role and function of voluntary trade as well as of the emergence of markets, which is linked to supply and demand in fixing prices.[104] It can be deduced that markets are part of the natural economic order and are needed for merchants to exchange their goods and services. Mutual exchange requires specialization as well as the division of labor to allocate available resources and goods. Due to self-interest, traders and participants are bound to establish profit-motivated behavior that might affect market forces, raising food prices, suggesting the prices "should be brought down by minimizing demand."[105]

According to Ghazanfar and Islahi,[106] al-Ghazālī correctly asserted the correlation between the evolution of markets and just price by stating the farmer sells his product at a low price when he does not have enough buyers or when food supplies are in low demand, indicating al-Ghazālī understood the supply and demand forces well (yet since food is a basic commodity, it has to be widely available).[107] He suggests the seller, out of benevolence, should not accept a high profit on a particular product just because the buyer is anxious to buy it. Al-Ghazālī does not clearly state the limit of profit; nevertheless, given the role of benevolence and the overall injunction of *Sharī'a*, the rate should not exceed 5–10 percent of the price of a good.[108] Since food is perceived as a basic human necessity, trading in food should not be motivated by profit, but rather to fulfill the needs of the community.[109] The accumulation of foodstuff

---

102 Al-Ghazālī, *Iḥyā'*, Vol. 2, 74.
103 Al-Ghazālī, *Iḥyā'*, Vol. 4, 91–92.
104 Al-Ghazālī, *Iḥyā'*, Vol. 3, 227.
105 Al-Ghazālī, *Iḥyā'*, Vol. 3, 227.
106 Ghazanfar and Islahi, *Economic Thought of al-Ghazali*, 20.
107 Al-Ghazālī, *Iḥyā'*, Vol. 3, 87.
108 Al-Ghazālī, *Iḥyā'*, Vol. 2, 73, 80.
109 Al-Ghazālī, *Iḥyā'*, Vol. 2, 73.

in order to increase the price in the market is thus unlawful, as is the human propensity to exploit those in need of it.[110] What stems from this proposition is that profit itself is not a necessity but rather a surplus of living conditions. Therefore, food has to be available at low prices so that everyone can afford it at any given time. Al-Ghazālī thus emphasized the illicit quality of exploiting food prices. Foodstuff is "to be consumed when one is in a need of it. This means that those who do not need it should give it out to those who do. [...] If someone who has foodstuff but does not need it is selling it as a commodity, he should [at least] sell it to those who need it."[111] On the nature of trade, al-Ghazālī states that:

> The māl should not be dirty or impious ("najs"). [...] Trade is allowed on reasonable profit but not at any cost. Accordingly marketing of undesirable objects like the mice, snakes, scorpions and other repelling menagerie is not permitted. [...] The third plausible condition is that a person can only sell that thing which may belong to him or he may be authorised to sell it by its legitimate owner. On the same principle the husband cannot sell any article belonging to his wife without her permission and vice versa. The fourth condition is that only those things can be sold whose physical possession may be handed over to the buyer. The fifth condition is that the quantity of goods and the standard of their quality should be specified. The sixth condition is that the articles bought should be taken into physical possession and then resold. Forward sale of imaginary goods on conjecture is not allowed.[112]

Necessities such as clothing, shelter, and medicine are placed in the same category of basic needs for which no extra profit should be extracted from the price. For such reasons, al-Ghazālī considers hoarding of these supplies unlawful, since it causes harm to the public good.[113]

The market has to function to supply basic needs according to ethical standards and principles of *Sharīʿa*, which would be beneficial for society as a whole. Hoarding foodstuff in order to increase food prices is prohibited, as everyone has the right to buy food directly from the market at affordable prices. If there are enough supplies in society, then it might be allowed under

110 Al-Ghazālī, *Iḥyāʾ*, Vol. 2, 72.
111 Al-Ghazālī, *Iḥyāʾ*, Vol. 4, 192–93.
112 Al-Ghazali, *Kīmiyā-yi Saʿādat*, 473–74.
113 He cites a *hadīth* of the Prophet Muhammad: "If a man is hoarding precious food supplies for forty days to obtain a higher price, he is displeased with God and God is displeased with him." Al-Ghazālī, *Iḥyāʾ*, Vol. 2, 72.

certain conditions, and the "hoarding of medicine and other items, which are not considered food or nutritious and hence not part of basic needs is not prohibited."[114] The merchant must be careful when selling supplies, for the capital (*r'as al-māl*) has to be known in the process of selling or purchasing a commodity.[115]

Determining the price of products is a sensitive matter, which is why al-Ghazālī pays close attention to the notion of truthfulness when declaring the price of goods during a transaction. "Economic truthfulness" is a prerequisite and a significant component of *Sharī'a*-based economic conduct. Since prices are set by market activity—which are, nonetheless, regulated by ethical norms—economic engagement should reflect the value of benevolence (*iḥsān*) by transcending purely material exchange of goods. Markets therefore ought not to function freely and prices are not to be set in advance; rather, benevolence should be exercised in the market when advertising a product's fair price.[116] Following this reasoning, no excessive profit made from a buyer by the seller can be justified as legally acquired. That is why when one purchases from a poor seller, one must exercise leniency. The possibility of cancelling an agreement or flexible repayment of debts is at one's disposal, as are fair repayments in paying one's debt. The extension of credit or deferred payment when selling to the poor are also optional, while denouncing debt from a poor buyer if one cannot afford to pay it back is cast as legitimate. In the same vein, selling a commodity in advance without expecting payment should be performed only if necessary.[117]

The concept of *iḥsān* hence presupposes that one should not set a high price for a commodity, avoid false advertisement, sell it for profit, or conceal its true price and status. From an economic perspective, in order for one to step on the path of the science of the hereafter, the following guidelines should be taken into account: the trader ought to act in accordance with ethical principles and have honest intentions; one should desire business in order to contribute to the public good (*maṣlaḥa*) by expanding one's trade; the attainment of the material should not precede the attainment of the spiritual (desires of the *dunyā* versus those of the *ākhira*); and one should restrict oneself from unlawful or illicit behavior in the market.[118] Overall, *dunyā* and the worldly pleasures of profit should not preoccupy a merchant, since one's profit cannot be utilized in the hereafter.

---

[114] Al-Ghazālī, *Iḥyā'*, Vol. 2, 73.
[115] Al-Ghazālī, *Iḥyā'*, Vol. 2, 69–70.
[116] Ghazanfar, *Medieval Islamic Thought*, 30.
[117] Al-Ghazālī, *Iḥyā'*, Vol. 2, 78–82.
[118] Al-Ghazālī, *Iḥyā'*, Vol. 2, 83–87.

Al-Ghazālī classifies economic development or production activities into five groups. All activities must ensure harmony of the socioeconomic environment and have to be carried out in a balanced fashion. They consist of farming, which includes producing food, grazing or producing food for animals, hunting or utilizing the natural environment, weaving or producing textiles, and construction or provision of shelter.[119] The specialization of professions and the division of industries stem from the human need to utilize various natural tools and metals through carpentry, leather production, and the iron industry. Furthermore, al-Ghazālī delineates three major categories of production—namely, agriculture, iron crafts, and that which is related to the supplementary activities of basic industries, such as grinding.[120] The division of industries is interrelated with various production modes, categorized into three main fields: agriculture, manufacturing, and services. The first is designated as the basic industry, which provides fundamental necessities for human life. The second means additional activities that expand on human welfare, while the third is complementary to the first two. The specialization of work and industry is due to the necessity of sharing common assets such as water, fire, natural resources, and the natural habitat, which potentially result in a more sustainable distribution of these resources.[121] Additionally, since the exchange of goods does not always bring about profit, bartering in the common market (along with money as a medium of exchange) is inevitable. The role of governmental authority, discussed in detail later, is crucial for promoting the cooperation of basic industries in markets. Socioeconomic harmony is achieved if all three industries are provided, since they represent a form of religious obligation linked to social responsibilities; the survival of human beings depends upon them.[122]

The notion of competition is, in al-Ghazālī's view, seen in its triple form: as obligatory, desirable, and permissible. Yet it is obligatory only within the framework of religious responsibilities when one strives for moral formation of the self through *'ibādāt*. It becomes desirable only through the process of acquiring necessities and comforts or to fulfill the needs of others as a form of munificence. It is permissible insofar as it relates to the acquisition of licit means of conduct according to *Sharī'a* stipulations. Competition in this context is seen as a means to acquire commodities when trading in a lawful manner and not as a rivalry or self-oriented engagement to boost personal interests

---

[119] Ghazanfar and Islahi, *Economic Thought of al-Ghazali*, 24.

[120] Al-Ghazālī, *Iḥyā'*, Vol. 1, 12–13; Vol. 3, 225; al-Ghazālī, *Mīzān*, 328–29.

[121] Al-Ghazālī, *Iḥyā'*, Vol. 3, 226–27.

[122] Al-Ghazālī, *Iḥyā'*, Vol. 2, 83; see also Ghazanfar and Islahi, *Economic Thought of al-Ghazali*, 24.

based on greed or lust for wealth. Lust for wealth brings us to the notions of *faqr* and *māl*.

3.5 *Faqr*, *Māl*, and Modes of Economic Gain

Along with al-Shaybānī, al-Muḥāsibī, Ibn Abi al-Dunyā, al-Mubārak, and al-Rāghib al-Iṣfahānī, al-Ghazālī's account on *māl* is often analyzed alongside *faqr* or poverty.

For al-Ghazālī, social poverty is not highly regarded, yet neither is lust for money nor begging compatible with a righteous character. Greed is considered poverty while despair is viewed as wealth.[123] Minimal economic gain is sometimes frowned upon, since it can mean lack of economic participation in society, leading to disbelief if it brings about social instability.[124] Moderation (*kifāya*) is encouraged as a preferred standard of living,[125] while poverty has to be abrogated; conversely, *faqr* can also be considered as a spiritual component over riches.[126] Wise men have "understood that the wealth according to need is panacea while what is more than that is a poison."[127] In discussing *faqr*,[128] al-Ghazālī invokes an earlier *ṣūfī* scholar, al-Muḥāsibī, who states that one must engage in praiseworthy economic activities by performing a set of spiritual exercises such as mindfulness, vigilance, remembrance of God, and purifying the heart of any ill thoughts (*ṭahārat al-qulūb*).[129] For al-Ghazālī, poverty "is not to possess what is necessary by removing wants. Not having that which is necessary is not considered poverty. If you have that which is necessary and have a command over it, you are not poor."[130] He categorizes poverty in five ways: (1) poverty of the one who renounces the world, which is regarded as the highest level because one does not indulge in riches; (2) poverty of the one who does not despise wealth, but possesses more than necessary; (3) poverty of the one who loves wealth, but does not strive to obtain it; (4) poverty of the greedy who desire to earn more wealth; and (5) poverty of the one who strives for wants, yet has no possession of wealth.[131] *Faqr* has thus an ethical merit and

---

123 Al-Ghazālī, *Iḥyā'*, Vol. 3, 239.
124 Al-al-Ghazālī, *Kīmiyā-yi Sa'ādat*, 928.
125 Al-Ghazālī, *Kīmiyāyi Sa'ādat*, 923.
126 Al-Ghazālī, *Iḥyā'*, Vol. 3, 264–65.
127 Al-Ghazālī, *Kīmiyā-yi Sa'ādat*, 939.
128 Al-Ghazālī, *Iḥyā'*, Vol. 3, 264–65.
129 For more, see al-Muḥāsibī, *al-Makāsib wa al-Wara'*.
130 Al-Ghazālī, *Iḥyā'*, Vol. 4, 190.
131 Al-Ghazālī, *Iḥyā'*, Vol. 4, 190–91.

is not simply a result of a particular destitution.[132] Practicing *faqr* is essential in forming one's moral order as a technique of self-transformation.

Likewise, money, wealth, or *māl* bear certain benefits and risks for an individual. Al-Ghazālī regards wealth as dangerous in one respect because it cannot completely satisfy anyone (*ḥub al-māl*), even if one possesses immense wealth.[133] Money is perceived as one of the most important inventions in economic affairs, and is for al-Ghazālī rendered as a benefit or a detriment if not handled right, depending on one's purposes and intentions (*niyya*).[134] Intentions, however, are never disassociated from the unveiling of the knowledge of God. The harms of wealth are of two kinds—namely, worldly and religious. While the former leads to various sins by indulgence, the latter means that even if one enjoys only that which is lawful, consequently one will still neglect the path to the hereafter. Al-Ghazālī regards *māl* as one of the five necessities (*al-ḍarūriyāt*) *Sharī'a* provides for safeguarding righteous conduct against any temptation (*fitna*), and claims no human being can survive without it.[135] To underpin the importance of the correct utilization of wealth, he cites many Qur'ānic verses and *aḥādīth*, stating wealth should not be praised. Miserliness is condemned, for it leads to tyranny if not handled correctly.[136] That is why spiritual predispositions or intentions are preconditions for using wealth, for if the intensions are good, so is wealth.[137]

In order to distinguish the importance of *māl* from its sinful implications if utilized under certain conditions, al-Ghazālī provides a description of *māl* according to its social function, concerning its ethical scope. *Māl* includes spiritual, bodily, and material benefits, yet it is only a means and not an end of human endeavor in carrying out economic conduct: "Wealth is the biggest temptation of them all,"[138] but also "the worldly wealth is good for a good man."[139]

Activities regarded as harmful to individuals and society at large, despite their widespread existence, are to be avoided, such as hoarding, counterfeiting coins, and not disclosing the true price of a commodity, as well as generating false statements in advertising a commodity in the market.[140] On various

---

132 See also the discussion in al-Ghazālī, *Iḥyā'*, Vol. 3, 264–74.

133 Al-Ghazālī, *Iḥyā'*, Vol. 3, 231, 232.

134 Al-Ghazālī, *Kīmiyā-yi Sa'ādat*, 932, 933; "*Fainnahu yanfa'u min wajhi wa yadru min wajhi.*" al-Ghazālī, *Mīzān*, 372.

135 Al-Ghazālī, *Iḥyā'*, Vol. 3, 231.

136 See Qur'ān 62:9, 64:14, 96:6–7; al-Ghazālī, *Iḥyā'*, Vol. 3, 232.

137 Al-Ghazālī, *Iḥyā'*, Vol. 3, 236.

138 Al-Ghazālī, *Iḥyā'*, Vol. 3, 234.

139 Al-Ghazālī, *Kīmiyā-yi Sa'ādat*, 930.

140 Al-Ghazālī, *Iḥyā'*, Vol. 2, 75.

occasions, al-Ghazālī stressed that "money is not a desire for its own sake."[141] The history of money indicates it was invented for the sake of exchanging goods, which led to the utilization of gold as a common denominator for transactions, due to its outstanding qualities such as high value, long-lasting durability, and easy minting and preservation. Mixing inferior metals (*fulūs*) with silver and gold is an illicit and unjust deed, because "dissemination of a single bad *dirham* is worse than stealing a thousand *dirhams*" since stealing is a sin that ends once carried out; however, disseminating bad money is a *bid'a* that can affect many who use it in transactions.[142] Counterfeiting coins is thus condemned because it affects the prices in markets. One should rather avoid selling broken coins and metals as *dirhams* or *dīnārs*, for their dissemination corrupts society.[143] If in possession of corrupted metals, a merchant has to dispose of them, know their source in order to avoid such occurrences, or make use of them only if some benefit is foreseen, for in society where trade is part of the social fabric, the honest merchant is superior to the believer.[144]

Since extravagant spending is undesirable, excessive expenditures also ought to be avoided. Extravagance is when money is spent "where it is not needed, at the time when it is not needed, and in the amount it is not needed."[145] Al-Ghazālī's observation of human behavior toward *māl* is that it is not praiseworthy unless put to use for the purpose of exercising righteous objectives (*maqāṣid*) pertaining to the hereafter. The twofold approach to *māl*—that is, as a tool to secure a righteous life and as a mechanism to counteract human inclination for lust—depends on one's objectives concerning wealth. He divided the benefits of *māl* into two categories—those pertaining to the mundane and those related to the *ākhira*. Yet both belong to the realm of ethical-economics, which is achieved by cultivating particular faculties in order to generate a virtuous character. Religious benefits of *māl* are further subcategorized as follows: money is beneficial if one spends it not only for the realization of one's religious endeavors and for other necessities that lead toward securing them, such as pilgrimage to *hajj*, but also for food, shelter, and clothing.[146] In other words, *māl* can be spent for "whatever is necessary for the accomplishment of a *wājib*" or that which is obligatory. Money can be advantageous if one spends it on other *Sharī'a*-prescribed or recommended matters, such as almsgiving or charity, and finally, if one spends it for public interest,

---

141 See, e.g., al-Ghazālī, *Iḥyā'*, Vol. 4, 114–15.
142 Al-Ghazālī, *Iḥyā'*, Vol. 2, 73–74.
143 Al-Ghazālī, *Iḥyā'*, Vol. 2, 68.
144 "*Al-tājir al-ṣadūq afḍal 'anda Allāhi min al-mut'bid.*" Al-Ghazālī, *Iḥyā'*, Vol. 2, 74.
145 Al-Ghazālī, *Mīzān*, 284; Al-Ghazālī, *Kīmiyā-yi Sa'ādat*, 922, 923.
146 Al-Ghazālī, *Kīmiyā-yi Sa'ādat*, 931–35.

such as religious endowments (*waqf*), the building of mosques, learning institutions, education, and public infrastructure.[147]

Money, however, also brings about parsimony and greed (*al-bukhl*). The remedy for miserliness is patience, knowledge, and action (performing good deeds). This includes choosing a middle path when dealing with earning a provision and expenditure, not being anxious for fortune and riches, knowing the merits of contentment and what honor is in not relying on others for financial support and understanding the disgrace of greed, thinking about the wealth of other religious denominations for comparisons, and not hoarding riches and foodstuff, since it can bring a fear of losing money.[148] Contrarily, the merits of generosity are associated with contentment, of which the highest level is altruism (*al-īthār*).[149] In the next subchapter, "Love for Wealth," in *Iḥyā'*, al-Ghazālī reasons there are two types of compulsory spending—spending in the name of *Sharī'a* and spending out of one's own chivalry (*al-marwa'*) and habit (*al-'āda*). If one does not spend in either way, one is regarded as a miser.[150] Benevolence is hence exercised only when one is generous in spending when one does not have to. Wealth has thus five charms a wealthy man should be aware of: to appreciate the benefits of wealth, why it has been created, and how it has to be earned; to examine the paths for righteous earnings; to avoid excess earnings; to maintain honest motives in expenditure and savings; and to confine one's acquisition to the service of the cultivation of the self through the knowledge of God.[151]

In *Kīmiyā*, al-Ghazālī lays down further instructions for how to utilize money: *māl* should not be spent on matters that might invoke impiety, and trading with such matters is disallowed. It is licit, however, to perform trade activity to gain some profit, but not at any cost. Trading with illicit goods themselves is illicit, such as purchasing prohibited animals; for instance, while a person can only sell a commodity that belongs to him or her, emphasizing the ownership of a good, for only those commodities that are in one's physical possession can be sold.[152] Such proceedings connote that the quantity and the quality of a commodity should be specified together with the date, venue, measure, and means of transaction, which is why goods have to be treated equally with respect to their status. Furthermore, the remuneration for one's service is to be specified, otherwise it is void. Mundane activities related to *māl*

---

147 Al-Ghazālī, *Iḥyā'*, Vol. 3, 235–36.
148 Al-Ghazālī, *Iḥyā'*, Vol. 3, 241–43.
149 Al-Ghazālī, *Iḥyā'*, Vol. 3, 257.
150 Al-Ghazālī, *Iḥyā'*, Vol. 3, 260.
151 Al-Ghazālī, *Iḥyā'*, Vol. 3, 263–64.
152 Al-Ghazālī, *Kīmiyā-yi Sa'ādat*, 474; see also Al-Ghazālī, *Iḥyā'*, Vol. 2.

can also involve illicit activities, since man is by nature greedy for wealth.[153] In this context, possessing wealth facilitates the enjoyment of illicit pleasures that can turn into habit and can thus also be acquired through unlawful means.

Since money is one of the most important tools of civilization, al-Ghazālī contends, it should be used only to facilitate the exchange of goods and economic transactions. Concomitantly, he firmly believes money has no intrinsic value, rather its value is known through the transaction of goods.[154] Value is thus inextricably related to commodities and not to money itself. All valuable commodities are differentiated according to their intrinsic value, as a means to an end, or both.[155] In relation to wealth and monetary value, gold *dīnārs* and silver *dirhams* are seen as a means to an end:

> Creation of *dirhams* and *dīnārs* is one of many bounties of God. Every aspect of economic activities relies on dealings with these two types of money. They are two metals that have no intrinsic benefit on their own, nonetheless, people need them, so that they can use them as [as a medium] for exchange for food, clothing, and other goods. Sometimes, one needs what one does not own and one owns what one does not need. For instance, if someone has saffron and needs a camel, and another person owns a camel but needs saffron, the two cannot carry out the exchange without using money [and a measure for things], for the one who owns a camel does not need the same amount of saffron.[156]

Due to the fact that money has no purpose on its own, but serves only as a medium to enable exchanges of commodities, the value of exchanged goods must be known in advance. Trading in gold and silver for the purpose of making profit is condemned, while selling gold for silver or vice versa is licit as an economic transaction.[157] Moderation in spending is a prerequisite for earning a just livelihood, while hoarding money goes against the very core of *Sharī'a*'s cultivation of the self and thus is illicit. Even if one has an inclination toward money, it can be utilized only for transactions in order to provide basic needs, and as a measure of value in exchange processes. Such reasoning intimates money should not be spent for its own sake,[158] since it does not bring

---

[153] Al-Ghazālī, *Iḥyā'*, Vol. 3, 290; Al-Ghazālī, *Kīmiyā-yi Sa'ādat*, 935.

[154] A similar approach can be observed centuries later in the writings of Karl Marx and Friedrich Engels.

[155] See also Ashker and Wilson, *Islamic Economics*, 248.

[156] Al-Ghazālī, *Iḥyā'*, Vol. 4, 91.

[157] Ashker and Wilson, *Islamic Economics*, 248.

[158] Al-Ghazālī, *Iḥyā'*, Vol. 3, 278.

about (social) good, leading people astray to achieve other purposes outside the *akhlāq* framework.[159] In other words, money should not be spent in order to gain more money, but rather it should be used as an indicator of balance in evaluating goods, since silver and gold coins were established for societies to benefit from mutual cooperation when engaging in economic activities. One is labeled unjust if one spends more wealth than needed and hoards it, while others might be in dire need.[160] This brings us to the conclusion that money carries only the value people attach to it and ought not to be desired simply for the sake of accumulation: "Anyone who utilizes money contrary to its objectives or functions is disregarding the bounty of God. If someone hoards *dirhams* and *dīnārs*, then he is a transgressor. [...] [*Dirhams* and *dīnārs*] are standards [for people] to know the value of goods. Anyone who turns them into tools is ungrateful to his Creator."[161]

Economic subjectivity is for al-Ghazālī encapsulated in an underlying foundation of the overall human experience based on the idea that the soul as the essence of selfhood serves the divine, but it is also cognizant of human needs. While affirming man's desire to accumulate wealth, he warns that through various practices and moral cognition within the self, one eventually acquires the path of eternal happiness. Man "does not become content despite possessing much [...] The Messenger of Allah (peace and blessings of Allah be upon him) said, 'If a man possesses gold of the quantity of [*sic*] equal to two valleys, he will be still greedy of the third valley.'"[162] Historic necessities and the expansion of trading activities have made money evolve into a social convention, without having a specific purpose of its own. In view of al-Ghazālī's theory of economics predicated on the moral self, one is inclined to guard one's wealth. Unlike wealth, however, knowledge does not need guarding, for by sharing knowledge it increases, whereas by spending wealth by illicit means it recedes.[163]

3.5.1 Ribā: An ill use of money

Societies engage in trade and exchange of goods in order to survive. As noted earlier, al-Ghazālī was cognizant of money as a particular measure of equivalence, which as a tool of exchange determines the value of a commodity. The Qur'ān and classical Muslim scholars demonstrated that exchange of goods

---

159 For examples, see Al-Ghazālī, *Iḥyā'*, Vol. 4, 91.
160 Al-Ghazālī, *Iḥyā'*, Vol. 4, 95.
161 Al-Ghazālī, *Iḥyā'*, Vol. 4, 91.
162 Al-Ghazālī, *Kīmiyā-yi Sa'ādat*, 940.
163 Al-Ghazālī, *Iḥyā'*, Vol. 4, 118.

takes place in an unjust or exploitative manner also through *ribā* (usually translated as *usury*). The prohibition of *ribā* is thus well known in the history of Islamic economic thought.[164] Generally, *ribā* can be viewed as a certain form of loan allocation that presupposes that money intrinsically possesses a certain value. In accordance with this view, it is inevitable to perceive interest on loans as an economic axiom. Since money only signifies the value it possesses, value is encapsulated not in money itself but in a commodity that is a result of the labor force. One can extrapolate from this that money cannot be the measure of value and cannot have an attached price. This further appertains to the notion of work in Islamic tradition. Unlike in a neoliberal economy, whereby productivity is utilized for the sake of consumption and in order to prompt (over)production, for al-Ghazālī, human work represents activity motivated by its usefulness or necessity for society at large.

By multiplying *dirhams* and *dīnārs* as an end in itself, the practice of *ribā* would then mean a transgression. Yet because of the practice of moneylending with interest, money became a source and tool of exploitative practices in the caliphate, despite the proliferation of many classical works on economic thought in Islamic tradition that address *ṣūfī* and ethical views on money as a medium of exchange in order to ensure just measure of goods. Or one could perhaps reverse the narrative and claim that those classical works, al-Ghazālī's included, point to the politico-ethical shortcomings of governmental authorities and learned men when dealing with economic stipulations. Since most scholars agree the Qur'ān prohibits (excessive) usury,[165] classical scholars aimed at detecting the exploitative nature of interest loans and tried to distinguish between interest on consumption loans and interest on production loans.[166] Ibn Taymiyya, for instance, who disagreed with al-Ghazālī on many points, states that "interest is forbidden because it is harmful to the needy and amounts to acquiring property by wrongful means. This motive is found in all usurious contracts."[167] This prohibition is based in essence upon the tradition of the Prophet Muḥammad advocating equity of barter exchange: "Gold for gold, silver for silver, wheat for wheat, barley for barley, dates for dates and salt for salt are to be exchanged, according to the same good and in equal amount. One who demanded extra or paid more indulged in usury."[168]

---

164 For more on *ribā*, see, e.g., Azhar, *Economy of Islamic Economics*, chapter 9.

165 See the Qur'ān 2:275, 2:276, 2:278, 3:130, 4:161, 30:39.

166 Islahi, *Contribution of Muslim Scholars to Economic Thought and Analysis*, 51.

167 Abdul Azim Islahi, *Economic Concepts of Ibn Taymiyya* (Leicester: Islamic Foundation, 1988), , 130.

168 See Ṣaḥīḥ Muslim, Book 10 (Book of Business Transactions), chapter 37 (Conversion of Currency and Selling of Gold for Silver on the Spot), No. 3852, accessible at

In *Iḥyā'*, al-Ghazālī does not address the problem of *ribā* in loans directly, but rather discusses nonmonetary transactions where interest might occur subtly. In his view, *ribā* is forbidden when carrying out exchange of currencies or food supplies. Subtle forms of *ribā* might occur when gold is exchanged for gold or other types of the same good but with differences in quantity or time of delivery. In this case, *ribā* might happen when the time of delivery is postponed and an excess quantity of the commodity might be cancelled. This is called *ribā al-nāṣi'a*. Interest is earned in this case due to late payment. The second example is when the exchanged quantity is not equal in value, which is called *ribā al-faḍl*. Interest in this case is due to overpayment for the commodity.[169] Both forms of *ribā* are illicit, since exchange of goods should occur simultaneously.[170] Since money has to circulate, usury would mean an end to its function and is hence associated with injustice (*ẓulm*).[171] By advocating fair exchange and the prohibition of *ribā*, al-Ghazālī is not only employing an indirect economic analysis of usury in his discussion but also criticizing the accumulation of wealth. The following quotation exemplifies the crux of his criticism of the utilization of money: "When someone is trading in *dirhams* and *dīnārs*, he is making them as his goal, which is contrary to their objectives. Money was not created to make more money, and doing so would be a transgression."[172] One can then infer that *māl* becomes an end and not a means, and hoarding it would go against the grain of what al-Ghazālī believed to constitute righteous conduct, since it violates the very nature of the function of money.[173]

---

www.sahihmuslim.com/sps/smm/sahihmuslim.cfm?scn=dspchaptersfull&BookID=10&ChapterID=629. See also No. 3845: "Do not sell gold for gold, except like for like, and don't increase something of it upon something; and don't sell silver unless like for like, and don't increase something of it upon something, and do not sell for ready money something to be given later."

169 Al-Ghazālī, *Iḥyā'*, Vol. 4, 192–93.

170 Various classical Muslim scholars, including Ibn Taymiyya and Ibn Rushd, wrote on the notion of money usage and usury. For the latter, the main aim of the prohibition is to prevent misuse in the barter exchange of commodities, gold, and silver. Since *ribā* opens the door for cheating, the prohibition enforces a just transaction and equivalence. *Dirham* and *dīnārs* were made for the sake of evaluation, and the justice in the exchange between various commodities lies not in their weight or measurement, but in proportionality. The ratio between two different kinds should be equal in respect to their kinds. See, e.g., Rushd, *The Distinguished Jurist's Primer*; Islahi, *Economic Concepts of Ibn Taymiyya*, chapter 5.

171 Ghazali and Sadeq, "Ghazalijevi pogledi na ekonomske probleme i neka etičko-pravna pitanja značajna za ekonomsko ponašanje," 156.

172 Ghazali and Sadeq, "Ghazalijevi pogledi na ekonomske probleme i neka etičko-pravna pitanja značajna za ekonomsko ponašanje," 31.

173 Al-Ghazālī, *Iḥyā'*, Vol. 4, 192–93.

Distribution is, apart from production, one of the primary market elements not only in classical economics but also in premodern economic thought in Islamic tradition. Since capital has to meet the terms of the participant and his share in circumstances of loss and profit, an interest rate is in theory absent, while price is dependent upon market forces.[174] Nonetheless, this attitude does not presuppose the logic of a free market economy, since classical Muslim scholars have always emphasized the observance of fair practices, considering ethically driven patterns of cooperation, in accordance with *Sharīʿa*'s moral law. Profit or remuneration should be a result of labor with a commensurate value, and not the outcome of mischief. One has to perform benevolence to the seller when purchasing a commodity, since small profit margins can create multiple transactions and bigger gains.[175] However, since profits relate to risk, al-Ghazālī contends, traders put their lives on the line while seeking profits.[176] Consequently, profit sharing should arise from the profit itself and not from the capital value of goods,[177] and the act of sharing is a result of the joint effort of all parties involved. True gain is rather in "the market of the hereafter (*ākhira*)," placing worldly economic affairs in service of achieving eternal happiness.[178]

3.5.2 Fair earnings and the distribution of goods

In *Iḥyāʾ*, al-Ghazālī divides society into three different groups concerning material gain. The first group consists of those who forget they will be brought back to life in the hereafter and thus concentrate on making earnings as the sole aim of their endeavors; they will perish. The second group comprises those whose sole aim in worldly life is the return to the hereafter at the expense of the mundane; they are to succeed. The last group belongs to the middle path, which is active in worldly (also economic) affairs and in following *Sharīʿa*; people in this group are to reach salvation.[179]

Each acquisition of wealth has to be earned lawfully and has to incorporate justice, kindness, and the fear of God.[180] Lawful earnings are of six

---

[174] See, e.g., Islahi, *Contribution of Muslim Scholars to Economic Thought and Analysis*, 38.

[175] Al-Ghazālī, *Iḥyāʾ*, Vol. 2, 80.

[176] Al-Ghazālī, *Iḥyāʾ*, Vol. 4, 118. Such a scheme (which could be seen as an alternative to interest in current economics) is the provision of sharing profit and loss, where none of the parties is entitled to profit guarantee; it is thus to be shared in a predetermined ratio, whereby a percentage is not earned on the capital supplied, hence the owner of the capital loses his capital and the worker his own labor.

[177] Al-Ghazālī, *Kīmiyā*, 480.

[178] Al-Ghazālī, *Iḥyāʾ*, Vol. 2, 75, 76, 84.

[179] Al-Ghazālī, *Iḥyāʾ*, Vol. 2, 62.

[180] Al-Ghazālī, *Iḥyāʾ*, Vol. 2, 64.

types: bargaining when buying and selling, trading, taking advance payment, working for a specific wage, conducting business through capital, and participating in joint business.[181] An individual can engage in economic conduct either by securing his or her necessary livelihood or through investment in one's wealth with the aim to increase it. The status of the latter is dependent on the means of gaining wealth. Al-Ghazālī informs us that if various trades and industries are diminished, then it will be difficult for people to manage their livelihood, since the majority will face hardship, and that "one particular group should be responsible for one kind of work."[182] Engagements pertaining to *maṣlaḥa* are praiseworthy objectives according to *Sharī'a*, because they protect the social fabric. Al-Ghazālī believes that:

> No one should neglect one's *dīn* and afterlife when engaging with trade, commerce, and earning a livelihood. If one does, then one will be ruined and regarded as one of those who is willing to replace the afterlife for this world. Yet, the wise is he who safeguards his capital, for his true capital is his *dīn* and matters related to the afterlife.[183]

Business transactions can generate harm if based upon unjust terms. Al-Ghazālī does not define harm or injustice per se; however, he describes the terms of economic behavior when making transactions.[184] Refraining from harmful behavior such as hoarding foodstuff in times of need, monopolizing a market, praising a commodity, not disclosing the price of a commodity, and other activities is lower in status when compared to acting benevolent in the first place. One should not obtain more profit than agreed upon at the time of the transaction, deliberately pay a poor seller more than the gross price for a commodity, reduce part of the amount for a commodity when selling to a poor seller, allow the seller more time for payment, extend the deadline of debt repayment, rescind the sale if the buyer asks for it, or sell foodstuff to the poor on credit (without interest) with no intention of demanding the cost from them, unless they become wealthy in the future.[185] Distinguishing between licit and illicit earnings is crucial for those who engage in economic activities, accentuating not legal materiality of economic interactions, but chiefly their composition in relation to one's underlying psycho-ethical predisposition.[186]

---

181 Al-Ghazālī, *Iḥyā'*, Vol. 2, 64, 65.

182 Al-Ghazālī, *Iḥyā'*, Vol. 2, 83.

183 Al-Ghazālī, *Iḥyā'*, Vol. 2, 83.

184 Quasem, *The Ethics of al-Ghazali*, 223–24.

185 Al-Ghazālī, *Iḥyā'*, Vol. 2, 79–80; Quasem, *The Ethics of al-Ghazali*, 225.

186 "Nobody shall carry on business in our markets who has got no knowledge of business. Otherwise he would involve in *ribā* willingly or unwillingly" (Caliph 'Umar).

To maintain a reasonable price for a commodity, al-Ghazālī advocates moderate profit rates as a form of *iḥsān*, even though high profits are not illicit per se. Their prohibition depends on the intention of the seller and the reason behind the earned money. It is, however, necessary that the seller avoids exploiting the buyer due to his lack of means, understanding, or information in respect to the commodity he is pursuing. Al-Ghazālī also mentions the notions of price and value in terms of prevailing prices in the market. Fairness and equity are related to social standards interrelated with market forces. If the standard or prevailing price violates norms of equity and justice (indicating one's financial monopoly, especially over basic human needs), then the governmental authority interferes.[187] This is why *dirhams* and *dīnārs* were established as a means of exchange for various useful goods. Profits are perceived as legitimate, yet one should be cautious how one obtains material gains. "Since profits represent an additional gain they should be generally sought as part of non-necessities,"[188] especially because one is inclined to accumulate wealth and property.[189]

3.6 Islamic Governance and the Question of Public Good (*Maṣlaḥa*) in Economic Affairs

This section aims to scrutinize the role of governmental authority in relation to economic conduct as well as analyze the main postulates put forward by al-Ghazālī, including the role of a *muḥtasib* or a public inspector in marketplaces.[190] Some of al-Ghazālī's inquiries on the nature of governance and its economic measures in Islamic tradition are found in *Iḥyā' Ulūm al-Dīn*, whereas his ideas on the role of the ruler and his moral stipulations are expressed in *Naṣīḥat al-Mulūk*.

One must meet certain requirements for the overall preservation of *dīn* while practicing economic conduct.[191] In this respect, one has to consider the overall well-being of society too by putting into practice the concepts of *'adl* (justice) and *iḥsān* (benevolence). In addition to man's fulfillment of

For examples from the Prophet Muhammad, as well as Caliph 'Umar's accounts of trading and other economic-related activities, see, e.g., Ashker and Wilson, *Islamic Economics*, and Ṣaḥīḥ Muslim.

187 Al-Ghazālī, *Iḥyā'*, Vol. 1, 17.

188 Al-Ghazālī, *Iḥyā'*, Vol. 2, 73.

189 Al-Ghazālī, *Iḥyā'*, Vol. 2, 280.

190 For more on the overview of al-Ghazālī's perception of government in his works, see Carole Hillenbrand, "Islamic Orthodoxy or Realpolitik? Al-Ghazālī's Views on Government," *Journal of the British Institute of Persian Studies*, Vol. 26 (1988): 81–94.

191 Al-Ghazālī, *Iḥyā'*, Vol. 2, 159–62.

the requirements of social utility in trade and commerce, the governmental authority has its own responsibilities to secure economic life, otherwise the repudiation of economic activities can become a threat to society. Al-Ghazālī cautions that the governmental authority—for him a necessary institution based on *Sharī'a*'s moral law and its ethical premise[192] for which he sometimes uses the terms *mulk* (kingdom), *sulṭān* (sultan), or *ḥukūma* (government)—is "the noblest of all basic industries [...] which must seek that which is good within society through cooperation and reconciliation."[193]

Various scholars claim that from its early beginnings, the caliphate aimed to protect the religious and political interests of the early Muslim community, stemming from the teachings of the Prophet Muḥammad and his understanding of the Qur'ānic social and metaphysical postulates. The Saljūqs, a Turko-Persian Sunni Muslim dynasty that ruled the region for more than 150 years, marked a new era with their political institutions. They attempted to cultivate an Islamic identity by recognizing the legitimacy of the caliphate and its divine origin and portraying themselves as the legitimate defenders of the Islamic faith.[194] "They enforced Islamic law, patronized the pilgrimage, endowed colleges of learning and religious activity, and sometimes waged jihad against non-Muslim populations in Anatolia and Central Asia. Nonetheless, these states were not considered inherently Islamic."[195] During the eleventh century, the masses were frequently identified with different Islamic schools of law that became important administrative as well as religious centers. In the Saljūq era during which al-Ghazālī lived, the political authority nurtured religious education.[196] Nevertheless, the political rule and religious realm were distinguished to a certain degree. Rule was slowly slipping from the hands of the caliphs into the hands of generals, administrators, and provincial figures. Governmental authorities were henceforth weaving together the political and the religious, in light of their (personal) commitments to the religion of Islam.[197] The members of the *'ulamā'*, being appointed as judges and advisors

---

[192] For more on governmental authority in Islamic tradition in English, see, e.g., Hallaq, *The Impossible State*, 2013; Mohammad Hashim Kamali, "Separation of Powers: An Islamic Perspective," *Islam and Civilisational Renewal*, Vol. 5, No. 4 (2014): 471–88; Safi, *Politics of Knowledge*.

[193] Al-Ghazālī, *Iḥyā'*, Vol. 1, 13.

[194] I. M. Lapidus, "State and Religion in Islamic Societies," *Past & Present*, No. 151 (1996): 3–27 at 13.

[195] Lapidus, "State and Religion in Islamic Societies," 13.

[196] For more on the Saljūq rule, see, e.g., Ann K. S. Lambton, "The Administration of Sanjar's Empire as Illustrated in the *'Atabat al-kataba*," *BSOAS*, Vol. 20, No. 1/3 (1957): 367–88.

[197] I. M. Lapidus, "The Separation of State and Religion in the Development of Early Islamic Society," *Journal of Middle East Studies*, Vol. 6, No. 4 (1975): 363–85 at 376.

to rulers, indeed regulated communal and religious life; however, this might also be perceived as an attempt to assert their religious power, since caliphates were doctrinally political institutions from their very inception.

For al-Ghazālī, governmental authority is a necessary institution for promulgating economic affairs and fulfilling *Sharī'a*-mandated social obligations.[198] The *sulṭān*'s authority and religion are indivisible foundations in a society. While religion forms society's basis, the ruler safeguards it. Al-Ghazālī continues that "if either of the two foundations is weakened, then society crumbles."[199] Certainly, an ideal governmental authority for him bases its rules upon *Sharī'a*'s teaching. Since jurisprudence promulgates order in society, the members of the community as its subjects, including the *'ulamā'*, are to be referred to by the ruler in order to promote justice. Yet the legal aspect of law is inextricably linked to moral behavior. Both the ruler and governmental authority are not above *Sharī'a*'s moral law, but, at least in theory, subsumed by it. The link between the political and ethical in classical economic thought is also focused on managing lust and one's negligence of moral conduct. While virtue is an individual matter, classical Muslim scholars emphasize individual attainment as a crucial element that can lead toward the overall restructuring of society and its sociopolitical fabric.[200]

3.6.1 *Kitāb Naṣīḥat al-Mulūk and Just Rulership*

Kitāb Naṣīḥat al-Mulūk, or the *Book of Counsel for Kings*, is a so-called Mirror for Princes, a distinctive literary genre that typically offers advice and outlines principles of conduct for leaders from the classical period, often written in Arabic and Persian. Mirror for Princes is not written in a systematic fashion, and political, moral, and juridical advice, accounts, examples, and anecdotes are stated rather interchangeably. The book is divided into two parts according to themes. The first part addresses rulership as a bestowed or predestined position for which one is accountable. The implication of the first part is that the ruler does not possess ultimate power and is thus responsible for the just reign of all subjects, whereas the second part tackles the qualities of appointed rulers, indicating principles of justice according to the examples of Muslim and non-Muslim rulers. The authorship of the second part of *Naṣīḥat al-Mulūk*

---

198 The political rulership of the sultanate (*sulṭāna*), however, is not stipulated by the knowledge of religion in the first degree, even though its reign certainly helps in matters that cannot exist without religion. Al-Ghazālī, *Iḥyā'*, Vol. 1, 17.

199 Al-Ghazālī, *Iḥyā'*, Vol. 1, 17; see also al-Ghazālī, *Iḥyā'*, Vol. 2, 312–15, 338; al-Ghazālī, *Counsel for Kings*, 59.

200 Quasem, *The Ethics of al-Ghazali*, 24.

has been disputed, since it displays inconsistencies with al-Ghazālī's earlier writings.[201] However, various scholars have confirmed its authenticity.[202] It is believed that *Naṣīḥat al-Mulūk* was composed in al-Ghazālī's birth town of Ṭūs upon his return from Nīshāpūr, after 1109, as a response to the criticism he received from a Ḥanafite *'ulamā'* and as a gift to Sulṭān Muḥammd ibn Malikshāh (d. 1092), who encouraged its composition.[203]

In *Naṣīḥat*, al-Ghazālī's ethical views of politics and livelihood are expressed,[204] addressing public ethics, political actions, and the role a ruler should play in securing a just socioeconomic life in his empire, laying down both practical and theoretical aspects. Given the nature of the genre and al-Ghazālī's intellectual investment, *Naṣīḥat* is ethical in essence—its politics comes second. For al-Ghazālī, public interest requires obedience to rulers, despite their personal or official shortcomings, since resistance against rulers might lead to a civil war and even greater social turmoil. Nonetheless, according to the Tradition of the Prophet Muḥammad, also referred to by al-Ghazālī, one has to be vocal if the ruler exercises injustice: "The best *jihād* is the utterance of what is just [i.e., truth] in the presence of the tyrant."[205] It is clear in *Naṣīḥat* that al-Ghazālī views justice (*'adl*) as sufficient for legitimizing the preordained Saljūq reign, and even attributes titles generally reserved for 'Abbāsid caliphs to Saljūq *sulṭāns*.[206] *Naṣīḥat* gives further incentives for the ruler, as the one who exercises political authority (*siyāsa*), to realize the importance of the role given to him, for the aim of the ruler is to obtain prosperity for his people, as he should both possess and exercise *siyāsa* or political authority in line with the principles of *Sharī'a*. The ruler, who is appointed by the governmental authority and supported by members of the community, must be devoted to his position, cooperate with *'ulamā'*, and not resort to injustice. Sanctions filed by the ruler should be justly reasoned—following the injunctions of

201 See, e.g., Patricia Crone, "Did al-Ghazālī Write a Mirror for Princes? On the Authorship of Naṣiḥāt al-Mulūk," *Jerusalem Studies of Arabic and Islam*, Vol. 10 (1987): 167–97.

202 See, e.g., Henri Laoust, *La politique de Ghazali* (Paris: Librairie Orientaliste Paul Geuthner, 1970); al-Ghazālī, *Counsel for Kings*, "Introduction."

203 Al-Ghazālī, *Counsel for Kings*, ix, xviii.

204 Al-Ghazālī, *Counsel for Kings*, xxxviii.

205 "*Afḍalu al-jihād kalimatu al-haqqi 'inda sulṭānin jā'irīn.*" Ghazali and Sadeq, "Ghazalijevi pogledi na ekonomske probleme i neka etičko-pravna pitanja značajna za ekonomsko ponašanje," 167.

206 For more on the notion of justice, see, e.g., Ann K. S. Lambton, "Justice in the Medieval Persian Theory of Kingship," *Studia Islamica*, No. 17 (1962): 91–119. On al-Ghazālī and the Saljūq authority, see, e.g., Ann K. S. Lambton, "The Theory of Kingship in the Naṣiḥāt ul-Mulūk of al-Ghazālī," *Islamic Quarterly*, Vol. 10, No. 1 (1954): 47–55; Ann K. S. Lambton, *State and Government in Medieval Islam* (New York: Oxford University Press, 1981); Garden, *The First Islamic Reviver*, chapter 1.

Sharī'a—and he should heed petitioners of his court.[207] Indulgence in passion, pride, and dominance of anger are prohibited, otherwise just policy will not be attainable. The governmental authority should keep all subjects satisfied and pleased with their rule. This suggests the masses ought to be satisfied, otherwise they can oppose the ruler.

In relation to prosperous economic development for all subjects, conditions for peace should be met:

> Efforts of those Kings to develop the world were undertaken because they knew that the greater the prosperity, the longer would be their rule and more numerous their subjects. They also knew that the religion depends on the authority, the authority on the army, and the army on the supplies, supplies and prosperity on justice.[208]

Sustainable economic growth is possible when all sectors of industry are balanced. Since economic development assumes a particular sociopolitical background, ethical stipulations in promulgating the common good in society are the main objectives for a healthy economic life.

In *Naṣīḥat*, al-Ghazālī discusses 10 principles of justice and the fair treatment of subjects in the caliphate. The ruler should fully comprehend the importance, responsibility, and danger of the role entrusted to him; he should seek cooperation with the devout *'ulamā* if in need of advice and avoid learned men with worldly ambitions aiming to flatter and please the authorities. The ruler should not be content with the personal combat of injustice, but should apply it at an institutional level and hence never tolerate injustice at any level. Authority must be exercised without any measure of pride, for this stipulates anger, which results in revenge and violence (discussed in detail in the book on "Destructive Evils/Things" in *Iḥyā'*). The ruler possesses the authority to hold himself responsible and accountable in given circumstances in which he reacts promptly without treasonable use of the role assigned to him. Moreover, he should not disregard petitioners of the court; this is viewed as intolerable. He must also not indulge in passions and must meticulously exercise his rulership and just conduct. The ruler should also avoid harsh governance and must fulfill these obligation, so as to keep his subjects pleased. Finally, he should not side with those contradicting *Sharī'a*.[209]

These principles and regulations offer examples of just rulership, and are based upon manners and moral codes for both Muslim and non-Muslim

---

207 Al-Ghazālī, *Counsel for Kings*, 13.
208 Al-Ghazālī, *Counsel for Kings*, 56.
209 Al-Ghazālī, *Counsel for Kings*, 13–31.

rulers. They do not represent the bulk of al-Ghazālī's theoretical stance on the intervention of governmental authority in exercising fair policies on economic conduct. In *Naṣīḥat*, al-Ghazālī did not directly address political conduct or the legal requirements of economic life, but he offered many insights into how a ruler should respond in accordance with *Sharī'a* norms in order to stipulate ethical-economic principles. Governmental authority is a necessary institution not only in regard to governance and leadership, but also in the fulfillment of *furūḍ kifāya* or *Sharī'a*'s obligations.[210] Ethical considerations are, at least in their exposition, hence inseparable from governmental ruling when it comes to moral conduct: "It is one's ability to obtain all his needs that convince him to remain in a society with cooperation. However, inclinations, such as jealousy, competition, and selfishness can cause antagonisms, and, as a consequence, it is necessary that certain conduct [in society] has to be checked and controlled," al-Ghazālī argues.[211] The responsibility of the ruler and the intervention of the authority are therefore intended to monitor (economic) conduct, if economic progress is anticipated and to bring about prosperity and secure conditions for mutual cooperation. From this perspective, governmental authority is perceived as the regulator of licit conduct while being a subject of that very regulation itself, because equitable rule is one of its main functions:

> When injustice and oppression are present, the people have no foothold, the cities and localities go to ruin, the inhabitants flee and move to other territories, the cultivated lands are abandoned, the kingdom falls into decay, the revenue diminishes, the treasury becomes empty, and happiness fades among the people. The subjects do not love the unjust king, but always pray that evil may befall him.[212]

This inevitably presupposes that Islamic governance regulates the market by imposing sanctions against false transactions, incorrect weights or illicit contracts, purchase of unlawful commodities, and fraud. The *sūq* was not only a marketplace meant for trading but it also encompassed other aspects of Muslim life through legal, economic, and ethical responsibility. Since exchanging goods was one of the primary economic activities in the classical period, marketplaces were common venues for trade and commerce. They facilitated economic growth and contributed to the expansion of cities, where rules were

---

210 E.g., al-Ghazālī, *Iḥyā'*, Vol. 2, 140; Al-Ghazālī, *Counsel for Kings*, 45, 46.
211 Al-Ghazālī, *Iḥyā'*, Vol. 4, 119.
212 Al-Ghazālī, *Counsel for Kings*, 55.

enforced and norms applied in commerce and trading under the banner of *ḥisba*.

3.6.2 Ḥisba Regulations

The literature on *ḥisba* is undeniably diverse, covering regions and cities from Andalusia to Baghdād. In classical Islamic tradition, the institution of *ḥisba* refers to the governmental monitoring of conduct, alluding to the domain of public ethics, politics, and economic affairs, in order to maintain righteousness and promote ethical principles.[213] This institution is believed to date back to the first Muslim community and the Prophet Muḥammad, himself a merchant who examined irregularities in the marketplace. With the expansion of the Muslim empire, Islamic governance, and market activities, the ruler appointed a special agent to ensure the security of trading activities. These state institutions were run by a *muḥtasib*, a public inspector or auditor who regularly checked market prices, false advertisements, incorrect weights, usurious transactions, contracts, and conduct that was not compliant with *Sharī'a* laws. The institution of *ḥisba*, as part of the Islamic governmental authority, controlled the functioning of the market and dealt with the commons through which political authorities exercised social, economic, and moral control over trade-related matters. The nature of control understandably differed across geographic regions, rulers' political motivations, and time periods.[214] While some caliphs imposed judicial stipulations according to Islamic law, others simply tried to sustain healthy economic growth.[215] Notably, writings on *ḥisba* are not intended for merchants but rather for state officials, to inform them about the regulation of marketplaces. The duties of *ḥisba* institutions encompassed the spiritual or religious as well as practical or financial domain,

---

213 See, e.g., Abū al-Ḥasan 'Alī Ibn Muḥammad Ibn Ḥabīb al-Māwardī, *Al-Aḥkām al-Sulṭāniyya* (Misr: al-Babi al-Ḥalabi, 1973); Ibn Taymiyya, *Al-Ḥisbah fī al-Islām*; Islahi, *Contribution of Muslim Scholars to Economic Thought and Analysis*, 59.

214 See Abbas Hamdani, "The Muhtasib as Guardian of Public Morality in the Medieval Islamic City," *Digest of Middle East Studies*, Vol. 17, No. 1 (2008): 92–104.

215 For more on the role of the *ḥisba*, see, e.g., Yassine Essid, *A Critique of the Origins of Islamic Economic Thought* (Leiden: Brill, 1995); Ibn Taymiyya, *Al-Ḥisba fi al-Islām*; R. P. Buckley (trans.), *The Book of the Islamic Market Inspector. Kitāb Nihāyat al-Rutba fī Ṭalab al-Ḥisba (The Utmost Authority in the Pursuit of Ḥisba) by 'Abd al-Raḥmān b. Naṣr al-Shayzarī* (Oxford: Oxford University Press, 1999); Muḥammad ibn Muḥammad ibn al-Ukhūwwah, *Ma'ālim al-Qūrbah fi Aḥkām al-Ḥisba*, ed. Reuben Levy (Cambridge: Cambridge University Press, 1938).

covering both *'ibādāt* and *mu'āmalāt*.[216] Often, regulations were based on discretionary power. Many treaties describe the *muḥtasib* as able to facilitate the welfare of an entire city by applying the aforementioned ethical principles. In *ḥisba* manuals, the link between society and piety is interrelated, hence the *muḥtasib* was perceived as a figure who regulates both realms. The role of the *muḥtasib*, as al-Ghazālī saw it, was to ensure provision of necessities, to supervise the development of various industries and trading, to resolve market-related disputes and fraud, and to standardize weights and measures of commodities in order to prevent further irregularities, hoarding (or counterfeiting) of money, fixed wages, and the establishment of monopolies at the market.[217] The multiple roles of *ḥisba* facilitated different state institutions and departments in diminishing illicit conduct in the market economy and abrogating the economic power of the few. Furthermore, the *muḥtasib* would distribute water throughout the city and take care of other social obligations, such as enforcing law at marketplaces, optimizing public safety, caring for prudent treatment of customers, and so forth. Caliph al-Ma'mūn (d. 833) was the first to replace the *sāhib al-sūq* or market inspector, who controlled practical economic matters (e.g., the measure of weights) in Baghdād, with the official *muḥtasib*, whose task was supervising market conduct and thereby mobilizing religious sentiments.[218]

Al-Ghazālī informs us that the institution of *ḥisba* is about *'amr bi al-ma'rūf wa nahy 'an al-munkar*, and consists of four components: the *muḥtasib*, the subjects at the market who are inspected by him, dishonorable deeds (*munkar*) that have to be sanctioned, and the very process of inspection or *iḥtisāb*.[219] The process of *iḥtisāb* is predicated upon several degrees and behaviors, commencing with identifying (*al-ta'ruf*) and defining (*al-ta'rīf*) what has to be sanctioned in the first place. The *muḥtasib* himself has to possess knowledge, piety, and good behavior (*ḥusn al-khulq*). He can, for instance, signal verbal warnings or give advice about particular conduct or alternatively impose the law by force.[220] The role of the *muḥtasib*, as al-Ghazālī described it, should not be perceived as a rigorously or rigidly conservative branch of authority trying to impose strict *Sharī'a* laws, but rather as a mechanism that promulgates *iḥsān* in order to achieve *maṣlaḥa* in society, especially in regard to securing common resources.[221] Furthermore,

---

[216] While the former was imposed on Muslims, it has been narrated that the latter impacted Muslims and non-Muslims alike.

[217] See, e.g., al-Ghazālī, *Iḥyā'*, Vol. 2, 338; Ibn Taymiyya, *Al-Ḥisba fi al-Islām*, 21–22.

[218] Essid, *A Critique of the Origins of Islamic Economic Thought*, 115; Lapidus, "The Separation of State and Religion in the Development of Early Islamic Society," 376.

[219] Al-Ghazālī, *Iḥyā'*, Vol. 2, 312.

[220] Al-Ghazālī, *Iḥyā'*, Vol. 2, 314.

[221] For instance, one cannot privatize water and other natural resources.

the *muḥtasib* promotes justice in the markets by preventing the previously listed harmful acts and by monitoring economic conduct; however, since he himself is part of this institution, he cannot demand from his subjects something he himself does not possess.[222] One of his most important tasks is setting the normal price of commodities at marketplaces by preventing merchants from hoarding or interfering with monetary policies, since the imposition of prices is unlawful not only because of the possible impoverishment of the merchant but also because of the potential disruption of order at the market. The view that the "natural regulation of the market corresponds to a cosmic regulation" holds in setting the price according to the current circumstances of the given time frame, the marketplace, and the city's economic stability.[223] The so-called cosmic regulation is not, however, detached from the moral law, but rather necessitated by it. Fixing prices only by market forces would mean not only to circumvent the ethical presuppositions but also to demean social functions by abusing the very nature of the market. Thus the *muḥtasib* is to restore what is believed to be the normal price of goods at the market, which is dependent on a certain criterion for setting prices, meaning "the price people are used to paying for a given product under normal market circumstances."[224] The normal price is thus labeled as the market price.

The practical impact of the *sāhib al-sūq* remained in place after the *muḥtasib* was introduced. However, the religious implications in inspecting moral behavior at the marketplace became much more frequent during the 'Abbāsid reign, seen as an attempt to assure a more religious sentiment at the market, which was often perceived as a sacred space in Muslim society.[225] Some historical accounts also indicate that a certain degree of corruption appeared in *ḥisba* institutions and government officials, linked also to tradesmen and the *muḥtasib* himself. This is probably one of the reasons al-Ghazālī insists on introducing ethical characteristics to the institution and its agents, to exact just payment of taxes and maintenance of fair prices, among other matters.

3.7 Taxes, Public Finances, and Expenditure

Al-Ghazālī differs from other classical scholars not only in clearly defining the functions and roles of the governmental authority and their relation to

---

[222] Al-Ghazālī, *Iḥyā'*, Vol. 2, 312.
[223] Essid, *A Critique of the Origins of Islamic Economic Thought*, 153.
[224] Essid, *A Critique of the Origins of Islamic Economic Thought*, 161.
[225] Essid, *A Critique of the Origins of Islamic Economic Thought*, 118.

Sharīʿa's ethical principles but also in that he focuses on both revenues and expenditures.[226]

Because the economy of his day was predominantly agriculture-based, it was believed that the land tax (*kharaj*) represented the chief source of public revenue. The system of levying a fixed land tax (*misāḥa*) had been introduced by the second caliph, ʿUmar bin al-Khattab (d. 644), after examining the productivity and capacity of the lands.[227] Al-Ghazālī informs us that revenues from all citizens, Muslims and non-Muslims alike, would be solicited accordingly. Valid sources of revenue relate to property and assets without heirs, whose owners cannot be identified. In addition, *zakāt* and *ṣadaqāt* are to be employed as well, while confiscation of property and bribery are perceived as illicit sources of revenue.[228] Al-Ghazālī affirms that public finances are based mostly on illicit sources, since the valid sources such as *zakāt*, *ṣadaqāt*, *fāi'*, and *ghanīma* were not prevalent in his time.[229] One reason is the system of taxation promulgated during the Saljūq dynasty, which was based on tradition and custom, and not exclusively on *Sharīʿa*'s law.[230] He was also in favor of the caliph's office collecting additional taxes in the interest of public welfare, in case resources would become deficient in the public treasury, when the governmental authority's security would be jeopardized, and in order to improve the conditions of orphans. The governmental authority would ensure the overall well-being of the subjects in a society.[231] As a general principle of just taxation, al-Ghazālī described his approach to pay-as-you-can taxation, proverbially speaking:

> When they (rulers) demand sums of money from the subjects for the well-being of the empire, they must demand them only at the proper seasons and times; they must know the usages and fix (tax) burdens in accordance with capacity and ability (to pay). They must be crane-slayers, not sparrow-slayers, at the hunt; that is to say, they must take

---

[226] Ghazanfar and Islahi claim al-Ghazālī provided an insight into what is today known as benefit-cost analysis. Ghazanfar and Islahi, *Economic Thought of al-Ghazali*, 38.

[227] See Ashker and Wilson, *Islamic Economics*, chapter 3; M. Kabir Hassan and Mervyn K. Lewis, *Handbook on Islam and Economic Life* (Cheltenham: Edward Elgar, 2014), chapter 2.

[228] Al-Ghazālī, *Iḥyā'*, Vol. 2, 139.

[229] *Fāi'* denoted different types of possession taken without any factual war, while *ghanīma* is confiscated from the enemy as spoils of war. *Jizya* or poll tax is collected from non-Muslims who have been granted rights under Islamic rule (*dhimmis*). Al-Ghazālī, *Iḥyā'*, Vol. 2, 139.

[230] Al-Ghazālī, *Counsel for Kings*, xliv.

[231] Al-Ghazālī, *Counsel for Kings*, 40.

> nothing from the poor; they must not covet the belonging and estates of deceased persons when there are heirs, but must shun such greed, as it is inauspicious; they must keep the hearts of the subjects and officials happy by granting them benefits and satisfying their petitions.[232]

While the notions of public finances and public expenditures were introduced into mainstream economics relatively late, the concept of a treasury or a central financial institution (*bayt al-māl*) was already known during the Rashidun caliphate (*al-khilāfa al-rāshida*; AD 632–61), which among other things administered taxes for public revenues in the caliphate.[233] Al-Ghazālī opposed the debasement of currency and the counterfeiting of money to meet a certain level of state expenditure for all citizens.[234] His theory of public expenditures constitutes part of his overall opinion of the governmental role in economic life, even related to public finances. For him, public expenditures have a direct link to sources of revenue and how they are allocated. The main criterion seems to be again the general welfare or common good. Al-Ghazālī links the impoverishment of people to deficient public services, which sets off a series of consequences from migration to general economic deterioration and culminates in the decline of security. Since it is probable that under such circumstances the poor would be exploited, in order to avoid civil disturbances and the general downfall of the economy, the very protection of society was dependent on regulations—both political and ethical—put forward by the caliph's office.[235] Poverty (as a social category) must be diminished in society if justice should prevail, and public expenditures should serve to increase the basic welfare. Public expenditures may be incurred for education, establishment of law, healthcare, and social and economic infrastructure; in this context, *fāi'* must be spent on activities that are beneficial to the whole community, such as building infrastructure, bridges, mosques, shelters, and other public spaces.[236] Public expenditures are intended for the establishment of security and economic development,[237] covering areas such as education, maintenance of law, healthcare, and social as well as economic infrastructure.[238]

Al-Ghazālī attributed the relevance of socioeconomic questions and the overall idea of human development to ethical teachings as part of his theory

---

232 Al-Ghazālī, *Counsel for Kings*, 112.
233 Islahi, *Contribution of Muslim Scholars to Economic Thought and Analysis*, 64.
234 Al-Ghazālī, *Iḥyā'*, Vol. 2, 73–74.
235 Al-Ghazālī, *Iḥyā'*, Vol. 2, 42.
236 Al-Ghazālī, *Iḥyā'*, Vol. 2, 130.
237 Al-Ghazālī, *Counsel for Kings*, 56, 76.
238 Al-Ghazālī, *Iḥyā'*, Vol. 2, 139–40.

of happiness, since the ethical self is defined by the knowledge of the divine linked to constant introspection. In other words, happiness is grounded in knowledge yet put in motion or materialized through action. For him, social duties are hence part of his ethical theory, in which the economy plays a crucial role in securing prosperity for society by means of fulfilling social obligations; if not fulfilled, members of society will face social disturbances.[239] This is why al-Ghazālī did not support only a provision of mere subsistence, but simultaneously argued against the acquisition of wealth: "If people stay confined to a mere sustenance and become very frail, then death will rise, all work and industry cease, and society will perish. Moreover, religion will be destroyed, since the mundane is only the preparation for the afterlife."[240]

In the following chapter, I turn toward classical economic thought as it emerged in early modern Europe in order to analyze its development and observe the considerable differences in al-Ghazālī's economic philosophy.

[239] Al-Ghazālī, *Iḥyā'*, Vol. 2, 32.
[240] Al-Ghazālī, *Iḥyā'*, Vol. 2, 108.

Chapter 4

CLASSICAL ECONOMICS AND ITS WORLDVIEWS

This chapter briefly introduces major postulates by classical economists and tries to position their theories in tandem with al-Ghazālī's formulations of the ethical-economic subjectivity. This serves as a building block for the next chapter, which discusses the convergences between, contradictions to, and possible approaches of reading al-Ghazālī's economic philosophy within the context of modern economics.

While scholars such as Benedikt Koehler suggest that early Islam envisioned and developed a rudimentary form of a capitalist society in how markets operated and were devised, and that the early Muslim scholars on economics did not differ from their European counterparts, it seems somewhat far-fetched to believe the economic philosophy of early Islam could accommodate what is nowadays known as a capitalistic mode of operation.[1] Timur Kuran, however, tried to explicate the reasons why Islamic culture did not produce an institution of corporation. In his view, a corporation was never established due to the rigid nature of *Sharī'a*, which obstructed the flourishing of such an institution and was not able to devise amendable corporate laws.[2] Both predicaments, however, are somewhat unsubstantiated, since *Sharī'a*'s moral laws—as major classical Muslim scholars and jurists conceived them—were never meant to empower individual (economic) gains over communal well-being, and as an extension of that, enable exploitation of natural resources as well as position competitive postures in the market above the idea of ethical human development. The exposition of mutual collaboration and the basic division of industries were well known to classical Muslim scholars such as al-Ghazālī, and they were formulated within the parameters of the science of the hereafter and *Sharī'a*'s moral law in order to stimulate economic activities and diversify

---

[1] See, e.g., Benedikt Koehler, *Early Islam and the Birth of Capitalism* (Lanham, MD: Lexington Books, 2014).

[2] Timur Kuran, "The Absence of the Corporation in Islamic Law: Origins and Persistence," *American Journal of Comparative Law*, Vol. 53, No. 4 (2005): 785–834.

economic outputs. Some of these approaches, despite the differences in their methodologies, were also known to pre-Enlightenment economic thinkers in Europe. In order to both comprehend and problematize the synergies and inflection points between al-Ghazālī and key early modern economists, in the following pages I examine classical economic theories, major philosophical trends, and some of their main representatives.

4.1 Classical Economic Theories, Positivism, and Utilitarianism

Classical economics as it emerged in early modern Europe is often portrayed as a school of thought in economics that asserts markets function best with limited government interference. It was developed in the late eighteenth and early nineteenth centuries in Britain by Adam Smith (d. 1790), David Ricardo (d. 1823), Jean-Baptiste Say (d. 1832), Thomas Malthus (d. 1834), and John Stuart Mill (d. 1873), who by and large envisioned theories of market economies governed by their own market forces during a period in which capitalism was emerging from feudalism and when the Industrial Revolution was one of the leading reasons for socioeconomic changes. Before presenting Adam Smith's and David Ricardo's views on economics below I briefly introduce major philosophical themes that impacted the development of economic science in Europe.

Classical economic thought stems from a particular historical and philosophical context and from corresponding epistemological considerations that made possible the transition to a secular economic (and political) doctrine. A turn toward a more secular orientation was necessary or even inevitable for various reasons,[3] which included the idea that the Enlightenment created a new stage in the evolution of human consciousness while rejecting traditional belief systems.[4] The development of the Enlightenment proceeds from Rene Descartes's (d. 1650) dualistic doctrine, which was succeeded by David Hume's (d. 1776) distinction between fact and value and by Jeremy

---

[3] See, e.g., Talal Asad, *Formations of the Secular* (Stanford, CA: Stanford University Press, 2003); Saba Mahmood, "Secularism, Hermeneutics, and Empire: The Politics of Islamic Reformation," *Public Culture*, Vol. 18, No. 2 (2006): 323–47; Charles Taylor, "Modes of Secularism," in *Secularism and Its Critics*, ed. Rajeev Bhargava (New Delhi: Oxford University Press, 1998), 31–53.

[4] See, e.g., David Hume, *A Treatise of Human Nature* (Auckland: Floating Press, 2009); Immanuel Kant, "Was ist Aufklärung?" *UTOPIE kreativ*, H. 159 (2004): 5–10. According to Roy Porter, Kant thought the Enlightenment was mankind's final stage and the emancipation of the human consciousness from ignorance. See also Roy Porter, *The Enlightenment* (London: Palgrave Macmillan, 1996).

Bentham's (d. 1832) psychological hedonism. Cartesian bifurcation of mind and body dissected matter from corporal body in the natural world, which eventually not only impacted philosophical trends but also defined social and political reality in Western thought, in that it constructed the image of the world as a mechanical reality, promoted facts as independent from values, and levitated quantity over quality by advancing a naturalist view that the external world can be explained in quantifiable measures.[5] Its ontological and epistemological rupture of the *knowing subject* and the *object to be known* further influenced philosophical rationalism and empiricism.[6] Mechanical perception of the cosmos and man's subjugation of the living habitat has also imparted the alienation of man from nature and a rather destructive approach to the natural environment.[7]

Closely related to Cartesian bifurcation is Hume's is/ought distinction and his philosophy, which promulgates the idea that all knowledge is found in experience.[8] The is/ought distinction lays the foundation for the difference between descriptive and normative statements. Hume's distinction presupposes all knowledge is based on observation, logic, and/or definition. This further asserts moral skepticism as part of metaethical theories that no one is or can be intrinsically moral.[9] As a forerunner of positivism, Hume's philosophy further influenced utilitarianism, Immanuel Kant's (d. 1804) philosophy, philosophy of science, and logical positivism. Jeremy Bentham's utilitarianism further exposes the definition of utility as "that property in any object whereby it tends to produce pleasure, good or happiness, or to prevent the happening of mischief, pain, evil or unhappiness to the party whose interest is considered."[10] Bentham's psychological hedonism attests humankind is governed by two sovereign motives—namely, pain and pleasure. As a critic of institutions, Bentham advanced the idea of virtue as a principle

---

5 See Rene Descartes, *Discours de la Méthode et Essais*, 3 vols. Ed. Marie Beyssade and Denis Kambouchner (Paris: Gallimard, 2009).

6 Seyyed Hossein Nasr, *The Need for a Sacred Science: The Gifford Lectures* (Edinburgh: Edinburgh University Press, 1981); Waleed El-Ansary, "The Quantum Enigma and Islamic Sciences of Nature: Implications for Islamic Economic Theory," in *Proceedings of the 6th International Conference on Islamic Economics and Finance* (Jeddah: Islamic Development Bank, 2005), 143–75.

7 Seyyed Hossein Nasr, *Knowledge and the Sacred* (New York: State University of New York, 1989).

8 Hume, *A Treatise of Human Nature*, 715.

9 Hume, *A Treatise of Human Nature*, Book 3, part 1.

10 Jeremy Bentham, *An Introduction to the Principles of Moral Legislation* (Kitchener, ON: Batoche Books, 2001), 14–15.

of utility that would ensure the greatest happiness to the greatest number of people.

In light of applying ideas from natural sciences into social sciences, the philosophical movement of positivism emerged in the nineteenth century, holding society operates according to similar laws as does the physical world. In general, positivism asserts that all authentic knowledge demands objectification and verification, proposing that only scientifically proven and quantifiable knowledge is valid.[11] Scholars such as Henri de Saint-Simon (d. 1825), Pierre-Simon Laplace (d. 1827), and Auguste Comte (d. 1857) believed the scientific method and its observation would eventually replace metaphysics in the study of human thought.[12]

One of Bentham's students was philosopher and economist John Stuart Mill, an exponent of utilitarianism who studied Adam Smith (whose thought is presented in more detail later in this chapter).[13] John Stuart Mill was influenced not only by Jeremy Bentham but also by Auguste Comte, Isaac Newton (d. 1727), John Locke (d. 1704), and David Hume, and he introduced (a modified version of Bentham's) utilitarianism to economic science, advocating a formulation of a logic of the human sciences—including history, psychology, and sociology—based on causal explanation as conceived by David Hume.[14] Mill's defense of freedom for man to pursue his own utility did not necessarily mean a strong support of laissez-faire, since he did not think of property rights as part of such a contract.

Turning more specifically to economics, Adam Smith was committed to the Enlightenment project, favoring reason, economic progress, and specialization of knowledge, and leaning toward a philosophy of particularism, stating that being virtuous in one situation might prove futile in another. For Smith, moral theory accompanies and guides one's actions. Smith distinguishes two types of normative guides to action—rules and virtues.[15] Moral rules prohibit certain types of behavior and are part of the notion of justice, whereas virtues stretch beyond the rules. His theory of moral philosophy is more a virtue ethic than an imposed rule of conduct, which would be linked to the thought of Immanuel Kant and utilitarian philosophers. Smith believed human moral faculties concern individual well-being and are not directed toward the

---

[11] See especially chapters 1 and 6 of Auguste Comte, *A General View of Positivism* (Cambridge: Cambridge University Press, 2009).

[12] Comte, *A General View of Positivism*, chapter 6.

[13] John Stuart Mill, *Utilitarianism* (London: Parker, Son and Bourn, 1863), 8–38.

[14] John Stuart Mill, *The Collected Works of John Stuart Mill, Volume IV: Essays on Economics and Society Part I*, ed. John M. Robson (Toronto: University of Toronto Press, 1967).

[15] See Adam Smith, *The Theory of Moral Sentiments*, MetaLibri, 2005, electronic edition.

preservation of material goods, which further connotes his idea that human decisions, deeds, and actions ought to aim at the greatest happiness for the greatest number of people.[16]

By the same token, thinking of Adam Smith as an economist and theoretician who sought a purely market-driven attitude of social engagement would be incorrect. As John Dwyer pointed out, "Smith's economics was subservient to his ethics."[17] Hence, Smith's political economy has to be read in tandem with his moral philosophy, and the *Wealth of Nations* in part fulfills that connection by describing a notion of justice in economics.[18] He thought states can foster economic growth and productiveness by the rule of law and should try to lift measures that restrict or encourage particular enterprises.[19] His economic manifesto indicates his leaning toward a restrained approach to economic intervention on the part of governing bodies; however, he did not favor a laissez-faire approach as some contemporary economists believe. Even if he encouraged industries over agriculture, providing for the poor and redistribution of wealth were two of Smith's political economic concerns. The idea that governance should be kept at a distance and not involved in business was based on the predicament that states are likely to advance and promote their particular interests and not provide for the well-being of ordinary citizens. Hence, the minimalist role states play in economic reality is predicated upon Smith's distrust in governance and political life, since for him political philosophy was not devised to promote moral conduct, and that morality does not stem from state authority but rather from one's own virtue. Smith's moral philosophy has little in common with David Hume's utilitarianism or Jeremy Bentham's psychological hedonism, and perhaps tries to assert that social institutions and policies have unintended consequences and that semi-controlled markets can function through their participants.

Despite Smith's faith in the Enlightenment project, he was also a skeptic concerning its progress and he believed social interactions shape human desires.[20] Smith argued man is more interested in a commodity's apparent function and propitiousness to utility rather than in its actual utility.[21] In

---

[16] See, e.g., Smith, *The Theory of Moral Sentiments*, section 2, chapter 3.

[17] John Dwyer, "Ethics and Economics: Bridging Adam Smith's Theory of Moral Sentiments and Wealth of Nations," *Journal of British Studies*, Vol. 44, No. 4 (2005): 662–87, doi:10.1086/431936.

[18] Adam Smith, *The Wealth of Nations*, MetaLibri, 2007, electronic edition, 157, 539, 687.

[19] Smith, *The Wealth of Nations*, chapter 2.

[20] Amartya Sen, "Progress and Public Reason," in *Performance and Progress: Essays on Capitalism, Business, and Society*, ed. Subramanian Rangan (Oxford: Oxford University Press, 2015), 151–73 at 162.

[21] Smith, *The Theory of Moral Sentiments*, part 6.

relation to that, justice cannot be delivered by a governing body alone, for "kindness or beneficence, however, cannot, among equals, be extorted by force."[22] It seems that, for Smith, virtue comes around if not enforced by state apparatus, since virtuous traits of character are profoundly related to deeds done out of one's own benevolence and not because of external commitment, an approach similar to al-Ghazālī's take on human righteousness. Smith's economic philosophy can thus be perceived as part of the Enlightenment project yet with different—that is, moral—ends.

Along with Adam Smith, David Ricardo developed and systematized early economic science, also by developing a theory of laws of distributions, while dividing community into property owners, workers, and owners of capital.[23] Ricardo concluded that profits rise inversely with wages, depending on the costs of necessities and production. Even though rudimentary labor theories of value existed prior to classical economists, such as St. Thomas Aquinas, Smith's and Ricardo's labor theories of value explain the value of a commodity in relation to the social labor invested in it in average terms. Ricardo sought to differentiate the quantity of labor necessary to produce a particular commodity from the wages paid to the laborers. Ricardo's theory was upheld by the proponents of laissez-faire capitalism, as well as by Karl Marx (d. 1883).

Since Karl Marx critiqued classical economists, he can be positioned outside the frame of classical economic theories; however, in line with the purposes of this book, he is analyzed within that category because of the similarity of topics he scrutinized in his texts and because he believed in the material make-up of the social world. Marx aimed to reveal the underlying economic mechanisms underpinning the capitalist mode of production, which, in addition to his defense of the proletariat, sets him apart from classical economists. Since owners of the means of production can claim certain rights linked to the surplus value—because their (property) rights are legally protected by the ruling class—wage labor becomes the focal point of a capitalist society. Technological and industrial developments increase material wealth while they diminish economic value, which leads to poverty in the midst of plentitude. Marx claimed it is not labor per se that creates the value of a commodity, but labor power sold by laborers to the owners of the means of production. Moreover, labor as such is not the source of all wealth, but also includes nature and the natural environment.[24]

---

22 Smith, *The Theory of Moral Sentiments*, 72.

23 David Ricardo, *On the Principles of Political Economy and Taxation* (Kitchener, ON: Batoche Books, 2001).

24 See Karl Marx, *Das Kapital* (Hamburg: Otto Meissner, 1894).

The following paragraphs discuss classical economic theories in relation to al-Ghazālī's ethical-economic thought by underlying certain parallels and distinctions between the major scholars.

4.2 Comparisons and Divergences

As indicated earlier in this chapter, the value theory of labor was advocated also by premodern Muslim scholars such as al-Ghazālī, Ibn Taymiyya, and Ibn Khaldūn who—unlike classical economists centuries later—discussed its mechanisms in light of *adab* as morals or good manners and the moral laws of *Sharīʿa* whereby material concerns are addressed within the broader ethical framework of one's benevolence. While classical economists resorted to empiricism, positivism, and/or materialist philosophy, classical Muslim scholars'—especially al-Ghazālī's—deliberations on economic thought have to be read as a moral yet no less scientific call to a spiritual-economic development in which fact and value, *ʿilm* and *amal*, and observation and faith supplement an economic life undergirded by broader metaphysical qualities. Unlike utilitarianists, al-Ghazālī believed economic activity must be based on higher goals of happiness in the hereafter and ought not to be performed out of one's own selfish orientation.[25] His thought allows for a harmonious intersection of logical reasoning, scientific dissecting, and the moral predicaments of *Sharīʿa* by covering basic concepts of economic behavior of individuals and other economic mechanisms, property, social welfare, market evolution, demand and supply, profits, barter, and the function of governmental authority.

Al-Ghazālī also argued about the development of the market, which should not be read in light of Adam Smith's theory of the invisible hand. Al-Ghazālī affirmed that markets evolve when there is a need for commodities and industries, and that the normal price on the market is the market price under common circumstances. His example of blacksmiths, carpenters, and farmers and their exchange of commodities in order to meet their respective needs indicates that markets are driven by profits, exchange, and economic activities.[26] This is very similar to Smith's example of butchers, brewers, and bakers. Nonetheless, while Smith claimed that "we address ourselves, not to their humanity but to their self-love"—which can also be read as Smith's

---

[25] E.g., al-Ghazālī, *Iḥyāʾ*, Vol. 2, 60.

[26] See al-Ghazālī, *Iḥyāʾ*, Vol. 3, 227; Tubagus Thresna Irijantoa, Mohd. Azlan Shah Zaidib, Abdul Ghafar Ismailc, and Noraziah Che Arshad, "Al Ghazali's Thoughts of Economic Growth Theory: A Contribution with System Thinking," *Scientific Journal of PPI-UKM*, Vol. 2, No. 5 (2015): 233–40.

critique and dissatisfaction with man's lust for his own utility—al-Ghazālī affirmed exchange and profits while regulating wants and illicit purchases in the name of spiritual goals that transcend individual endeavors.[27] Moreover, Marx was critical of the ruling class whose ownership of the means of production facilitated unbalanced and impoverished socioeconomic relations among different classes in society, a thought similar to—despite the lack of class division theories in the Islamic milieu—al-Ghazālī's scheme of the prohibition of hoarding money because it would eliminate its inherent function and enable monopoly in the community by certain groups. Marx's theory nonetheless stems from a particular historical and intellectual context that favors materialist philosophy and equates metaphysics with ideology. For Marx, human nature or *Gattungswesen* exists as a function of human labor, which pinpoints the very narrow and technical nature of human relations and centers on economic determinism whereby subject–object relations occupy the central position.[28] While Marx rejected Comte's positivism, he nonetheless advocated for a scientific study of society. Despite the similarities between Marx's theory of money and al-Ghazālī's views on money as a medium of exchange, scholars of the classical Islamic milieu aimed to transcend class relations. While accumulation of capital indeed shapes social systems, al-Ghazālī's philosophy showcases that social change can also occur through spiritual-economic development and not exclusively via a technical-legal understanding of economic postulates.

In spite of some of the important voices that opposed the empirical study of social phenomena in the Western economic tradition while emphasizing understanding (*Verstehen*) as the key notion to study humanities and intellectual history, such as Wilhelm Dilthey (d. 1911)[29] and George Simmel (d. 1918),[30] the orientation that proceeded the classical theories reigned supreme—namely, neoclassical economics.

---

27 Smith, *The Theory of Moral Sentiments*, 16.

28 Marx, *Das Kapital*, Vol. 1, chapter 7.

29 See Wilhelm Dilthey, *Einleitung in die Geistwissenschaften*, 26 vols. (Leipzig: Verlag von Duncker & Humblot, 1883); Wilhelm Dilthey, *Gesammelte Schriften* (Leipzig und Berlin: Verlag von B. G. Teubner, 1921).

30 See George Simmel, *Einleitung in die Moralwissenschaft*, 2 vols. (Stuttgart and Berlin: J. G. Cotta'sche Buchhalndlung Nachfolger, 1904).

Chapter 5

CONTEMPORARY DEBATES

AL-GHAZĀLĪ AND MODERN ECONOMICS

5.1 The Emergence of Neoclassical and the Rise of Heterodox Economics

This chapter outlines the variations of neoclassical economics in order to set forth an engagement with contemporary debates on economic thought and the locale of Islamic economic postulates that have been forgotten, under-researched, or cast as unscientific. The fundamental idea of reinvigorating classical scholars such as al-Ghazālī connotes that economic doctrine cannot be studied on its own terms and has to be reshaped in relation to other human fields, including ethical principles. Such a standpoint also asserts that ethics as virtuous traits of character have to be brought back to the table in contemporary economic discourse.

Despite the significant variations of and within neoclassical economics, it is widely accepted as part of the so-called mainstream or orthodox economic theories taught at universities across the world.[1] Following rational choice theory and supply and demand, neoclassical economics favors an individual's rationality and one's ability to maximize utility or profit, while also resorting to mathematical equations and evolutionary methods in the study of the economy. Neoclassical economics was developed in the late nineteenth century, based on the theories of William Stanley Jevons (d. 1882),[2] Léon Walras (d. 1910),[3] Carl Menger (d. 1921),[4] and Alfrid Marshall (d. 1924),[5] and became

---

[1] See Tony Lawson, "What Is This 'School' Called Neoclassical Economics?" *Cambridge Journal of Economics*, Vol. 37 (2013): 949–83 at 949, 950.

[2] W. Stanley Jevons, *The Theory of Political Economy* (New York: Augustus M. Kelley, 1960).

[3] Léon Walras, *Éléments d'économie politique pure, ou théorie de la richesse sociale* (Paris: Lausanne, 1926).

[4] Carl Menger, *Principles of Economics*, trans. James Dingwall and Bert F. Hoselitz (Auburn, AL: Ludwig von Mises Institute, 2007).

[5] Alfrid Marshall, *Principles of Economics* (London: Macmillan, 8th edn., 1920), accessed online April 25, 2017.

popularized in the early twentieth century. It is widely believed that Thorstein Veblen (d. 1929) first used the term *neoclassical economics* as it sprang out of demand and supply theory or the so-called Marginal Revolution.[6] Despite diverse theories and approaches within neoclassical economics, its philosophy primarily focuses on consumers' maximization of personal satisfaction, which also employs mathematical deductivism. This theory coincides with the objectives of rational behavior theory that man's economic decisions are rationally induced. While classical economists maintain that a value of a commodity is the result of the cost of material and the cost of labor, neoclassical economists hold there is also a perceived value of a commodity by a consumer that has a direct effect on price and demand. Furthermore, generally neoclassical economists advance competition in the market, oppose governmental involvement, and uphold that savings determine investment and its economic equilibrium.

The success of neoclassical (or mainstream) economics is largely associated with the "mathematization" of economics in the twentieth century.[7] Early Marginalists and economists of the late nineteenth and early twentieth centuries aimed at legitimizing economics as a scholarly discipline, which also presupposes that social goals are attainable if one applies scientific principles. Conversely, Keynesian economics is a contrast to laissez-faire in that John Maynard Keynes (d. 1946) advocated borrowing money from a government in order to stabilize the market economy, while he believed demand, not supply, drives production.[8] Despite that distinction, Keynesian economists advocate for a managed market economy.

With the rise of heterodox (or nonconventional) economics as the analysis and study of various economic principles and mechanisms considered outside of orthodox or mainstream economics, diverse economic schools of thought emerged, including post-Keynesian and Austrian economic schools of thought, which varied between Keynesian economics and the critique of neoclassical economic doctrine. One of the responses to Keynesian economics and the intellectual divisions of Keynesianism, in addition to external political factors, was the neoliberal economic doctrine, which upholds transfer of economic factors from the public to the private sector. While rooted in nineteenth-century classical liberalism, which defines socioeconomic aspects

---

[6] For a critical reading of Veblen's understanding and definition of neoclassical economics as an economic school that is different from the Austrian, see Lawson, "What Is This 'School' Called Neoclassical Economics?" 966, 967.

[7] Lawson, "What Is This 'School' Called Neoclassical Economics?" 953, 954.

[8] John Maynard Keynes, *The General Theory of Employment, Interest and Money: The Collected Writings of John Maynard Keynes*, Vol. VII (Cambridge: Cambridge University Press, 2013).

of society, it took off in the second half of the twentieth century. This model of economics builds upon the fundamental premises of neoclassical economics while advocating for reforming tax law, limiting protectionism, opening up markets for international trade, abolishing regulation, and privatizing state-run businesses. Neoliberalism is often associated with laissez-faire economics and the idea that continued economic growth will lead to human progress.

Positive economics is a pervasive methodological view in contemporary economic discourse, despite its various trends and subdivisions. One such school of economics is the Chicago school, focusing on the concept of usefulness in economics. Despite, for instance, Milton Friedman's (d. 2006) argument against the is/ought distinction, he underpinned methodological positivism.[9] Yet dissatisfaction with the neoclassical and neoliberal economic theories prompted the rise of mainstream economics' critics, which include, for instance, Ernst F. Schumacher (d. 1977),[10] Tony Lawson,[11] and numerous other scholars and economists who explore the notion of value in economic development and the status of ontological economics, respectively. Some of these theories build upon ethical values as axioms of economic subjectivity.

5.2 The Desideratum for Ethical Economics

Despite the fact that neoclassical economics denoted a new ontology of economics in comparison to the classical economic school, as stated by Veblen, that ontology employed similar methodological inconsistencies. Instead of studying social reality as a historical process, economists continued utilizing methods that rendered economic science taxonomic, referring to deductivism to explain economic correlations.[12] This reiterates that economists are ill prepared to study social and human reality and further limits the scope of economic science to a particular and localized field of economic ontology. Even if neoclassical economics denotes a new ontology of economic thinking, it nonetheless persists on dominant features and methods of classical economics.

The primary concern of ethical-economic development goes against the common belief that economic science ought to be solely defined as positivistic or that it cannot and should not accommodate ethical theories of metaphysical proportions. Given the birth and historical development of economic science as a discourse born out of the division of social and natural sciences, while simultaneously adapting to the methodologies of natural sciences, it often omits the

---

9 Milton Friedman, *Essays in Positive Economics* (Chicago: University of Chicago Press, 1953).
10 See Ernst F. Schumacher, *Small Is Beautiful* (London: Perennial Library, 1973).
11 Tony Lawson, *Reorienting Economics* (London: Routledge, 2003).
12 Lawson, "What Is This 'School' Called Neoclassical Economics?" 971.

very sciences of nature and the positioning of human moral agency. Islamic economic intellectual history also implies, however, that "a theory of spiritual values or ethics is logically prior to a theory of exchange," aiming at economic engagement with spiritual ends through which economic equilibrium can be achieved.[13] Spiritual-economic equilibrium gives further incentives for economic efficiency, opposing single-level utility function while introducing a combination of economic, moral, and metaphysical qualities.[14] El-Ansary claims that "some spiritual and ethical 'goods' such as love and friendship require non-market exchange, and non-market institutions such as households and states that are necessary for markets to exist require these 'goods,'" which implies a need for nonmarket transactions in market institutions.[15] An economic theory of market transactions and market institutions premised on the necessity of a theory of ethics entails and is imbued with reverberations of human virtue. While neoclassical economics reduces values to a utility-based object of desire and denies metaphysical qualities as well as spiritual considerations, as shown by Schumacher, the modern economy is unsustainable, in part because of the unrestricted usage of nonrenewable natural resources.[16] A mechanical vision of the universe coincides with secular science, which further denies qualitative aspects of nature, as it does not require multidimensional theories of ethics oriented toward achieving higher ends.

In the context of classical Islamic economic thought, ethics and morality are not set apart but linked by and integrated in the Qur'ānic metaphysic and moral laws. Thinking of *Sharīʿa* as a moral entity whose laws are rooted in metaphysical qualities expounds an atypical and, more importantly, inexorable outlook on economic subjectivity. Against the backdrop of classical Islamic economic thought, the Arabic term *iqtiṣād* (often translated as *economy*) entails qualities of ethical dimensions and does not convey only economic growth, and hence should be in the service of wider socio-ecological predicaments.[17] While in classical economics value is linked to human desires against economic and political constraints, whereby the market functions as a space to resolve such issues, classical Muslim scholars, such as al-Ghazālī, al-Maqrīzī, and Ibn Taymiyya, among many others, affirm that the *sūq* or market is not

---

[13] Waleed El-Ansary, "Recovering the Islamic Economic Intellectual Heritage," Proceedings of the Third Harvard University Forum on Islamic Finance: Local Challenges, Global Opportunities. Cambridge, Massachusetts, Center for Middle Eastern Studies, Harvard University, 1999, 2.

[14] El-Ansary, "Recovering the Islamic Economic Intellectual Heritage," 2.

[15] El-Ansary, "Recovering the Islamic Economic Intellectual Heritage," 2.

[16] See Schumacher, *Small Is Beautiful.*

[17] See Adi Setia, "The Meaning of 'Economy': Qasd, Iqtisad, Tadbir Al-Manzil," *Islamic Sciences*, Vol. 14, No. 1 (2016): 117.

only a place for trade but a space where broader socioeconomic and moral advances are scrutinized and are therefore closely associated with one another. Market mechanisms and governmental intervention—whenever necessary—also extend to the concept of well-being and welfare that al-Ghazālī put forward. Every individual act might have a communal effect that can potentially harm the public good (*maṣlaḥa*), since it might cause imbalances in the market, including hoarding of money, counterfeiting of coins, and dealing with illicit goods.[18] The contention that money has no intrinsic value apart from being a medium of exchange or a tool to achieve higher ends is paradigmatic for an ethically oriented conceptualization of economic development. The purpose of producing and using money is to circulate it back into the community and to prevent a monopoly over it. This invites us to rethink not only how sophisticated the classical Islamic milieu was on economic affairs but, more importantly, how we perceive money as a commodity in twenty-first-century financial transactions.

An ethical-economic subjectivity combines individual utility with social relationality in order to achieve righteous living predicated upon self-knowledge and divine sensibility. This is a sharp contrast to neoclassical economic postulates and its economic agent as being divorced from moral considerations. Al-Ghazālī's "individual-in-community" personality is founded upon the notion of *tawḥīd*, which further dictates not only self-oriented endeavors but also community-centered responsibilities.[19] By the same token, al-Ghazālī's notion of good governance—based on the Islamic social contract—fosters *Sharī'a*'s moral premise of commanding the good and forbidding the harmful.

As one of the forefathers of economic thought in Islamic tradition, al-Ghazālī presents a culmination of ethical approach to economic system by providing an analytical approach to economic activities based upon philosophical and *ṣūfī* principles, and was predated by al-Shaybānī, al-Muḥāsibī, and Ibn Abi al-Dunyā, to name but a few scholars. Al-Ghazālī and other classical Muslim scholars have not been analyzed sufficiently by modern (Muslim) economists, despite their efforts to establish a new economic system as a "third way" that would oppose both neoclassical economics and its various offshoots.[20] Certainly, al-Ghazālī cannot be read in the light of modern economic theories; however, since he provided theoretical patterns

---

[18] Al-Ghazālī, *Iḥyā'*, Vol. 1, No. 17; see also Vol. 2.

[19] Ozay Mehmet, "Al-Ghazzali on Social Justice Guidelines for a New World Order from an Early Medieval Scholar," *International Journal of Social Economics*, Vol. 24, No. 11 (1997): 1203–18 at 1206.

[20] See, e.g., the writings of Umer Chapra, Alam Choudhury, Nejatullah Siddiqi, Muhammad Akram Khan, Muhammad Fahim Khan, and so forth.

for the study of moral behavior in economic engagements, he has to be read within the context of intellectual history and an ethical framework, in particular the ethical-economic genre—part of which is also deeply indebted to *ṣūfī* teachings—which displays a seemingly different economic philosophy in comparison to neoclassical economic orientation. Delving further into the discourse of modern Islamic economics, it is obvious that contemporary Muslim economists have not devised an epistemologically underlined long-term solution to economic problems for several reasons.[21] The most apparent one is that modern Islamic economics established its own niche within neoclassical theory and adapted similar methods despite the deployment of ethical theories. Further, modern Muslim economists have in most cases failed to understand and analyze classical economic scholarship in Islamic tradition and its epistemological considerations, and finally, contemporary Islamic economics has been criticized as nonscientific.

Denying purely individual endeavors in the market while constructing a marketplace based on intricate relations between moral action and economic development can assist us in reorienting current modes of economic operations toward a more humane and efficient system that would consider financial, legal, and technical variables as subsidiary to higher aspiration. Instead of inverting spiritual qualities and diminishing the ethical bias, al-Ghazālī's economic thought reassures and teaches that one way of recovering the current debates of modern economic issues is to resort to (Islamic) intellectual heritage—that very heritage that also helped shape the modern world, including its moral philosophy. Competitiveness, overproduction, annihilation of natural resources, uninformed consumerism, and purely rational economic decisions geared toward fulfilling wants and not needs can be overcome, at least in part, by reinvigorating sciences of nature and attending to individual needs in the light of communal well-being.

[21] For a more detailed account on the development and critique of modern Islamic economics, see Al-Daghistani, "The Making of Islamic Economics."

CONCLUSION: CONUNDRUM OF ETHICS IN ECONOMICS

A FEASIBLE POSSIBILITY OR VAIN ATTEMPT?

The link between ethical teachings and economic reasoning is often difficult to find in modern economic science. The reasons lie in both internal and external forces that have influenced the development of economics as a field, a science, and a human endeavor. Virtue economics, in that it places human moral value in rational reasoning on the path to achieve happiness, is fundamental to human well-being like any other human endeavor—it leads to the realization of personal goals and the fulfillment of social obligations. Al-Ghazālī's economic epistemology teaches us that economic endeavors are, in essence, about moral self-preservation, realized by both knowledge and action. While the conventional market economy encourages impersonal economic gains and selfish behavior by maximizing profits, the market from al-Ghazālī's point of view not only coordinates people's interests but also aims to protect the social welfare of the community by creating production forces directed as human needs. This does not imply that the conventional economic models are immoral, but rather that the market economy produces *amoral* behavioral patterns, and hence delinks ethics from economics on the individual level. This leads us to the following inquiries: what constitutes economic thought, and what is the very nature of human value in this context?

In this work, I aimed to examine al-Ghazālī's legal, *ṣūfī*, and ethical views through his economic and moral philosophies. This book has focused primarily on his ethical contributions to the field of economic thought in Islamic tradition, al-Ghazālī's understanding of *Sharīʿa* and *fiqh*, and his stance on governmental authority in relation to economic conduct. The book's aim is hence threefold. First, it highlights al-Ghazālī's theoretical contributions to economic thought as indispensable to the understanding of the overall development of economic tradition in Islam. Second, it contends that the impartment of (Islamic) ethical teaching extracted from *Sharīʿa* and al-Ghazālī's economic subjectivity and rooted in his theory of happiness constitute the core of his approach to economic behavior. This latter point has been chronically absent from discussions in modern economic science including contemporary Islamic economics. Third, this book positions al-Ghazalı's economic philosophy in the context of modern economic thought and offers a comparative analysis.

A pious man, a jurist by training, and a *ṣūfī* by conviction, al-Ghazālī envisioned that knowledge was best handled through the valence of spiritual care. While some Western scholars acknowledge the historical importance of classical Muslim economic scholarship, al-Ghazālī's ethical teaching along with that of numerous other classical scholars has yet to be implemented in academic discursive reasoning, especially in economic history. Despite his religious imprint (or perhaps exactly because of it), as a forerunner of classical Islamic economic thought who also influenced European scholastics, he bears significance not only for reviving the neglected history and contributions of classical Muslim scholars on economic thought but also for exploring the notion of applied ethics within the field of economics as a human science.[1] Muslim scholars' main contributions on economic thought had already reached medieval Europe, relying too on Aristotle and Bryson. Their work contributed not only to the development of scholastics but also to the rise of mercantilism.[2] Indeed, the Greeks laid down the foundations of early economic science, addressing important economic issues such as the barter system and the concept of money.[3] Yet classical Muslim scholars went beyond these concepts when analyzing the Hellenic legacy and, where necessary, intertwining them with Islamic ethical precepts. They devised a twofold economic narrative by, one, advancing a detailed account of economic aspects within the field of Islamic jurisprudence, and two, merging its moral law with ethical teachings—often through the tradition of *taṣawwuf*.

Classical Muslim scholars neither encouraged an ascetic perception of worldly life nor shunned the acquisition of wealth; rather, they joined the two by emboldening moral standards in commerce and trade, advocating social justice, and imposing ethical restrictions necessary for the establishment of

---

1 S. M. Ghazanfar and A. Islahi, "A Rejoinder to 'Economic Thought and Religious Thought,'" in *Medieval Islamic Thought: Filling the "Great Gap" in European Economics*, ed. S. M. Ghazanfar (London: Routledge, 2003), 53. The traditional dogmatic views of Christianity did not favor economic engagement because of the belief that it is not in accordance with religious stipulations. Schumpeter, *History of Economic Analysis*, 72.

2 Islahi, *Contribution of Muslim Scholars to Economic Thought and Analysis*, 97. For more on the compatibility of the economic ideas of al-Ghazali and Thomas Aquinas, see, e.g., Abdul Azim Islahi, "The Economic Ideas of Muslim Scholars and Christian Scholastics: Linkages and Parallels," *Islam and Christian–Muslim Relations*, Vol. 25, No. 1 (2014): 49–66; Ghazanfar, "The Economic Thought of Abu Hamid Al-Ghazali and St. Thomas Aquinas."

3 Schumpeter, *History of Economic Analysis*, 60.

social cohesion and the preservation of community life. This can be seen as both a supreme economic ideal to be attained by learned men and an implicit critique of the sociopolitical life of the time. Al-Ghazālī's economic teachings in particular were also socially relevant in that they came to reflect ethical prepositions put forward in seminal works on *fiqh*, theology, and Islamic mysticism. For instance, al-Ghazālī, and later on Ibn Taymiyya and Ibn Khaldūn, perceived money as a medium of exchange with no intrinsic value. Hence, "Muslim economic thought was never to deviate from this conception regarding the place that economic factors should occupy within society."[4]

Through various channels, classical Muslim scholars transmitted acquired knowledge and influenced economic thought in medieval Europe. The first channel was the translation process that took place in various centers, such as Aragon and Toledo, and during the reign of Emperor Fredrick II in Sicily. Even Schumpeter recognized the importance of the Arabic translation of economic ideas; however, he perceived the writings of Muslim scholarship only in the light of transmitting economic ideas and not in actively contributing to its expansion.[5] The second channel was the oral transmission of Islamic thought at European universities, while the third comprised trade and commerce.[6] The aforementioned Muslim scholars believed trade was a mutual benefit and not an advantage of the privileged; therefore, the application of economic ethics appeared crucial when participating in commercial life. Al-Ghazālī's teachings suggest that precedence is given to the moral restructuring of an economic agent in the light of the ethics of happiness, out of which social justice, equity, and other ethical norms emerge. It is also closely associated with the training of the self or self-transformation through contemplation or reason (*tafakkur*) and obtaining divine knowledge associated with epistemological, ethical, and psychological sensibilities. His theory indicates a rather different reading of economic science, emphasizing ethical functions of the purification of the heart and the observance of the moral law through the concepts of *zuhd*, *kasb*, *faqr*, and *riyāḍa al-nafs*, among others that enable the highest ethical principles.

Al-Ghazālī's economic theory, encompassing jurisprudential-*ṣūfī* ethics, can be divided into several branches consisting of the development of markets and production activities; the very meaning of economic provision as nonmaterial gain, detachment from the world, and the role of poverty and wealth in society; and the significance of governmental authority and public inspectors in managing markets, taxes, and public finances. In the context of

---

[4] Yassine, *A Critique of the Origins of Islamic Economic Thought*, 5.

[5] Schumpeter, *History of Economic Analysis*, 87.

[6] Islahi, *Contribution of Muslim Scholars to Economic Thought and Analysis*, 90.

the theory of eternal happiness, the pursuit of individual gains is frowned upon. Unlike Aquinas who believed trade was generally base despite its usefulness, al-Ghazālī put forward an idea that the very essence of trade is to sell, buy, and make profits. Yet these activities are carried out in accordance with the moral integrity of the self—as part of the natural order of things in how one engages with and simultaneously surpasses worldly possessions. Al-Ghazālī hence affirmed that the motivation behind trade and commerce was making profits, although this was linked to metaphysical aspirations and hopes for eternal happiness since "excessive" profits were illicit. Similar was his view on private property: while ownership of goods is permitted, those same goods can also be used to further the common good, for ultimately all goods and resources belong to a higher order. In other words, if gaining goods and wealth leads to a lessening of spiritual qualities and the increase of personal whims, then such gains ought to be condemned. He considered property in the context of the doctrine of stewardship (*khalīfa*), which can traditionally be linked to the question of ownership and a different usage of material possessions.

Building upon past scholarship, al-Ghazālī argued there are five compulsory *Sharī'a*-based foundations for a just social life—*dīn*, *nafs*, *nasl*, *'aql*, and *māl*.[7] *Māl* is especially significant for his theory of preserving the common good and for developing ethical-economic subjectivity. Whether a merchant or ruler, one must follow the path of righteous economic conduct. One who engages in economic activity has to trade in basic human necessities not for profit but to fulfill the needs of the community, for the public good is to be upheld. Profit is therefore licit under certain regulations, while the market has to function along the lines of moral standards found in *Sharī'a* principles. He specified that the hoarding of foodstuffs is illicit, especially at times of shortage, and that the level of consumption should vary between necessity and extravagance. Similar constraints can be applied to *ribā* since money does not possess intrinsic value and should therefore not be utilized for profit but as a medium in trade relations. Money ought not to become an end but rather a means in securing transactions. Since one who possesses wealth is exposed to its risks, s/he must have good intentions before engaging in economic conduct, for intentions based in actions form the ethical self. Al-Ghazālī believed the division of labor would uphold mutual cooperation among various industries. Rather than conveying a hierarchical social structure, the division of labor in his view is a sign of the natural development of markets; it is a provision for society's needs under the assumption that all labor is ethical in essence.

Understandably, al-Ghazālī did not discuss the specifics of modern economics as they emerged in modern Europe, but nonetheless he deeply

---

7 Ghazanfar and Islahi, *Economic Thought of al-Ghazali*, 7.

engaged with the notion of the public good and the utilization of money alongside his discussion of the fluctuation of prices and the evolution of markets.[8] He warned the ethical epistemology of economics, encompassing jurisprudential-*ṣūfī* principles, was bound to both individual introspection and societal regulations. One of the key concepts on which al-Ghazālī based his economic analysis is the overriding notion of *maṣlaḥa*, or the common good upon which society rests. It encompasses the mundane as well as religious affairs and is seen as a link between individual and socioeconomic needs.[9] This instrument regulates the development of market and industries according to what is necessary or beneficial for society. The members of the community, al-Ghazālī cautioned, should heed the religious laws as encapsulated in the Qur'ān and the Prophetic Tradition. Despite al-Ghazālī's deeply rooted piety, which trickled down into his views on economics, he cannot be simply regarded as the defender of orthodoxy in the sense that he supported the implementation of a rigid legal culture within theological or economic matters. In fact, he fought against *taqlīd*, or blindly following the religious knowledge of one's predecessors. He indeed incorporated ethical-economic stipulations into a governmental framework from an ideal point of view. Still, his approach to economic issues appears to be structural in its critique of governmental officials.

In *Counsel for Kings*, al-Ghazālī's ethical views of livelihood and politics are explained in relation to rulers and governmental authority, where he also discusses public finances and sources of revenue. He firmly believed that a ruler should never tolerate injustice on any level and ought to cooperate with learned men in the community. Governmental authority is crucial for the maintenance of a prosperous and just society. Governmental authority should monitor economic conduct through the institution of *ḥisba*, and the sources of the caliphate's revenue should be collected from all members of society. In order to avoid societal impoverishment, public services should be increased.

Al-Ghazālī warned of two economic practices that are now widely present in the contemporary economy—the concealment of sufficient quantities of goods and the deliberate utterance of false statements in order to gain profit.[10] This, however, does not presuppose his writings should be perceived through the lenses of modern economics. The practice of concealing commodities can

---

8 Paul Ostington, "Economic Thought and Religious Thought: A Comment on Ghazanfar and Islahi," in *Medieval Islamic Thought: Filling the "Great Gap" in European Economics*, ed. S. M. Ghazanfar (London: Routledge, 2003), 48.

9 Al-Ghazālī, *Iḥyā'*, Vol. 1, 284; Vol. 2, 109.

10 Ghazali and Sadeq, "Ghazalijevi pogledi na ekonomske probleme i neka etičko-pravna pitanja značajna za ekonomsko ponašanje," 164.

be dangerous when medical supplies, foodstuffs, or means of transportation are at stake, which appears to be relevant nowadays through the expansion of commerce. For sustainable economic growth, all sectors of industry should be balanced. In al-Ghazālī's view, the institution of *ḥisba* might be a solution to the problem by which members of society can become acquainted with the methods of deception at the hands of sellers and industries. False claims about the quantity and quality of products on the market can occur. The role of the *muḥtasib*, or public auditor, is thus to ensure the healthy functioning of the market.

Al-Ghazālī's work is very much needed in today's economic discourse on wealth, trade, and the function of markets, showcasing how intimately tied economic postulates are to both human actions and conditions of the soul. The gap between metaphysics and economic science can be narrowed by synthesizing economic epistemology with the insights derived from *taṣawwuf* and *fiqh* as part of the economic subjectivity of the ethical self. In al-Ghazālī's understanding, the market is not only a meeting place where one conducts purchases and sales, but a space where market forces of demand and supply are confronted with practices of personal management. The market does not represent only the material realm—which can be perceived as idolatry if means are substituted for ends—but as a polyfunctional environment where the material meets the moral.

Ethical-economic principles critique the technical functioning of economic postulates and advocate one's relation to wealth, accumulation, and welfare by comprehending the very knowledge and action that leads toward happiness in this world and in the afterlife. Looking back into intellectual history does not mean that one needs to replicate classical Islamic economic thought in modern times; it can instead serve as a discursive reminder and a source of inspiration about how to apply certain ethical principles in economics as an overall human endeavor. The first step would be to recover ethical-economic teachings of a higher order, while critically reassessing the existing (neoclassical and Islamic) economic theories and models. Economic thought then, in the classical Islamic milieu, is part and parcel of moral engagements, since it deals with the virtuous traits of the human character. Hence, a "revival" of al-Ghazālī signifies rather an alternative approach to the economic world, one in which an ethical dimension of economic activity is constantly heeded.

APPENDIX 1

HISTORICAL DEVELOPMENT OF SOME OF THE MOST PROMINENT CLASSICAL MUSLIM SCHOLARS ON ECONOMIC THOUGHT

The following table presents two major trends in classical Islamic economic thought. The left column indicates scholars who incorporated various conceptualizations from an ethical standpoint and the tradition of *taṣawwuf*. The scholars in the right column wrote more specifically, yet certainly not exclusively, on technical-legal aspects of economics. Scholars from both groups often overlap in defining and delineating righteous economic engagement as an ethical category.

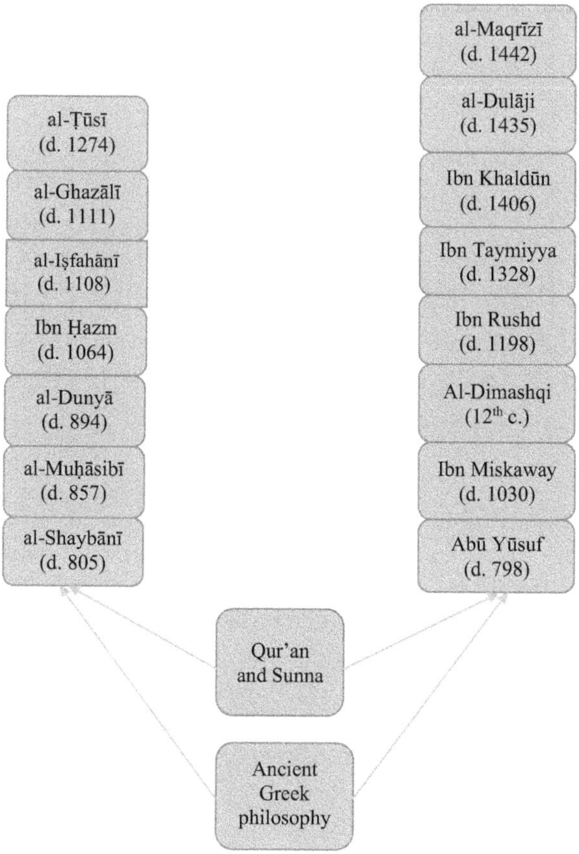
al-Maqrīzī
(d. 1442)
al-Dulāji
(d. 1435)
Ibn Khaldūn
(d. 1406)
Ibn Taymiyya
(d. 1328)
Ibn Rushd
(d. 1198)
Al-Dimashqi
(12th c.)
Ibn Miskaway
(d. 1030)
Abū Yūsuf
(d. 798)
al-Ṭūsī
(d. 1274)
al-Ghazālī
(d. 1111)
al-Iṣfahānī
(d. 1108)
Ibn Ḥazm
(d. 1064)
al-Dunyā
(d. 894)
al-Muḥāsibī
(d. 857)
al-Shaybānī
(d. 805)
Qur'an
and Sunna
Ancient
Greek
philosophy

APPENDIX 2

SELECTED QUOTATIONS OF AL-GHAZĀLĪ'S ECONOMIC TEACHINGS IN THE ENGLISH LANGUAGE

From *Iḥyā'*:

Take only that much of goods from the world as are absolutely necessary for your earthly sojourn. If you want to be saved from the mischief of the world, then consider your wealth and dust as equal.

Revival of Religious Sciences, 100 (translated by Bankery Behari)

The *zakāh* in merchandise, like that in gold and silver, [is one-fourth of 10 percent for the year].

The Mysteries of Almsgiving, 11 (translated by Nabih Amin)

If a person decides to invest a part of his income, the year will not be reckoned until he actually purchases something with it, for the mere intent to invest is not enough.

The Mysteries of Almsgiving, 12 (translated by Nabih Amin)

The *zakāh* due on the profits which accrue to the money-lender is due on the lender himself, i.e. on his share of the profit, even before the division of the shares takes place. This is the most regular practice.

The Mysteries of Almsgiving, 13 (translated by Nabih Amin)

Know that the payer of the *zakāh* should observe five things: Intention, which means that the person should purpose in his heart the payment of the ordained *zakāh*, but he does not have to specify the property for which he pays the *zakāt*. [...] Promptness in paying *zakāh* at the end of each year and on breaking the fast of Ramadān. [...] That no substitute based on the value of the *zakāt* be offered in its stead. [...] That the *sadaqah* should not be transferred from one town to another. [...] Consequently, let the *zakāh* be spent in the town wherein it was collected. [...] That the payer of the *zakāh* should divide the sum which he pays among the different groups of beneficiaries found in his home-town.

The Mysteries of Almsgiving, 17–23 (translated by Nabih Amin)

Know that he who seeks the road of the hereafter through the *zakāh* has certain duties to fulfill. These are as follows: The first duty is to understand the reasons why the *zakāh* is obligatory, to comprehend its significance, to find out how it constitutes a criterion wherewith man's devotion to God is tested and tried, and finally why it has been made one of the [five] pillars of Islam although it is merely a financial transaction and does not form a part of bodily worship. [...] Property and wealth are much loved by all people because they are means by which they enjoy the pleasure of this world, and because of them they love life and hate death, although through it they will meet [God] the beloved. [...] But giving up wealth is easier than giving up oneself. [...] The second meaning is to purify oneself from the stigma of niggardliness which is one of the destructive matters of life. [...] The stigma of niggardliness is removed by the practice of giving money away, since the love of a thing is overcome by compelling oneself to stay away from it until abstention becomes habitual. According to this meaning the *zakāh* is purity because it purifies the person who fulfills it from the destructive impurities of niggardliness. The extent to which the person is purified from the stigma of niggardliness is proportional to the amount of his giving and the degree of his pleasure in giving and in his delight in spending in the care of God. [...] The third meaning is gratitude for the blessing of God for he has blessed man in his own self and in his possessions. The bodily acts of worship [196] are man's gratitude for the bodily blessings which God has bestowed upon him, while the financial acts of worship are his gratitude for the financial gifts. [...] The second duty concerns the time of payment. One of the signs of etiquette among religious people is to pay [*zakāh*] before it is already due, in order to show their desire to conform willingly to the law. [...] The third duty is secrecy. It is farther removed from the desire to be seen and heard. [...] Whenever the giver's aim in giving is fame, his good deed will prove useless since the purpose of the *zakāh* is to banish niggardliness and weaken the love of wealth, yet the love of position and rank is more insidious than the love of wealth.

[…] The fourth duty is that the giving of alms be made public, if in so doing men are induced to do likewise and give. […] The fifth duty is that man should not make his alms (*sadaqah*) void by taunts and injury. […] The outward manifestation of injury are rebuke, derision, rough speech, stern looks, putting to shame by exposure, and all manner of ridicule. Its inward nature wherefrom its outward manifestations spring is made up of two things: the one is man's unwillingness to give up any of his wealth and the extreme pain which it causes him when he parts with any of it. This [attitude] makes a man inevitably short tempered. The second is his belief that he is superior to the poor who, by reason of his need, is inferior. Both these things are the result of ignorance. […] The sixth duty is that man should belittle his gift because if he should make much of it he would be led to feel well-pleased with it, and vanity is one of the destructive matters of life and renders all good works useless. […] Hence the manner of his giving should be one of humility and shame. […] The seventh duty is that the person should, [when giving], select from his wealth the portion which is best and dearest unto him. […] The eighth duty is to seek for his *sadaqah* one worthy of it rather than simply be content that the recipient is one of the rank and file of the eight groups of beneficiaries.

The Mysteries of Almsgiving, 25–47 (translated by Nabih Amin)

Know that to no one is the *zakāh* due except to a free Moslem belonging to one of the eight groups mentioned in the Book of God. […] The first group comprises the paupers (*al-fuqarā'*). The pauper (*al-faqīr*) is he who has no wealth and is unable to earn a living. If the person possesses his daily food and clothing, he will not be a pauper but a poor man (*miskīn*). If he possesses half his daily food then he is a pauper. […] Therefore, begging is not considered a means of earning a living. […] If he were able to earn his living by means of an instrument which he does not possess, then he would be a pauper. […] The second group comprises the poor (*al-miskīn*). A poor man (*miskīn*) is he whose income is not sufficient to cover his expenses. Thus, a person may possess a thousand dirhams and yet be poor, while another may own nothing more than an ax and a rope and yet be rich. […] The third group comprises the agents (*al-'āmilūn*). These are the workers who collect the *zakāh* except the caliph and the judge. […] The fourth group comprises those whose hearts are reconciled [to Islam] (*al-mu'allafah qulūbuhum*). These are the nobles who embraced Islam. […] The fifth group comprises those in captivity (*al-mukatabūn*). […] The sixth group comprises those in debt (*al-ghārimūn*). […] The seventh group comprises the warriors (*ghuzāh*) who are not inscribed in the commissary registry. [...] The eighth group comprises the wayfarers (*ibn al-sabīl*).

The Mysteries of Almsgiving, 56–62 (translated by Nabih Amin)

It is obligatory on the merchant to learn about money (*ta'allum al-naqd*), not for his self-interest per se, but [also] so that he can avoid giving [even] a counterfeit coin to a Muslim out of heedlessness, lest he should be sinful due to his shortcoming in learning his science of money.

"Al-Ghazālī on the Proprieties of Earning and Living," 26 (translated by Adi Setia)

The second matter is to intend, through one's craft, commerce, or work, the discharge of one of the obligations of sufficiencies (*furūḍ al-kifāyāt*). If the crafts and the business should be abandoned, the livelihoods of people would be disrupted, and most people would perish [as a consequence]. Therefore the well-ordering of the affairs of all is realized through the cooperation of all (*intiẓām amr al-kull bi-ta'āwan al'kull*), while each group assumes an occupation. If all of them were to be devoted to a single vocation (*ṣinā'a*), then the rest of the vocations would be left unattended and people would be destroyed. It is in the light of this reality that some of the scholars have interpreted the saying of the Prophet—Allah bless and give him peace—"The diversity of my Community is a mercy (*ikhtilāf ummatī raḥma*)" as referring to the diversity of their occupations in the various crafts and vocations.

"Al-Ghazālī on the Proprieties of Earning and Living," 31 (translated by Adi Setia)

The earner is in need of the science of earning (*al-muktasib yaḥtāj ilaa 'ilm al-kasb*). And when he has acquired knowledge of this topic, he will pause at practices that corrupt transactions (*mufsidāt al-mu'āmala*) and guard himself against them. [...] This is because if the earner does not know in general the causes of corruption [of transactions] (*asbāb al-fasād*), then he will not be aware when he is obliged to pause and to enquire.

"Al-Ghazālī on the Proprieties of Earning and Living," 37 (translated by Adi Setia)

Anything by which the transactor is harmed is oppression. Justice (*al-'adl*) is that a Muslim is not harmed by his brother. [...] One should not engage other people in any transaction that would have caused hardship to him or burden his heart were he himself to be engaged in it. Rather, one should view as equally valuable one's own dirham and the dirham of one's brother.

"Al-Ghazālī on the Proprieties of Earning and Living," 52
(translated by Adi Setia)

Commerce is the touchstone of true men (*miḥakk al-rijāl*), by which a person's religion is put to the test, along with his scrupulousness (*warʿ*).

"Al-Ghazālī on the Proprieties of Earning and Living," 56
(translated by Adi Setia)

If people confine to subsistence level (*sadd al ramaq*) and become very feeble, deaths will increase, all work and industry will come to halt, and the society will be ruined. Further, religion will be destroyed, as the worldly life is the preparation for the Hereafter.

Economic Thought of al-Ghazali, 9 (translated by Ghazanfar and Islahi)

It happens that farmers live in a place where farming tools are not available. And blacksmiths and carpenters live where farming does not exist. So the farmer needs blacksmiths and carpenters and they in turn need the farmers. Naturally, each will want to satisfy his needs by giving up in exchange a portion of what he possesses. But it is also possible that when the carpenter wants food in exchange for some tools, the farmer does not need the tools. Or, when the farmer needs the tools from the carpenter, the carpenter does not need food. So such situations create difficulties. Therefore, there emerge forces leading to the creation of trading places where all kinds of tools can be kept for exchange and also the creation of warehouses where farmers' produce can be stored. Then customers come to obtain these goods and markets and storehouses are established. Farmers bring their produce to the markets and if they can't readily sell or exchange what they possess, they sell them at a lower rate to the traders who in turn store the produce and try to sell to the buyers at a profit. This is true for all kinds of goods and services. […] Then such practices extend to different cities and countries. People travel to different villages and cities to obtain tools and food and transport them. People's economic affairs become organized into cities which may not have all the tools needed and into villages which may not have all the foodstuffs needed. People's own needs and interests create the need for each other and for transportation. Then a class of professional traders who carry goods from one place to another is created. The motive behind all these activities is the accumulation of profits, no doubt. These traders exhaust themselves by traveling to satisfy others' needs and wanting to make profits and these profits too are then eaten by others—like robbers or a tyrant ruler. This seems their ignorance and foolishness, but in these activities Allah has provided a system for the welfare of the people and the formation of communities. Really speaking, all worldly affairs are based on ignorance and meanness of some people. If people were wise and had higher and nobler intentions, they would discard the mundane life. However, if they would do this, then the means of livelihood would perish and people would perish including the pious too.

Economic Thought of al-Ghazali, 18
(translated by Ghazanfar and Islahi)

Industries and businesses represent a religious duty because if people abandon them, then human beings could not survive. It is one of the blessings of Allah that people have skills to undertake different occupations. This is one of the interpretations of the Prophet's (PBUH) sayings that "differences of my people are blessing."

Economic Thought of al-Ghazali, 24
(translated by Ghazanfar and Islahi)

The farmer produces grain, the miller converts it into flour, the baker prepares bread from the flour [...] further, the blacksmith makes the tools for the farmer's cultivation, and the carpenter manufactures the tools needed by the blacksmith. Same goes for all those who engage in the production of tools and equipment needed for production of foodstuffs. [...] You should know that the plants grown from the earth and the animals cannot be eaten and digested as they are. Each of them needs some transformation, cleaning, mixing, and cooking, before consumption. For a bread, for example, first the farmer prepares and cultivates the land, then the bullock and tools are needed to plough the land. Then the land is irrigated for a period of time. It is cleared from weeds, then the crop is harvested and grains are cleaned and separated. Then there is milling into flour before baking takes place. Just imagine how many tasks are involved and we here mention only some. And imagine the number of people performing these various tasks, and the number of various kinds of tools, made from iron, wood, stone, etc. If one investigates, one will find that perhaps a single loaf of bread takes its final shape with the help of perhaps more than a thousand workers.

Economic Thought of al-Ghazali, 25
(translated by Ghazanfar and Islahi)

When people live in a society and their desires for different things develop, there tends to be a struggle in acquiring the fulfillment of those desires. […] There is competition, but a balance can be maintained through the exercise of authority and maintenance of justice.

Economic Thought of al-Ghazali, 26
(translated by Ghazanfar and Islahi)

Creation of dirhams and dinars (i.e., gold and silver coins) is one of the bounties of Allah. The entire world of economic activities is based on transactions with these two kinds of money. They are two metals with no benefits in themselves. However, people need them in order to exchange them for different things—food, clothing, and other goods. Sometimes a person needs what he does not own and he owns what he does not need. For example, a person has saffron but needs a camel for transportation and one who owns a camel does not presently need that camel but he wants saffron. Thus, there is the necessity for a transaction in exchange. However, there must be a measure of the two objects in exchange, for the camel owner cannot give the whole camel for a quantity of saffron. There is no similarity between saffron and camel so that equal amount of that weight and form can be given. Likewise is the case of one who desires a house but owns some cloth or desires a slave but owns socks, or desires flour but possesses a donkey. These goods have no direct proportionality so one cannot know how much saffron will equal a camel's worth. Such barter transactions would be very difficult.

Various forms and types of goods such as these need a medium which could rule justly and determine their value or worth according to their place in exchange. When their place and grades are ascertained, it is then possible to distinguish which one is equal to each other and which is not. Thus, Almighty Allah created dinars and dirhams as two rulers and mediums of exchange for all goods and the value of goods is measured through them. So it is said a camel is, say, equal to 100 dinars and this much quantity of saffron is worth 100 dinars. Since each of them is equal to a given amount, the two quantities are equal to each other. This equality of worth or value becomes conveniently possible through dinars only because those dirhams and dinars are not needed for themselves. […] Allah created dirhams and dinars to change hands (to circulate) and to establish rules between exchanging of goods with justice and buying goods which have usefulness. A thing (such as money) can be exactly linked to other things if it has no particular special form or feature of its own—for example, a mirror which has no color but can reflect all colors.

Same is the case with money—it has no purpose of its own, but it serves as medium for the purpose of exchanging goods.

Economic Thought of al-Ghazali, 27–28
(translated by Ghazanfar and Islahi)

Anyone who uses money contrary to its objectives or functions is ungrateful to the bounty of Allah. If someone hoards dirhams and dinars, he is a transgressor. He would be like a person who imprisons a ruler, thus depriving the society of the benefits of his benevolence. Dirhams and dinars are not created for any particular persons; they are useless by themselves; they are just like stones. They are created to circulate from hand to hand, to govern and to facilitate transactions. They are symbols to know the value and grades of goods. Anyone who converts them into utensils of gold and silver is ungrateful to his Creator and worse than the hoarder of money, for such a person is like one who forces the ruler to perform unsuitable functions—as weaving cloth, gathering taxes, etc. Hoarding of coins may be preferable to such conversion of coins into utensils. Why? Because there are other metals and materials—copper, bronze, iron, clay—which can be used to make utensils instead of gold and silver, for the storage and drinking of liquids, etc. But clay and iron cannot be used for the functions performed by dirhams and dinars—they are not meant for that purpose. If anyone does not appreciate this fact, he should try to convince himself of remembering the saying of the Prophet (PBUH), "One who drinks in gold and silver utensils, he is like one who takes the fire of hell in his stomach."

Economic Thought of al-Ghazali, 29
(translated by Ghazanfar and Islahi)

Similar is the position of foodstuffs. They are created to be used as nutrition, so they should not be misused. If exchange within them is freely allowed, it will result in their longer stay in hands and delay their use as nutrition for which they are created. Foodstuffs are created by Allah to be eaten which is a dire need. This requires that they should go from the hands of that who does not need them to one who needs them. Only that person will do a transaction on food who does not need it. Because if a person has food why does he not eat it if he is in need of that; why is he using it as a trade commodity? If he wants to make it a trade commodity, he should sell it to that who needs it with something other than the same foods. If someone is buying with exactly same food, he is also not in need of it; this is the reason that *Sharīʿa* cursed the hoarder.

Economic Thought of al-Ghazali, 31
(translated by Ghazanfar and Islahi)

From *Kīmiyā-yi Sa'ādat*:

The first element is the *'Aqid*, the seller [...] the seller should not deal with the following five categories of people. A minor. A mad or insane person. [...] A (slave person, male or female). A blind person. A person who earns illegally and eats unlawful food. [...] The second element is the *Māl* (the good). Six things are necessary for it. The *Māl* should not be dirty or impious (*Najs*). [...] Trade is allowed on reasonable profit but not at any cost. Accordingly marketing of undesirable objects like mice, snakes, scorpions and other repelling menagerie is not permitted. [...] Likewise, buying and selling of beautiful birds like parrots and peacocks is permitted. [...] But sale and purchase of musical instruments [...] is forbidden for obvious ethical reasons. Children's toys in the shape of animals, generally made of clay, are not allowed. The third plausible condition is that a person can only sell that thing which may belong to him or he may be authorized to sell it by its legitimate owner. On the same principle the husband cannot sell any article belonging to his wife without her permission and vice versa. The fourth condition is that only those things can be sold whose physical possession may be handed over to the buyer. Under the circumstances the goods that are loaded on the camel's back, the milk that has not been yielded cannot be sold. [...] The fifth condition is that the quantity of goods and the standard of their quality should be specified. [...] The sixth condition is that the articles bought should be taken into physical possession and then resold. Forward sale of imaginary goods on conjecture is not allowed. The third element is the *Aqd*—i.e. the agreement. It should be pronounced clearly by the buyer and the seller.

Alchemy of Eternal Bliss, 474 (translated by Muhammad Asim Bilal)

To give goods on credit and charge more for them is *Haram*. Same applies to payment of goods in gold.

Alchemy of Eternal Bliss, 476 (translated by Muhammad Asim Bilal)

Only those things should be given, sold, whose status may be clear, especially in terms of assessment of their value. [...] In time-stipulated bargains the date of maturity of transactions should be absolutely clear. [...] Likewise the place of delivery must be specified, to forestall controversy later.

Alchemy of Eternal Bliss, 478 (translated by Muhammad Asim Bilal)

The remuneration to be paid must be clearly specified, otherwise the *Ijara* (the remuneration) or profit will be invalid.

Alchemy of Eternal Bliss, 479 (translated by Muhammad Asim Bilal)

As for the profit, the following five considerations are of essence. The first condition is that the thing on which a beneficial remuneration is accepted or a gain obtained should not be a sinecure. Commensurate value, work or labor should be involved in it. [...] The second condition is that the *Ajara* or profit sharing should be from the profit itself and not on the capital value of goods. [...] The third condition is that the assignment to perform a job should be allocated to a suitable person fit to discharge its obligations. [...] The (*Ijara*) remuneration for the following is *Haram* according to *Shariat*. To side with, aid and abet a tyrant. To suppress evidence willfully. To give a wrong statement as a witness or as a paid agent. According [to] *Shariat* to accept *Ijara* for the following is not allowed. To pay a *Mujahid*. To pay a *Qazi* for giving a just decision or to pay a witness to tell the truth. To pay somebody to say prayers on his behalf or to pay someday on normal conditions to keep a (*Roza*) fast for him. [...] The fifth condition is that if an animal is hired to carry weight, there should be no cruelty to the animal. [...] The sixth condition is that if a third party is involved in a transaction, his *Ijara* should be stipulated and clearly foreseen. [...] The seventh element is that whereas the profit sharing between the parties in partnership should be at the ratio of their investment, in case one of the partners is a managing partner and others are not, the additional remuneration eligible to him should be decided right at the beginning.

Alchemy of Eternal Bliss, 480–85 (translated by Muhammad Asim Bilal)

Hoarding of goods for profiteering is a sickness of thought (*Fikr*) and very treacherous. [...] The second vicious thing is passing a bad coin.

Alchemy of Eternal Bliss, 486–88 (translated by Muhammad Asim Bilal)

Furthermore in the man's dealings with others there should be nothing miserly spiteful or based on egotism. It is equivalent to (*Zulm*) cruelty to others. [...] Also, there should be no deceit in selling. The merchandise being sold should not be overpraised. Such qualities should not be attributed to a thing which may not be present in it. If the thing being sold is really praiseworthy, the buyer has not to be told. He divines it automatically.

Alchemy of Eternal Bliss, 490 (translated by Muhammad Asim Bilal)

The (*Rizq*) livelihood is in the hands of Allah. He increases it or decreases it as He wills. All that man can do is to be hard working and honest. Deception and dishonesty never pay. On the contrary it takes away all the *Barakt*—i.e. the virtue and bountifulness out of the transaction and from his livelihood too.

Alchemy of Eternal Bliss, 492 (translated by Muhammad Asim Bilal)

It is more becoming to try and not charge a profit to a person who may not be able to afford a thing but may be going in for it perforce majeur in a state of distress. [...] The second propriety is wantonly buying the goods from the not so well off, poor or destitute at a higher price than its value, like cotton wool from a widow or an orphan.

Alchemy of Eternal Bliss, 498–500 (translated by Muhammad Asim Bilal)

The world is very engaging and the man is weak. Therefore it is of the utmost importance that the man does not forget that this world is merely a transitory phase in his existence. [...] Hence to get absorbed in frivolous playful activities in transit is to mar the very purpose for which he had undertaken this arduous journey.

Alchemy of Eternal Bliss, 504–5 (translated by Muhammad Asim Bilal)

Man should not prefer the bazaar of (*Dunya*) this world to the Bazaar (the passage way: a marketplace) of the *Akhirat.*

Alchemy of Eternal Bliss, 507 (translated by Muhammad Asim Bilal)

BIBLIOGRAPHY

Works by al-Ghazālī

al-Ghazālī, Abū Ḥāmid. *Kīmiyā-yi Sa'ādat Alchemy of Eternal Bliss.* Translated by Muhammad Asim Bilal. Lahore: Kazi, 2001.

———. *Al-Ghazali's Moderation in Belief.* Translated by Aladdin M. Yaqub. Chicago: University of Chicago Press, 2013.

———. *Al-Iqtisād fī al-I'tiqad.* Damascus: Dār Kutayba, 2003.

———. *Al-Munqidh min al-Ḍalāl.* Beirut: Dār-al Mandas, 1967.

———. *Al-Mustasfā fi 'Ilm al-Usūl.* Medina: Intisharāt Dār al-Dhahā'ir, 1993.

———. *Briefe und Reden des Abu Hamid Muhammad al-Gazzali.* Translated by Dorothea Krawulsky. Freiburg im Breisgau: K. Schwarz, 1971.

———. *Counsel for Kings.* Translated by F. R. C. Bagley. London: Oxford University Press, 1964.

———. *Criterion of Action.* Translated by Muhammad Hozien, edited by S. Dunyā. Cairo: Dār al-Ma'ārif, 1964.

———. *Das Kriterium des Handelns.* Translated by Abd-Elsamad Abd-Elhamid Elschazli. Darmstadt: WBG, Wissenschaftliche Buchgesellschaft, 2006.

———. *The Faith and Practice of al-Ghazālī (Deliverance from Error).* Translated by Montgomery Watt. London: G. Allen and Unwin, 1967.

———. *Fayṣal al-Tafriqa.* Edited by Maḥmūd Bījū. Damascus: Maḥmūd Bījū, 1993.

———. *Iḥyā' 'Ulūm al-Dīn.* 4 vols. Beirut: Dār al-Ma'rifa, 1982.

———. *Kitāb Naṣīḥat al-Mulūk.* n.d.

———. *Letters of al-Ghazali.* Translated by Abdul Qayyum. New Delhi: Kitab Bhavan, 1992.

———. *Maqāṣid al-Falāsifa: Maqāṣid al-Falāsifah: fī al-Manṭiq wa al-Ḥikmah al-Ilāhīyah wa al-Ḥikmah al-Ṭabī'īyāh.* Cairo: al-Matba'ah al-Mahmudiyah al-Tijariyah bi-al-Azhar, 1936.

———. *Mishkāt al-Anwār.* Edited by 'Abd al-'Azīz al-Sīrawān. Beirut: 'Ālam al-Kutub, 1986.

———. *Mīzān al-'Amal.* Edited by S. Dunyā. Cairo: Dār al-Ma'ārif, 1964.

———. *On the Boundaries of Theological Tolerance in Islam.* Translated by Sherman A. Jackson. Oxford: Oxford University Press, 2002.

———. *Revival of Religious Learning.* Translated by Fazl-ul-Karim. Karachi: Darul-ishaat, 1993.

———. *The Revival of Religious Sciences.* Translated by Bankery Behari. Vrindaban: Mata Krishna Satsang, 1964.

———. *Tahāfut al-Falāsifa.* Edited by S. Dunyā. Cairo: Dār al-Ma'ārif, n.d.

———. *Uber Rechtgläubigkeit und religiose Toleranz. Eine Ubersetzung der Schrift Das Kriterium der Unterscheidung zwischen Islam und Gottlosigkeit.* Translated by Frank Griffel. Zurich: Spur, 1998.

Works on al-Ghazālī

Abū-Sway, Mustafa. *Al-Ġazālī: A Study in Islamic Epistemology*. Kuala Lumpur: Dewan Bahasa dan Pustaka, 1996.

al-Qaradaghi, ʿAlī Muḥī al-Dīn. "ʿAṣr al-Ghazālī." In *Al-Waṣīt fī al-mathhab*, Abū Ḥāmid al-Ghazālī, 21–293. Cairo: Dār al-Anṣār, 1983.

al-Qaraḍāwī, Yūsuf. *Al-Imām Ghazālī bayna Mādiḥī wa-Nāqidhī*. Beirut: Mūʾassat Al-Risāla, 1994.

al-Shamī, Ṣāliḥ Aḥmad. *Al-Imām Ghazzālī: Ḥujjat al-Islām wa-Mujaddid al-Miʾah al-Khāmisa*. Damascus: Dār al-Qalam, 1993.

Al-ʿAsam, ʿAbd al-ʾAmīr. *Al-Faylasūf al-Ghazālī*. Beirut: Dār al-Andulus, 1988.

Badri, Malik. *Contemplation: An Islamic Psychospiritual Study*. London: Human Behaviour Academy, 2000.

Bauer, Hans, trans. *Islamische Ethik, Das 37. Buch von al-Ghazali's Hauptwerk*. Halle: Verlag von Max Niemeyer, 1916.

Bouyges, Maurice. *Essai de chronologie des oeuvres de al-Ghazali*. Edited by Michel Allard. Beirut: L'Institute de Letters Orientalles de Berouth, 1959.

Campanini, Massimo. *Al-Ghazali and the Divine*. London: Routledge, 2019.

Crone, Patricia. "Did al-Ghazālī Write a Mirror for Princes? On the Authorship of *Naṣīḥat* al-Mulūk." *Jerusalem Studies of Arabic and Islam*, Vol. 10 (1987): 167–97.

Diaw, Abdou. "Imam Al-Ghazali's Views on Economic Activities." Paper presented at the International Centre for Education in Islamic Finance: The International Conference on Islamic Economics and Economies of the OIC Countries, Kuala Lumpur, Malaysia, April 28–29, 2009.

Frank, Richard M. *Al-Ghazālī and the Ash'rite School*. Durham, NC: Duke University Press, 1994.

Garden, Kenneth. *The First Islamic Reviver: Abū Ḥāmid al-Ghazālī and His Revival of the Religious Sciences*. New York: Oxford University Press, 2014.

Ghazanfar, S. M. "The Economic Thought of Abu Hamid Al-Ghazali and St. Thomas Aquinas: Some Comparative Parallels and Links." *History of Political Economy*, Vol. 32, No. 4 (2000): 857–88.

———. *Medieval Islamic Thought: Filling the "Great Gap" in European Economics*. London: Routledge, 2003.

Ghazanfar, Mohammad and Islahi Abdul Azim. *Economic Thought of al-Ghazali*. Jeddah: Scientific Publishing Centre, King Abdulaziz University, 1997, second edition 2014.

———. "Economic Thought of an Arab Scholastic: Abu Hamid Al-Ghazali." *History of Political Economy*, Vol. 22, No. 2 (1990): 381–403.

———. "A Rejoinder to 'Economic Thought and Religious Thought,'" in *Medieval Islamic Thought*, ed. S. M. Ghazanfar, 53.

Gianotti, Timothy J. *Al-Ghazali's Unspeakable Doctrine of the Soul: Unveiling the Esoteric Psychology and Eschatology of the Ihya'*. Leiden: Brill's Studies in Intellectual History, Book 104, 2001.

Gilʿadi, Avner. "On the Origins of Two Key Terms in Al-Ġazzālī's Iḥyāʾ ʿUlūm al-Dīn." *Arabica*, Vol. 36, No. 1 (1989): 81–93.

Gramlich, Richard. "Muḥammad al-Ġazzālīs kleine islamische Fundamentaldogmatik." *Saeculum*, Vol. 31 (1980): 380–98.

Griffel, Frank. *Über Rechtgläubigkeit und religiöse Toleranz. Eine Übersetzung der Schrift Das Kriterium der Unterscheidung zwischen Islam und Gottlosigkeit (Fayṣal at-tafriqa bayna l-Islam wa-z- zandaqa)*. Translated, introduced, and annotated by Frank Griffel. Zurich: Spur Verlag, 1998.

———. *Al-Ghazālī's Philosophical Theology*. Oxford: Oxford University Press, 2009.

———. ed. *Islam and Rationality: The Impact of al-Ghazālī. Papers Collected on His 900th Anniversary*, Vol 2. Leiden: Brill, 2016.

Hillenbrand, Carole. "Islamic Orthodoxy or Realpolitik? Al-Ghazālī's Views on Government." *Journal of the British Institute of Persian Studies*, Vol. 26 (1988): 81–94.

Hourani, George F. "Ghazālī on the Ethics of Action." *Journal of the American Oriental Society*, Vol. 96, No. 1 (1976): 69–88.

Irijantoa, Tubagus Thresna Mohd, Azlan Shah Zaidib, Abdul Ghafar Ismailc, and Noraziah Che Arshad. "Al Ghazali's Thoughts of Economic Growth Theory, A Contribution with System Thinking." *Scientific Journal of PPI-UKM*, Vol. 2, No. 5 (2015): 233–40.

Jabre, Farid. *Essai sur le lexique de Ghazali*. Beirut: Publications de L'Universite Libanaise, 1985.

Kojiro, Nakamura. "Was Al-Ghazali an Ash'arite?" Originally published as "Gazali and Ash'arite Theology." *Isuramu Sekai* (*The World of Islam*), Vol. 41 (1993).

Krawulsky, Dorothea, trans. *Briefe und Reden des Abū Ḥāmid Muḥammad al-Ġazzālī*, Freiburg: Klaus Schwarz, 1971.

Lambton, Ann K. S. "The Theory of Kingship in the Naṣīḥat ul-Mulūk of al-Ghazālī." *Islamic Quarterly*, Vol. 10, No. 1 (1954): 47–55.

Laoust, Henri. *La politique de Ghazali*. Paris: Librairie Orientaliste Paul Geuthner, 1970.

Mehmet, Ozay. "Al-Ghazzali on Social Justice: Guidelines for a New World Order from an Early Medieval Scholar." *International Journal of Social Economics*, Vol. 24, No. 11 (1997): 1203–18.

Moosa, Ebrahim. *Ghazālī and the Poetics of Imagination*. Chapel Hill: University of North Carolina Press, 2005.

Nabih Amin, trans. *The Mysteries of Almsgiving, Book VI*. Lahore: Sh. Muhammad Ashraf, 1980.

Obermann, Julian. *Der philosophische und regligiöse subjektivismus Ghazalis: ein Beitrag zum Problem der Religion*. Vienna: W. Braumuller, 1921.

Ormsby, Eric L. *Ghazali: The Revival of Islam*. Oxford: Oneworld, 2007.

———. "The Taste of Truth: The Structure of Experience in al-Ghazali's Munqidh min al-dalal." In *Islamic Studies Presented to Charles J. Adams*. Edited by Wael B. Hallaq and Donald P. Little, 133–52. Leiden: Brill, 1991.

———. *Theodicy in Islamic Thought: The Dispute over Al-Ghazali's "Best of All Possible Worlds."* Princeton, NJ: Princeton University Press, 1984.

Setia, Adi. "Al-Ghazālī on the Proprieties of Earning and Living: Insights and Excerpts from His *Kitāb Ādāb al-Kasb wa-al-Ma'āsh* for Reviving Economies for Communities." *Islamic Sciences*, Vol. 11, No. 1 (2013): 19–62.

———. *The Book of the Proprieties of Earning and Living*. Kuala Lumpur: IBFIM, 2013.

Shehadi, Fadlou. *Ghazali's Unique Unknowable God*. Leiden: Brill, 1964.

Sherif, Mohamed Ahmed. *Ghazali's Theory of Virtue*. Albany: State University of New York, 1975.

Smith, Margaret. *Al-Ghazālī: The Mystic*. Lahore: Hijra International Publishers, 1983.

Tamer, Georges, ed. *Islam and Rationality: The Impact of al-Ghazālī. Papers Collected on His 900th Anniversary*. Leiden: Brill, 2015.

Treiger, Alexander. "Al-Ghazālī's Classifications of the Sciences and Descriptions of the Highest Theoretical Science." *Divan*, Vol. 2011, No. 1 (2011): 1–32.

———. *Inspired Knowledge in Islamic Thought: Al-Ghazali's Theory of Mystical Cognition and Its Avicennian Foundation*. London and New York: Routledge, 2012.

'Umaruddin, M. *The Ethical Philosophy of al-Ghazzālī*. Delhi: Adam, 1996.

Watt, Montgomery. *Muslim Intellectual: A Study of al-Ghazali*. Edinburgh: Edinburgh University Press, 1963.

Other Primary and Secondary Works

'Abd Muhammad, 'Abd Allah. *Wilāyat al-Ḥisba fī al-Islām*. Cairo: Maktaba al-Zahrā', 1996.

Abu-Lughod, Janet L. *Before European Hegemony*. New York: Oxford University Press, 1989.

Abed Al Jabri. *Arab-Islamic Philosophy: A Contemporary Critique*. Austin: University of Texas, Center for Middle East Studies, 1999.

Ahmed, Shahab. *What Is Islam?*. Princeton, NJ: Princeton University Press, 2016.

al-Attar, Mariam. *Islamic Ethics: Divine Command Theory in Arabo-Islamic Thought*. London: Routledge, 2010.

Ahmed, Abdel Rahman Yousri, "The Scientific Approach to Islamic Economics: Philosophy, Theoretical Construction and Applicability," in *Theoretical Foundation of Islamic Economics*, ed. Habib Ahmed (Jeddah: Islamic Development Bank, Islamic Research and Training Institute, No. 3, 2002), 19–58.

Al-Daghistani, Sami. "The Making of Islamic Economics." PhD diss., Leiden University, 2017.

———. "Semiotics of Islamic Law, Maṣlaḥa, and Islamic Economic Thought." *International Journal for the Semiotics of Law—Revue internationale de Sémiotique juridique*, Vol. 29, No. 2 (June 2016): 389–404. Accessible at https://doi.org/10.1007/s11196-016-9457-x.

———. "The Time Factor: Toshihiko Izutsu and Islamic Economic Thought." *Asian Studies*, Vol. 6, No. 1 (2018): 55–71.

al-Dimashqī, Abū al-Faḍl Ja'far. *Al-Ishāra ilā Maḥāsin al-Tijāra*. Cairo: Maktabah al-Kulliyyat al-Azhariyyah, 1977.

al-Dunyā, Ibn Abī. *Iṣlāḥ al-Māl*. Beirut: Mu'assasa al-Kutub al-Thaqāfiyya, 1993.

Ali-Karamali, Shista P. and Fiona Dunne. "The Ijtihad Controversy." *Arab Law Quarterly*, Vol. 9 (1994): 238–57.

al-Jāḥiẓ, 'Amr ibn Baḥr al-Kinānī al-Baṣrī. *Al-Tabassur bi al-Tijāra*. Tunis: Dār al-Kitāb al-Jadid, 1966.

al-Juwaynī, Imām al-Ḥaramayn. *A Guide to the Conclusive Proofs for the Principles of Belief*. Translated by Paul E. Walker. Reading, UK: Garnet, 2001.

al-Makkī, Abū Ṭālib. *Qūt al-Qulūb*. Cairo: Maktaba Dār al-Thurāth, 2001.

al-Māwardī, Abū al-Ḥasan 'Alī Ibn Muḥammad Ibn Ḥabīb. *Al-Aḥkām al-Sulṭāniyya*. Misr: al-Babi al-Ḥalabi, 1973.

al-Mawdudi, Abul 'Ala. *The Economic Problem of Man and Its Islamic Solution*. Lahore: Islamic Publications, 1947.

al-Muḥāsibī, al-Hārith. *Al-Makāsib wa al-Wara'*. Beirut: Mu'ssasa al-Kutub al-Thaqāfiyya, 1987.

———. *Al-Ri'āya li-Ḥuqūq Allāh*. Edited by 'Abd al-Ḥalīm Maḥmūd and 'Abd al-Qādir 'Aṭā. Cairo: Dār al-Kutub al-Ḥadītha, 1970.

al-Rāghib al-Iṣfahānī, Abū al-Ḳāsim al-Ḥusayn b. Muḥammad b. al-Mufaḍḍal. *The Path of Virtue*. Translated by Yasien Mohamed. Kuala Lumpur: International Institute for Islamic Thought and Civilization, 2006.

al-Ṣadr, Muḥammad Bāqir. *Iqtiṣādunā*. 3 vols. Beirut: Dār al-Ta'ārif, 1987.

al-Shaybānī, Muḥammad bin Ḥasan. *Al-Iktisāb fī al-Rizq al-Mustaṭāb*. Beirut: Dār al-Kutub al-Ilmiyyah, 1986.

al-Tūsi, Abū Naṣr al-Sarrāj. *Kitāb al-Luma' fī al-Taṣawwuf*. Edited by Reynold Alleyne Nicholson. Leiden: Brill, 1914.

Ameer, Ali and Thompson Herb. "The Schumpeterian Gap and Muslim Economic Thought." *Journal of Interdisciplinary Economics*, Vol. 10 (1999): 31–49, available at www1.aucegypt.edu/faculty/thompson/herbtea/articles/jie3.html.

Aquinas, St. Thomas. *Summa Theologica*. Translated by Fathers of the English Dominican Province. Perrysburg, OH: Benziger Bros. edition, 1947.

Aristotle. *Nicomachean Ethics*. Translated by F. H. Peters. London: Kegan Paul, Trench, Trübner, 1906.

Arkoun, Mohammed. "Deux epitres de Miskawqyh." *Bulletin d'Etudes Orientales* (Institute Français de Damas), Vol. 17 (1961–62): 7–74.

Asad, Mohammed. *Islam na raspuću*. Sarajevo: El Kalem, 2002.

Asad, Talal. *Formations of the Secular*. Stanford, CA: Stanford University Press, 2003.

———. "The Idea of an Anthropology of Islam." *Qui Parle*, Vol. 17, No. 2 (2009): 1–30.

Ashker, Ahmed El- and Rodney Wilson. *Islamic Economics: A Short History*. Leiden: Brill, 2006.

Attas, Muhammad. *Prolegomena to the Metaphysics of Islam*. Kuala Lumpur: Dar al-Risala, 2001.

Ayubi, Zahra. *Gendered Morality: Classical Islamic Ethics of the Self, Family, and Society*. New York: Columbia University Press, 2019.

Azid, Toseef. "The Concept and Nature of Labour in Islam: A Survey." *Review of Islamic Economics*, Vol. 9, No. 2 (2005): 93–122.

Baeck, Louis. *The Mediterranean Tradition in Economic Thought*. London: Routledge, 1994.

Bartol, Vladimir. *Alamut*. Ljubljana: Sanje, 2001.

Bauer, Thomas. *Die Kultur der Ambiguität. Eine andere Geschichte des Islams*. Berlin: Verlag der Weltreligionen, 2011.

Bell, J. F. *A History of Economic Thought*. New York: Ronald Press, 2nd edition, 1967.

Bentham, Jeremy. *An Introduction to the Principles of Moral Legislation*. Kitchener, ON: Batoche Books, 2001.

Buckley, R. P., trans. *The Book of the Islamic Market Inspector. Kitāb Nihāyat al-Rutba fī Ṭalab al-Ḥisba (The Utmost Authority in the Pursuit of Ḥisba) by ʿAbd al-Raḥmān b. Naṣr al-Shayzarī*. Oxford: Oxford University Press, 1999.

Chapra, Umer Muhammad. *Islam and the Economic Challenge*. Herndon, VA: International Institute of Islamic Thought, 1992.

———. "Islamic Economics: What It Is and How It Developed." Paper written for EH.NET's Online Encyclopedia of Economic and Business History, http://eh.net/encyclopedia/article/chapra.islamic (accessed April 17, 2013).

Choudhury, Masudul Alam. "A Critique of Modernist Synthesis in Islamic Thought: Special Reference to Political Economy," *American Journal of Islamic Social Sciences*, Vol. 11, No. 4 (1994): 475–506.

———. *Islamic Economics and Finances: An Epistemological Inquiry*. Bingley: Emerald, 2011.

———. *The Islamic World-System: A Study in Polity–Market Interaction*. New York: Routledge, 2004.

———. *The Islamic Worldview*. London: Kegan Paul International, 2000.

———. *The Principles of Islamic Political Economy: A Methodological Enquiry*. New York: Macmillan, 1992.

———. *Studies in Islamic Social Sciences*. London: Palgrave Macmillan, 1998.

———. "Theory and Practice of Islamic Political Economy." In *Islamic Political Economy in Capitalist-Globalization: An Agenda for Change*. Edited by M. A. Choudhury, M. Z. Abdad, and M. S. Salleh. Kuala Lumpur: Utusan Publications, 1997.

———. "Towards Islamic Political Economy at the Turn of the Century." *American Journal of Islamic Social Sciences*, Vol. 13, No. 3 (1996): 366–81.

Comte, Auguste. *A General View of Positivism*. Cambridge: Cambridge University Press, 2009.

Descartes, Rene. *Discours de la Méthode et Essais*. 3 vols. Edited by Marie Beyssade and Denis Kambouchner. Paris: Gallimard, 2009.

Dilthey, Wilhelm. *Einleitung in die Geistwissenschaften*. 26 vols. Leipzig: Verlag von Duncker & Humblot 1883.

———. *Gesammelte Schriften*. Leipzig und Berlin: Verlag von B. G. Teubner, 1921.

Dwyer, John. "Ethics and Economics: Bridging Adam Smith's Theory of Moral Sentiments and Wealth of Nations." *Journal of British Studies*, Vol. 44, No. 4 (2005): 662–87, doi:10.1086/431936.

El-Ansary, Waleed. "The Quantum Enigma and Islamic Sciences of Nature: Implications for Islamic Economic Theory." *Proceedings of the 6th International Conference on Islamic Economics and Finance*, 143–75. Jeddah: Islamic Development Bank, 2005.

———. "Recovering the Islamic Economic Intellectual Heritage." Proceedings of the Third Harvard University Forum on Islamic Finance: Local Challenges, Global Opportunities. Cambridge, Massachusetts, Center for Middle Eastern Studies, Harvard University, 1999.

———. "Linking Ethics and Economics for Integral Development: The Need for a New Economic Paradigm and the Three Dimensions of Islam," Al-Alwani Lectures 202, Washington Theological Consortium. Accessible at https://washtheocon.org/wp-content/uploads/2012/11/Ansary-2012-Lecture.pdf.

The Encyclopaedia of Islam, s.v. "*Tawḥīd*." Leiden: Brill, 2010.

Essid, Yassine. *A Critique of the Origins of Islamic Economic Thought*. Leiden: Brill, 1995.

Fakhry, Majid. *A History of Islamic Philosophy*. New York: Columbia University Press, 2004.

Foucault, Michel. *The Archeology of Knowledge*. New York: Pantheon Books, 1972.

Friedman, Milton. *Essays in Positive Economics*. Chicago: University of Chicago Press, 1953.

Garaudy, Roger. *Živi islam* (*Islam vivant*). Sarajevo: El Kalem, 2000.

Ghazali, Aidit and Abul Hasan Muhammad Sadeq, eds. *Pregled islamske ekonomske misli* (*An Overview of Islamic Economic Thought*). Sarajevo: El-Kalem, 1996.

Hallaq, Wael B. "From Fatwās to Furū': Growth and Change in Islamic Substantive Law." *Islamic Law and Society*, Vol. 1, No. 1 (1994): 29–65.

———. "Groundwork of the Moral Law: A New Look at the Qur'ān and the Genesis of *Sharī'a*." *Islamic Law and Society*, Vol. 16, No. 3/4 (2009): 239–79.

———. *The Impossible State*. New York: Columbia University Press, 2013.

———. "On the Origins of the Controversy about the Existence of Mujtahids and the Gate of Ijtihad." *Studia Islamica*, Vol. 63 (1986): 129–41.

———. *The Origins and Evolution of Islamic Law*. Cambridge: Cambridge University Press, 2005.

———. *Sharī'a: Theory, Practice, Transformations*. Cambridge: Cambridge University Press, 2009.

———. "Was the Gate of Ijtihad Closed?" *International Journal of Middle East Studies*, Vol. 16 (1984): 3–41.

Hamdani, Abbas. "The Muhtasib as Guardian of Public Morality in the Medieval Islamic City." *Digest of Middle East Studies*, Vol. 17, No. 1 (2008): 92–104.

Haneef, Mohamed Aslam and Hafas Furqani, "Developing the Ethical Foundations of Islamic Economics: Benefitting from Toshihiko Izutsu," *Intellectual Discourse*, Vol. 17, No. 2 (2009): 176.

Hanifa, Abu. *Al-Fiqh al-Akbar. Die Fundamente des Glaubens vom Imam Abu Hanifa*. Translated by Ali Ghandour. Istanbul: Kalbi Kapital, 2009.

———. *Imām Abū Ḥanifa's al-Fiqh al-Akbar*. Translated by Abdur-Rahman ibn Yusuf. Santa Barbara, CA: White Thread Press, 2007.

Hassan, M. Kabir and Mervyn K. Lewis. *Handbook on Islam and Economic Life*. Cheltenham: Edward Elgar, 2014.
Heckscher, Eli F. *Mercantilism*. Translated by Mendal Shapiro. London: George Allen and Unwin, 1954.
Hourani, Albert. *A History of the Arabs Peoples*. London: Faber and Faber, 2002.
Huff E. Toby and Wolfgang Schluchter, eds. *Max Weber and Islam*. New Brunswick, NJ: Transactions, 1999.
Hume, David. *A Treatise of Human Nature*. Auckland: Floating Press, 2009.
Hussin, Iza. *The Politics of Islamic Law*. Chicago: Chicago University Press, 2016.
Ibn ʿĀshūr, Muḥammad al-Ṭāhir ibn Muḥammad. *Maqāṣid al-Sharīʿah al-Islāmiyyah*. Edited by Muḥammad al-Ṭāhir al-Masāwī. Amman: Dār al-Nafā'is, 2001.
———. *Treatise on Maqāṣid al-Sharīʿa*. Translated by Muḥammad al-Ṭāhir al-Masāwī. London: International Institute of Islamic Thought, 2006.
Ibn al-Ukhūwwah, Muḥammad ibn Muḥammad. *Maʿālim al-Qūrbah fī Aḥkām al-Ḥisba*. Edited by Reuben Levy. Cambridge: Cambridge University Press, 1938.
Ibn Khaldūn. *The Muqaddimah*. 3 vols. Translated by Franz Rosenthal. London: Routledge and Kegan Paul, 1958.
———. *Muqaddimah*. 3 vols. Beirut: Dār al-Fikr, 1967.
———. *Muqaddimah*. Sarajevo: IRO Veselin Masleša, 1982.
Ibn Manẓūr. *Lisān al-ʿArab*, 1979.
Ibn Miskawayh. *Refinement of Character* (*Tahdhīb al-akhlāq*). Translated by Constantine Zuryak. Chicago: Kazi, 2002.
Ibn Rushd. *Bidāyat al-Mujtahid*. Beirut: Dār al-Maʿrifa, 1988.
———. *The Distinguished Jurist's Primer*. Translated by Imran Ahsan Khan Nyazee. Reading: Centre for Muslim Contribution to Civilization, 1996.
Ibn Taymiyya. *Al-Ḥisbah fī al-Islām*. Cairo: Dār al-Sha'b, 1976.
———. *Majmūʿ Fatāwa Shaykh al-Islām Aḥmad Ibn Taymiyya*. Edited by al-Najdi, ʿAbd al-Raḥmān b. Muḥammad. Al-Riyāḍ: Matabi' al-Riyāḍ, 1963.
———. *Public Duties in Islam: The Institution of the Hisbah*. Translated by Muhtar Holland. Leicester: Islamic Foundation, 1982.
Irwin, Robert. *Ibn Khaldun: An Intellectual Biography*. Princeton, NJ: Princeton University Press, 2018.
Islahi, Abdul Azim. *Contribution of Muslim Scholars to Economic Thought and Analysis, AH 11–905/AD 632–1500*. Jeddah: Islamic Economics Research Centre, King Abdulaziz University, 1425/2004.
———. *Economic Concepts of Ibn Taymiyya*. Leicester: Islamic Foundation, 1988.
———. "The Economic Ideas of Muslim Scholars and Christian Scholastics: Linkages and Parallels." *Islam and Christian–Muslim Relations*, Vol. 25, No. 1 (2014): 49–66.
———. *History of Economic Thought in Islam*. Aligharh, India: Department of Economics, Aligharh Muslim University, 1996.
Izetbegović, Alija. *Islam između istoka i zapada* (*Islam between East and West*). Novi Pazar: El Kelimeh, 1996.
———. *Moj bijeg u slobodu* (*My Escape into Freedom*). Sarajevo: Izbrana djela OKO, 2003.
Jevons, W. Stanley. *The Theory of Political Economy*. New York: Augustus M. Kelley, 1960.
Kamali, Mohammad Hashim. "Separation of Powers: An Islamic Perspective." *Islam and Civilisational Renewal*, Vol. 5, No. 4 (2014): 471–88.
Kant, Immanuel. "Was ist Aufklärung?" *UTOPIE kreativ*, H. 159 (2004): 5–10.
Karić, Enes. *Ibn Khaldun—Uvod u čitanje Al-Muqaddime*. Sarajevo: El Kelem, 2008.

Keynes, John Maynard. *The General Theory of Employment, Interest and Money: The Collected Writings of John Maynard Keynes*, Vol. VII. Cambridge: Cambridge University Press, 2013.

Khan, Muhammad Akram. *An Introduction to Islamic Economics*. Islamabad: International Institute of Islamic Thought and Institute of Policy Studies, 1994.

———. *What Is Wrong with Islamic Economics? Analysing the Present State and Future Agenda*. Cheltenham: Edward Elgar, 2015.

Khan, Muhammad Fahim. "Theorizing Islamic Economics: Search for a Framework for Islamic Economic Analysis." *Islamic Economics*, Vol. 26, No. 1 (2013): 209–42.

Khan, Muhammad Tariq. "Historical Role of Islamic Waqf in Poverty Reduction in Muslim Society." *Pakistan Development Review*, Vol. 54, No. 4, (2015): 979–96.

Knysh, Alexander. *Islamic Mysticism: A Short History*. Leiden: Brill, 2000.

———. *Sufism*. Princeton, NJ: Princeton University Press, 2017.

Koehler, Benedikt. *Early Islam and the Birth of Capitalism*. Lanham, MD: Lexington Books, 2014.

Korkut, Besim, trans. *Al Qur'an Al Karim, Kur'an s prevodom* (*Qur'an with Translation*). Sarajevo: El Kalem, 1989.

Kuran, Timur. "The Absence of the Corporation in Islamic Law: Origins and Persistence." *American Journal of Comparative Law*, Vol. 53, No. 4 (2005): 785–834.

———. *Islam and Mammon* (Princeton, NJ: Princeton University Press, 2005).

Lambton, Ann K. S. "The Administration of Sanjar's Empire as Illustrated in the *'Atabat al-kataba*." *BSOAS*, Vol. 20, No. 1/3 (1957): 367–88.

———. "Justice in the Medieval Persian Theory of Kingship." *Studia Islamica*, No. 17 (1962): 91–119.

———. *State and Government in Medieval Islam*. New York: Oxford University Press, 1981.

Langholm, Odd. *The Legacy of Scholasticism in Economic Thought*. Cambridge: Cambridge University Press, 1998.

Lapidus, Ira M. "The Separation of State and Religion in the Development of Early Islamic Society." *International Journal of Middle East Studies*, Vol. 6, No. 4 (1975): 363–85.

———. "State and Religion in Islamic Societies." *Past & Present*, Vol. 151, No. 1 (1996): 3–27.

Lawson, Tony. *Reorienting Economics*. London: Routledge, 2003.

———. "What Is This 'School' Called Neoclassical Economics?" *Cambridge Journal of Economics*, Vol. 37 (2013): 949–83.

Layish, Aharon. "Islamic Law in the Modern World Nationalization, Islamization, Reinstatement." *Islamic Law and Society*, Vol. 21 (2014): 276–307.

Lowry, Todd and Barry Gordon, eds. *Ancient and Medieval Economic Ideas and Concepts of Social Justice*. Leiden: Brill, 1998.

Mahmood, Saba. "Secularism, Hermeneutics, and Empire: The Politics of Islamic Reformation." *Public Culture*, Vol. 18, No. 2 (2006): 323–47.

Malik, Muhammad Usman. *Mensch und Gesellschaft im Islam: eine Analyse unter besonderer Berücksichtigung der Religionskritik bei Karl Marx und der religionssoziologischen Untersuchungen Max Webers (Human being and Society in Islam: an Analysis in regard to Karl Marx's Critique of Religion and Max Weber's religious-sociological Analysis)*. PhD diss., Universität Köln, 1969.

Manfred, Gangl. "Judentum, Katholizismus, Protestantismus und der 'Geist' der Kapitalismus." In *L'ethique protestante de Max Weber et l'esprit de la modernite' (Max Webers protestantische Ethik und der Gesit der Moderne)*. Edited by Groupe de recherche sur la culture de Weimar, 121–45. Paris: Collection Philia, 1997.

Marshall, Alfrid. *Principles of Economics*. London: Macmillan, 8th ed. 1920, at https://oll.libertyfund.org/title/marshall-principles-of-economics-8th-ed, accessed online April 25, 2017.

Marx, Karl. *Das Kapital.* Hamburg: Otto Meissner, 1894.
Marx, Karl and Friedrich Engels. *Kapital und Politik.* Deutschland: Zweitausendeins, 2009.
———. *Manifesto of the Communist Party.* In *K. Marx and F. Engels, Selected Works, Vol. 1.* Moscow: Foreign Languages Publishing House, 1962.
———. *Marx. Economic and Philosophical Manuscripts of 1844.* Translated by Martin Milligan. Moscow: Foreign Languages Publishing House, 1959.
Maxime, Rodinson. *Islam et capitalisme.* Paris: Éditions du Seuil, 1996.
McKane, William, trans. *Book of Fear and Hope.* Leiden: Brill, 1965.
Menger, Carl. *Principles of Economics.* Translated by James Dingwall and Bert F. Hoselitz. Auburn, AL: Ludwig von Mises Institute, 2007.
Mill, John Stuart. *The Collected Works of John Stuart Mill, Volume IV: Essays on Economics and Society Part I.* Edited by John M. Robson. Toronto: University of Toronto Press, 1967.
———. *Utilitarianism.* London: Parker, Son and Bourn, 1863.
Mirakhor, Abbas. "Muslim Scholars and the History of Economics: A Need for Consideration." *American Journal of Islamic Social Sciences*, Vol. 4, No. 2, (December 1987): 245–76.
Muslim, Ṣaḥīḥ, Book 10 (Book of Business Transactions), chapter 37 (Conversion of Currency and Selling of Gold for Silver on the Spot), No. 3852, accessible at www.sahihmuslim.com/sps/smm/sahihmuslim.cfm?scn=dspchaptersfull&BookID=10&ChapterID=629
Myers, Eugene A. *Arabic Thought and the Western World.* New York: Fredrick Unger, 1964.
Nakissa, Aria. "An Epistemic Shift in Islamic Law: Educational Reform at al-Azhar and Dār al-ʿUlūm." *Islamic Law and Society*, Vol. 21 (2014): 209–51.
Naqvi, Syed Nawab Haider. *Ethics and Economics: An Islamic Synthesis.* Leicester: Islamic Foundation, 1981.
———. *Islam, Economics, and Society.* London: Kegan Paul International, 1994.
Nashat, M. A. *Ibn Khaldun: Pioneer Economist.* Le Caire: Imprimerie Nationale Boulac, 1945.
Nasr, Seyyed Hossein. *Knowledge and the Sacred.* New York: State University of New York, 1989.
———. *The Need for a Sacred Science: The Gifford Lectures.* Edinburgh: Edinburgh University Press, 1981.
Newman, Philip, Arthur Gayer, and Milton Spencer, eds. *Source Readings in Economic Thought.* New York: W. W. Norton, 1954.
Nomani, Farhad and Ali Rahnema. *Islamski ekonomski sistemi* [*Islamic Economic Systems*]. Sarajevo: El Kalem, 1996.
Nyazee, Imaran Ahsan Khan. *Theories of Islamic Law: The Methodology of Ijtihad.* Kuala Lumpur: Other Press, 1994.
O'Brien, George. *An Essay on Medieval Economic Teaching.* London: Longman, 1920.
Opwis, Felicitas. *Maṣlaḥa and the Purpose of the Law: Islamic Discourse on Legal Change from the 4th/10th to the 8th/14th Century.* Leiden: Brill, 2010.
Ostington, Paul. "Economic Thought and Religious Thought: A Comment on Ghazanfar and Islahi." In *Medieval Islamic Thought: Filling the "Great Gap" in European Economics.* Edited by S. M. Ghazanfar. London: Routledge, 2003.
Ouda, Jasser. *Maqāṣid al-Sharīʿa.* Herndon, VA: al-Ma'had al-ʿālami lil fikr al-Islāmī, 2012.
Peters, F. E. *Allah's Commonwealth.* New York: Simon and Schuster, 1973.
Popper, Karl. *The Logic of Scientific Discovery.* London: Routledge, 1977.
Porter, Roy. *The Enlightenment.* London: Palgrave Macmillan, 1996.
Pribram, Karl. *A History of Economic Reasoning.* Baltimore, MD: Johns Hopkins University Press, 1983.

Quasem, Muhammad Abdul. *The Ethics of al-Ghazali*. Petaling Jaya: Quasem, 1975.

———. *On Islamic Guidance*. Malaysia: National University of Malaysia, 1979.

Ricardo, David. *On the Principles of Political Economy and Taxation*. Kitchener, ON: Batoche Books, 2001.

Ritter, Helmut. "Ein Arabiches Handbuch Der Handelswissenshaf." *Der Islam*, No. 7 (1917): 1–91.

Rosenthal, F., trans. *Muqaddimah of Ibn Khaldum (An Introduction to History)*. 3 vols. Princeton, NJ: Princeton University Press, 1967.

Safi, Omid. *The Politics of Knowledge in Premodern Islam*. Chapel Hill: University of North Carolina Press, 2006.

Saheeh International. *The Qur'an*. Jeddah: Almunatada Alislami; Abul Qasim Publishing House, 1997.

Schumacher, Ernst F. *Small Is Beautiful*. London: Perennial Library, 1973.

Schumpeter, Joseph. *History of Economic Analysis*. New York: Oxford University Press, 1997.

Sen, Amartya. *On Ethics and Economics*. Oxford: Basil Blackwell, 1987.

———. "Progress and Public Reason." In *Performance and Progress: Essays on Capitalism, Business, and Society*. Edited by Subramanian Rangan, 151–73. Oxford: Oxford University Press, 2015.

Setia, Adi. "Al-Muḥāsibī: On Scrupulousness and the Pursuit of Livelihoods: Two Excerpts from His al-Makāsib wa al-Wara'." *Islamic Sciences*, Vol. 14, No. 1 (2016): 67–90.

———. "Imam Muḥammad Ibn al-Ḥasan al-Shaybāni on Earning a Livelihood: Seven Excerpts from his Kitāb al-Kasb." *Islam & Science*, Vol. 10, No. 2 (2012): 99–116.

———. *Kitāb al-Makāsib (The Book of Earnings) by al-Hārith al-Muḥāsibī (751–857 C.E.)*. Kuala Lumpur: IBFIM, 2016.

———. "The Meaning of 'Economy': *Qaṣd, Iqtiṣād, Tadbīr al-Manzil*." *Islamic Sciences*, Vol. 14, No. 1 (2016): 117–24.

———. "The Restoration of Wealth: Introducing Ibn Abī al-Dunyā's *Iṣlāḥ al-Māl*." *Islamic Sciences*, Vol. 13, No. 2 (2015): 77–94.

Shatzmiller, M. *Labour in the Medieval Islamic World*. Leiden: Brill, 1994.

Siddiqi, Mohammad Nejatullah. *Muslim Economic Thinking*. Jeddah: International Centre for Research in Islamic Economics and Leicester, Islamic Foundation, 1981.

Simmel, George. *Einleitung in die Moralwissenschaft*. 2 vols. Stuttgart und Berlin: J. G. Cotta'sche Buchhalndlung Nachfolger, 1904.

Smailagić, Nerkez. *Leksiokon islama (Lexicon of Islam)*. Sarajevo: Svijetlost, 1990.

Smith, Adam. *The Theory of Moral Sentiments*. MetaLibri, 2005. Electronic edition.

———. *The Wealth of Nations*. MetaLibri, 2007. Electronic edition.

Spengler, Joseph J. "Economic Thought of Islam: Ibn Khaldun." *Comparative Studies in Society and History*, Vol. 6 (1964): 268–306.

Swedberg, Richard and Ola Agevall. *The Max Weber Dictionary: Key Words and Central Concepts*. Stanford: Stanford University Press, 2005.

Taylor, Charles. "Modes of Secularism." In *Secularism and Its Critics*. Edited by Rajeev Bhargava, 31–53. New Delhi: Oxford University Press, 1998.

———. *A Secular Age*. Cambridge, MA: Harvard University Press, 2007.

Turner, Bryan. *Weber and Islam: A Critical Study*. London: Routledge & Kegan Paul, 1974.

Udovitch, Abraham L. *Partnership and Profit in Medieval Islam*. Princeton, NJ: Princeton University Press, 1970.

Walras, Léon. *Éléments d'économie politique pure, ou théorie de la richesse sociale.* Paris: Lausanne, 1926.

Watt, Montgomery. *The Influence of Islam on Medieval Europe.* Edinburgh: Edinburgh University Press, 1972.

Worland, Stephen Theodore. *Scholasticism and Welfare Economics.* Notre Dame, IN: University of Notre Dame Press, 1967.

Yazaki, Saeko. *Islamic Mysticism and Abū Ṭālib al-Makkī: The Role of The Heart.* London: Routledge, 2013.

Zarqa, Anas. "Islamic Economics: An Approach to Human Welfare." In *Studies in Islamic Studies.* Edited by Khurshid Ahmed, 3–118. Markfield: Islamic Foundation, 1980.

INDEX

Lightning Source UK Ltd.
Milton Keynes UK
UKHW041822250221
379332UK00001B/34

9 781785 275302